For George Warburg,
fellow-Freuhänder, with
best wishes from
Joshua Lederman
New York, 15 November 1979

M. M. WARBURG & CO.: 1798–1938

Max M. Warburg (1867–1946)

E. ROSENBAUM
A. J. SHERMAN

M. M. WARBURG & CO.

1798–1938

MERCHANT BANKERS OF HAMBURG

HM

HOLMES & MEIER PUBLISHERS, INC.
New York

First published in German as
Das Bankhaus M. M. Warburg & Co. 1798–1938

First published in the United States of America 1979 by
HOLMES & MEIER PUBLISHERS, INC.
30 Irving Place, New York, N.Y. 10003

Chapters I–IV, written in German by E. Rosenbaum, were translated into English by A. J. Sherman. Chapters V–X were originally written in English.

Library of Congress Cataloging in Publication Data
Rosenbaum, Eduard, 1887–
M. M. Warburg & Co., 1798–1938, merchant bankers of Hamburg
Translation of Das Bankhaus M. M. Warburg & Co.
Bibliography: p.
Include index.
1. Warburg (M.M.)–Brinckmann, Wirtz & Co.
I. Sherman, Ari Joshua, joint author. II. Title.
HG3060.H24W371713 1979 332.1′0943′515 79–511
ISBN 0–8419–0477–4

PRINTED IN GREAT BRITAIN

CONTENTS

PLATES

PREFACE TO THE ENGLISH EDITION

A good bank, particularly in the small international world of merchant and investment bankers still known collectively as the *haute banque*, has been likened to a virtuous woman who occasions 'no talk, either in praise or criticism'.* If we have nonetheless ventured to write a history of M. M. Warburg & Co. from its foundation to the day when its fortunes were confided to those who secured its survival beyond the Nazi era, it was in the hope that the story of this individual firm, aside from its intrinsic interest, might serve to illuminate some of the complex factors that have enabled a fortunate handful of European private banking houses to survive and prosper amid the many changes of the past two centuries.

That M. M. Warburg & Co. still carries on a multi-faceted banking business in Hamburg, from premises it has occupied for more than a century, is in itself worthy of remark; even more unusual in this age of huge joint-stock banks and anonymous financial conglomerates is the fact that descendants of the original founders still control and manage the firm. With the advantage of hindsight, we may observe that the comparatively long story of M. M. Warburg & Co. reflects to a large degree the fortunate availability at times of need of the appropriate successors, whether drawn from within or outside the Warburg family. Continuity was in fact based primarily on family ties: sons were schooled in the bank, in due course succeeded to responsibility for its management, and ultimately in their turn transmitted the enterprise to the next generation. The emphasis was throughout on prudence, thorough personal knowledge of clients and fellow-members of the banking fraternity, the deliberate accumulation of small profits on a series of continuing transactions. Only very gradually, in the bank's second century of existence, was there a cautious expansion beyond dealings in foreign exchange and in trade bills to the long-term financing of industrial and colonial enterprises.

Down the years, the firm's success was far more a product of steady common sense and the confidence built up over generations of dealings

* David Landes, *Bankers and Pashas* (New York, 1969), p. 35.

than the occasional daring coup or brilliant transaction. Reliability and trustworthiness born of long experience; a certain agility in obtaining and acting on information; some of that 'enlightened nepotism' that has often been remarked among private bankers; a self-restraining discipline that looked askance at ostentation and spectacular bonanzas: all these were part of the firm's tradition, and explain in some measure its continuing life.

But that is not of course the entire story. Warburgs was and remains a Hamburg house: its rise reflects accurately the modern economic history of that proud trading city with its Hanseatic traditions and close dependence on international commerce. As Hamburg prospered, so too did Warburgs; the earnings of both, however, fluctuated according to the vagaries of the world's markets in commodities and manufactured goods. Hamburg's chief trading partners were Great Britain and the United States: its cosmopolitan merchants traditionally looked outward, cultivating trade links that extended far beyond the North Sea and the Atlantic. For Warburgs too, international connections strengthened by ties of marriage and religious community were of prime importance: as the balance of international economic power shifted from Europe to the United States, these links enabled the firm to mobilize substantial new financial resources that contributed significantly to its wealth and standing.

Within Germany, however, the weight of Berlin as a financial and political centre increased steadily under Bismarck and his successors, compelling Warburgs eventually to meet this competitive challenge by establishing a Berlin office. The strongest competitors for Warburgs and their fellow private bankers were the joint-stock banks and finance companies whose rise in the last half of the nineteenth century fuelled the extraordinary growth in railroads and new industry of all kinds. Private bankers retained their substantial niche within the wider circle of international banks, but their numbers steadily dwindled, particularly after 1900, as financial power was increasingly concentrated in the largest of the joint-stock banking institutions.

By far the most serious challenge to the continued existence of M. M. Warburg & Co. was political, a menace that grew following the unparalleled destruction of the First World War, the raging inflation that ensued in Germany, and the subsequent worldwide slump. Despite the position Warburgs had attained near the very centre of political power under both the Wilhelmine Empire and the Weimar Republic, they were unable to deflect the onrushing catastrophe. Their many contributions to

German economic, social and cultural life, their patriotic sacrifices throughout the war and afterward, their political prestige in Hamburg and Berlin were all to no avail: with the rise of Nazism and the eventual appointment of Hitler as Reich Chancellor, the Warburg family and the bank itself became targets for anti-Semitic abuse, boycotts, a slow strangulation that culminated at last in their exclusion from the Reich loan consortium, the inner fraternity of major German banks. Despite a stubbornly gallant rearguard action, the Warburgs eventually stood alone and were compelled to accept the inevitable, fleeing into exile and handing over the bank to faithful stewards who by dint of remarkable tenacity and good fortune were able to preserve it throughout the war.

With this caesura our story ends; but the bank, now under the style M. M. Warburg-Brinckmann, Wirtz & Co., continues in its Hamburg home to pursue all aspects of the banking business.

The history of this study itself was outlined by my friend and colleague Dr. Eduard Rosenbaum in his preface to the original German edition: there too he explained our joint approach to the subject, and the aims we attempted to achieve. As he indicates, we jointly bear responsibility for this book. I should like here to express my gratitude for Dr. Rosenbaum's unfailing generosity, patience and good humour. His willingness to share his insights and experiences with a younger colleague and his warm encouragement have made for a collaboration of rare harmony. Dr. Rosenbaum and I have been fortunate in the care our London publisher, Mr. Christopher Hurst, devoted to the preparation of this edition; we are most grateful for his valuable assistance. I should also like to acknowledge with thanks the generous assistance of Mr. Eric M. Warburg throughout the preparation of this book. I am indebted to him for a timely research grant, permission to consult family and firm papers, many valuable introductions, and the warm hospitality that made my visits to Ferdinandstrasse 75 so memorably agreeable.

New York, September 1978 A. J. SHERMAN

PREFACE TO THE GERMAN EDITION

This book was written by my friend A. J. Sherman and me, and we jointly bear the responsibility for its contents. Since however we do not need to speak formally of the 'right-hand signer' and the 'left-hand signer' – as is the case with joint holders of power of attorney – this preface is signed only by me, particularly because I am in a position, alas, to look back and report on a very much longer period of the pre-history of this work.

This book was not commissioned by the firm, nor is it a *Festschrift* with the usual selection of illustrations; it is a work freely undertaken by the authors. It should nonetheless be obvious that such a study cannot be written without the knowledge of the firm and its permission to use the available primary sources. But in addition to the cooperation of the firm, for which our thanks will later be expressed more fully, there is a further justification for this work that should not be overlooked without comment.

On 7 April 1921 I received a letter from Max M. Warburg that began as follows:

> Dear Doctor, I have now spoken with my partners, and we have decided to write a history for the 125th anniversary of our firm which will be celebrated on 1 January 1923. It is appropriate for you in the first instance to look over the available material. It will be delivered to you and put in order here. I do not want these papers to be worked on outside the office, and should like the entire project to be carried out in the closest touch with me.

If after this typical formulation I had still entertained doubts as to who the real author of this work was to be, these were laid to rest following receipt of a shower of communications that Max M. Warburg sent me in quick succession from his holiday retreat in Kissingen. I was given work-space in the 'small meeting-room' in which I collected measured dosages of material. It rapidly transpired, however, that the papers which had been arranged either disappeared overnight or were taken away from me during the day, since they were required for the current conduct of business. In an address which he made to the staff on 1 January 1923, Max Warburg referred humorously to these interruptions, saying that they proved the firm was still too young and lively for a historical examination. At the same time, moreover, the serious crises of the German currency led to the decision to devote all energies to current problems, and to defer historical considerations to a future time.

Be that as it may, here are two examples of the ideas that occurred to Max Warburg in Kissingen; they are typical of him, and were not overlooked in the present study:

> I should set great store on demonstrating how large a role chance plays in the development of such a business, and indeed how much more economic development altogether is to be ascribed to chance opportunities and naturally occurring growth than to the so-called working toward a goal of some individual. Throughout the work there should be a certain respect for these spontaneous developments; for most people suffer from exaggerated notions of their importance, and bank directors especially, when they write their annual reports three to six months after year-end, ascribe to their acts after the event a foresight that in fact never existed.

Just as characteristic of Max Warburg and the matter itself is this remark of 26 April 1921 from Bad Kissingen:

> I therefore think that one cannot begin with much of this family history, and that it should not be excessively indulged for vanity's sake; that would, I believe, only do violence to history. After all, we all have ancestors, and the further one can trace them back as people of accomplishment or wealth, the more probably will degeneracy begin to make its appearance. I therefore attach relatively little importance to this part of the work.

These comments were borne very much in mind even in the first English study on the firm, written in 1962 for the *Year Book* of the Leo Baeck Institute, London;* they led to a definition of the work that excluded purely family history and any exaggeration of the importance of a single firm. When Eric M. Warburg asked me, in connection with the short 1962 study, whether I was prepared in accordance with his late father's wishes to undertake a more comprehensive history of the firm, I agreed, with the intention of writing not family history but a contribution to the history of private banking.

* E. Rosenbaum, 'M. M. Warburg & Co., Merchant Bankers of Hamburg – A Survey of the First 140 Years, 1798 to 1938', *Year Book VII*, Leo Baeck Institute (London, 1962).

The possible value of this study consists not in the universal applicability of its conclusions, but in the description through business documents that have survived of how transactions were conducted, and how they fitted into more general economic developments – instead of the customary *Festschrift* approach of sonorous but thinly-documented observations. In that process, without touching up the figures, the private banker's special obligation of discretion was not overlooked. Mistakes and losses were not suppressed; but nothing derogatory was reported about third parties and their successors in interest, in accordance with the norms governing possible damage to the credit standing of firms or individuals. As Max Warburg once said to me: 'A grandson would not like to read that we supported his grandfather in the crisis of 1857 [that also endangered the Warburg bank itself].'

The bibliography of works consulted in addition to the bank's files indicates the sources used, but is not exhaustive; it should permit the informed reader to follow up matters of interest. The footnotes with specific references are therefore to be considered an integral part of the text.

Since I was unable for personal reasons to carry out the study beyond the year 1890, Dr. A. J. Sherman, a member of a younger generation, was recruited for the task, and his participation was made possible by a research grant from Mr. Eric M. Warburg. Dr. Sherman, who studied law at Harvard University, politics and history at Columbia and Oxford, and was for eight years with Kuhn, Loeb & Co., investment bankers in New York, wrote his part in English. Thanks for the translation of this section into German are due to Mr. Wolfgang Rittmeister of Hamburg.

Our thanks for making this entire work possible are bound up with memories that recall Conrad Ferdinand Meyer's verse:

Wir Toten, wir Toten sind grössere Heere
*als ihr auf der Erde, als ihr auf dem Meere.**

The book is dedicated to the memory of Max M. Warburg and Rudolf Brinckmann.

Max M. Warburg was, with his friend Albert Ballin, among the leading personalities of public life in Hamburg in those years which one may call without historical value-judgment the Wilhelmine era. Eric M. Warburg wrote definitive words of reminiscence about him when he printed privately a selection of the memoirs his father had left in manuscript form.

* 'We dead, we dead are greater armies
Than you on earth, than you on the seas.'

A comprehensive evaluation of what Rudolf Brinckmann contributed to the bank and its preservation through the dark years of the Third Reich must be deferred to that time when the present firm, M. M. Warburg-Brinckmann, Wirtz & Co., has become an appropriate subject for a history. Perhaps a younger generation can accomplish this in 1998 with a view towards the further future. But even at this point one must draw attention to the extraordinary accomplishment of Rudolf Brinckmann; having joined the firm in 1920, he held its power of attorney from 1938 onwards and, assisted by Paul Wirtz, saved the firm from destruction under the National Socialist regime. His comprehensive expertise and remarkable knowledge of foreign languages and customs were but valuable adjuncts to his qualities of personal courage, diplomatic skill and tenacious perseverance. There was symbolic significance in the fact that the end of his life came on 2 January 1974, one day after he had transferred leadership to the younger partners.

A similar symbolism is connected with the death of Carl Melchior, who died as early as December 1933 as he spent his last strength in efforts on behalf of those Jews left in Germany. Sustained by a high ethical standard, his distinguished intellect, both sensitive and tough-minded, wore itself out in the struggle with forces whose inhuman power he had not conceived possible.

The name of Charles (Karl) Warburg (1907–72) must be recalled with warm thanks; it is he who made possible the reliance of this study on original sources. Soon after 1933 he emigrated to England, and brought there a comprehensive collection of business documents and personal papers that had been assembled by his father, Aby S. Warburg, which he permitted us to use freely and without pre-conditions. He later left this material to Eric M. Warburg for inclusion in the Hamburg archives of the bank (see Note on Unpublished and Restricted Sources).

Our thanks must also be expressed to Dr. Peter Freimark, Director of the Institut für die Geschichte der deutschen Juden, Hamburg, and to Miss Marianne Engel for supervising the printing and preparation of the manuscript; and not least to our publisher Kurt Christians for his patience and helpful understanding of the purpose of our work.

London, 1976 EDUARD ROSENBAUM

I

THE BANK'S EARLY YEARS: THE BACKGROUND

According to an adequately verified tradition, the Hamburg banking house M. M. Warburg and Co. was founded in the year 1798 when Gumprich Marcus Samuel Warburg turned over to his sons Moses Marcus and Gerson Warburg the running of his business as a money changer.

Since their predecessors, who will be discussed in a later section, had also been in the business of money exchange and advancing loans secured by pledges and goods, the firm, unlike others founded around the same time, was from the beginning purely a banking enterprise and did not evolve from a general merchandising business, as for example did such Hamburg firms as L. Behrens & Söhne, Conrad Hinrich Donner* (founded 1798) and Joh. Berenberg, Gossler and Co.

For this last firm too, whose beginnings go as far back as 1590, 1798 was the decisive year, the year in which the new partner Johann Heinrich Gossler built up the financial side of the enterprise into a 'Discount and Acceptance House'.†

Since the beginnings of the banking houses Mendelssohn (1795), Salomon Oppenheim jun. & Co. (1798 in Bonn, from 1799 in Cologne), and Bleichröder (1803), as well as the transformation of the Düsseldorf

* Richard Tilly writes about the Rhineland that the beginning of specialized private banking can be traced to the last decades of the eighteenth century, but that it is frequently not easy to say when somebody was a banker and when not, since this function was often only a part of another form of business. *Financial Institutions in the Rhineland 1815–1870* (Madison, 1967), pp. 46 ff.

† M. Möring, *Joh. Berenberg, Gossler and Co.* (Hamburg, 1962); printed as manuscript without pagination. A presentation, full of insight, of the history of the banking house Conrad Hinrich Donner (1798–1973) is given by Maria Möring (Hamburg 1973). The often misunderstood significance of Altona as a Danish harbour on the Elbe is described convincingly with its cultural background.

firm C. G. Trinkaus* (1785) from a merchandising business into a bank business, and finally the beginnings of the Rothschild dynasty (around 1803) can all be found in this period, we may justifiably seek certain general conditions for this development precisely in the time of the Napoleonic Wars. For our purposes we may limit the scope of our inquiry to the shaping factors that are of particular importance for northern Germany and especially Hamburg. We shall presume acquaintance with the early history of Hamburg, its position on the edge of the Atlantic and of a national economy whose integration into a world economy was by no means yet complete, as well as the location of Hamburg in the middle of transportation routes which reached then from the Baltic North down to the Mediterranean South, and later included connecting routes to both Americas and to other continents.

To gain a preliminary view of the special position of Hamburg in the second half of the eighteenth century, we can reach back to a source of a unique kind. In 1806, as the globe crowning the church tower of St. Peter's was being repaired, an essay on 'The State of Trade in Hamburg during the Last Fifty Years' by Johannes Ernst Friedrich Westphalen was placed in the globe, along with other documents intended for the information of posterity'. The study could scarcely have fulfilled this aim in that rather inaccessible spot if a church official, Jürgen Suhr, had not made a copy of it on the occasion of another repair of the tower in the spring of 1840. This copy remains in the possession of the Commerz-bibliothek in Hamburg. The author was in 1800 president of the Commercium, a forerunner of the Chamber of Commerce, and in 1806 president of the Hamburg Bank; in 1809 he was elected to the Senate, to which he belonged until his death in 1833. The manuscript has never been published, but has been used by several historians: Adolph Soetbeer,† Adolf Wohlwill and Heinrich Sieveking. With the aid of this 'tower essay' we shall first consider the main characteristics of Hamburg's economic situation at the end of the eighteenth century, and then complement this survey by reference to other sources. The first and most important fact in this period was that Hamburg maintained its neutrality: 'thus it was

* *175 Jahre C. G. Trinkaus. Tradition und neue Aufgaben* (Düsseldorf, 1960), p. 15. Besides the history of the firm written by Carl Otto Heuser, this volume contains excellent monographs by Achterberg, Palyi, Röpke and Schmölders on the development and functions of the German private banking house.

† A. Soetbeer, *Beiträge und Materialien zur Beurtheilung von Geld- und Bank-Fragen mit besonderer Rücksicht auf Hamburg* (Hamburg, 1855), p. 55.

used by nations at war for the furtherance of their trade.'* In practical terms, this meant that during the years 1795 to 1800, when England blockaded the French and Dutch ports, 'both republics had to carry on the largest part of their trade through Hamburg.' The decline of the credit of the Bank of Amsterdam brought the Dutch discount business to Hamburg. 'Russia paid the interest on its loans from Holland here. England paid its subsidies to foreign powers here. Thus, all factors coincided to increase the banking business here, and one can assume that in general bank funds must have increased five, ten or even fourteen times more than in earlier times.'† Moreover, there was the influx of emigrants and their wealth, as well as the transfer of unaccompanied flight capital. We perceive in the description of the increased import of goods and the resultant 'trade confusion' of 1799, that the discount rate rose to over 15 per cent, but by December 1799 had already fallen back to 3 per cent. Fifty-nine firms, with altogether 36 million Mark Banco‡ of liabilities, became insolvent.§ There is no indication in either documents or in family tradition that the firm M. M. Warburg & Co. was noticeably affected by these happenings.

As a last factor, and one particularly important for Hamburg as a banking centre, we read in Westphalen's essay remarks about the growth of the insurance business and the investment of premium funds in bills of exchange: 'In order to keep monies held by the insurance companies usefully invested, bills were discounted or advances made against sub-pledges on goods. In this way the discount market was greatly enlarged. ... The importance of the discount business transacted by the insurance companies may be gauged by considering the fact that the year-end accounts of these companies revealed discount earnings that amounted to 15, 30, 60, indeed even 80,000 Mark Banco.'‖

Of the themes suggested by the 'tower essay' let us first consider the question of Hamburg's neutrality, since it is particularly in times of war that the neutral status of a trade centre is of decisive importance for the flow of goods and funds.

* J. Westphalen, p. 3, according to the copy by Suhr.

† Ibid., pp. 8 ff. On Russia's drafts, cf. Johann Georg Büsch in his original essay *John Bull der jüngere oder über die neuesten Vorfälle der Londoner Bank* (Hamburg, 1797), p. 28.

‡ The Mark Banco was the unit of account with the Hamburgische Bank, and was equal to M1.20.

§ Joh. Westphalen, ibid., p. 16.

‖ Ibid., p. 30. Cf. J. G. Büsch, *Versuch einer Geschichte der Hamburger Handlung* (Hamburg, 1797), pp. 151 ff: 'Die in Hamburg entstandenen Assekuranz Kompanien'.

In respect of the Continental blockade, the English economic historian C. R. Fay says of this period: 'Hamburg became the headquarters of an illicit trade which was so normal that the risk of breaking the French cordon was evaluated exactly and added to the price of goods.'* But trade in these times was by no means so normal that the difficulties could have been overcome merely with risk-free calculations. Right at the outbreak of the first war of the Coalition with France, Hamburg received as early as December 1792 'an Imperial edict prohibiting trade with the enemies of the Empire'. It was not a general trade interdiction, but the difference between what was allowed and what prohibited was not made very clear, and for the first time grain and other foodstuffs were declared contraband of war.† Another problem arose for Hamburg when it was required by the Directorate of Lower Saxony to expel the French Ambassador accredited to it who resided in Hamburg. This Ambassador was very popular in Hamburg and belonged to the circle of friends of Georg Heinrich Sieveking (1751–99) who, like many progressive thinkers in western Germany, followed the ideas of 1789 with great sympathy. In the year 1793 he was the president of the Commerce Deputation and with his colleagues arrived at a solution to the dilemma. They feared that an actual expulsion would be regarded by the French as an act of war, which would mean the end of Hamburg's conditional neutrality. So a substantial sum of money was collected from among the merchants (2,000 gold ducats), which was to be given to M. Lehoc as a parting gift when he decided on his own to leave Hamburg. The 'Imperial and Prussian ministers residing here' were to receive 1,000 gold ducats each 'in order to ensure the good will of both towards the city'.‡ This delicately managed affair finally had a successful ending; the Ambassador left Hamburg 'with clear signs of emotion', refused to accept the gift for himself but later consented to have the 12,000 Mark Banco turned over to his daughters Sophie and Justine, who expressed appropriate thanks in letters of 27 July 1793.§

* C. R. Fay, *Great Britain from Adam Smith to the Present Day* (3rd ed., London, 1932), p. 32.

† J. G. Büsch, op. cit, pp. 184 ff.

‡ This description is based on: *Dokumente zur Geschichte der Handelskammer Hamburg* (Hamburg, 1965), pp. 45 ff. For the larger connections however see the chapter 'Das hansische Spiel um Freiheit und Handel', in Hermann Tiemann, *Essays, Vorträge und Aufsätze aus vier Jahrzehnten* (Hamburg, 1975), pp. 165–99.

§ *Dokumente*, op. cit., p. 54.

We have dealt with this special sort of diplomacy and money trafficking in such detail because it was only a prelude to the mingling of financial factors in further developments and because these factors later had a far weightier significance.

When after the Peace of Basel in 1795 the neutrality of Hamburg was secured and Karl Friedrich Reinhard appointed by the French government as the new Ambassador in Hamburg, the Court in Vienna warned against recognizing him, while the French government demanded that he be formally accredited within thirty days. We cannot go into the details of the deliberations here. In order to settle the matter, Georg Heinrich Sieveking travelled to Paris on 17 March 1796 armed with the full authority of the Senate and the Commerce Deputation for the purpose of calming the infuriated Directory. For this particular purpose he had with him 'for the freest use' 300,000 Mark Banco, which had been collected by the Commerce Deputation 'with great difficulty'. Of this sum Barras, the leading member of the Directory, alone received 161,000 Mark Banco; the administrative head of the foreign office, Flassan, another 55,000 Mark Banco; other amounts went to Mme. Buonaparte, Mme. Tallien, Mme. Condorcet and Lehoc.* Moreover, larger sums had to be paid in addition to the French treasury; but good relations with the French were re-established.

It is worth recalling, in connection with this mixture of *raison d'état* and money transfer, the judgement passed by the historian François Crouzet on the very limited effectiveness of the Continental blockade: 'C'est le cas d'abord de la corruption des douaniers, consuls, fonctionnaires et militaires de tous grades qui furent chargés de l'application du Blocus;' it was an 'énorme coalition de cupidités, de trahison et de complicités'. Matters were somewhat simpler – 'moins choquantes' – as far as trade with Holland was concerned, since King Louis did not approve of the blockade policy of his brother and during his brief reign (1806–10) permitted licences to be distributed to anyone willing to pay.†

In addition to these non-economic distortions to the price structure, there were also the payments, mentioned by Westphal, of subsidies to England's Continental allies. These were of essential importance for the money market in Hamburg, and thus also for banking business, since the

* Ibid., p. 67. The receipts are still in the possession of the Chamber of Commerce.

† F. Crouzet, *L'économie Brittanique et le Blocus Continental 1806–1813* (Paris, 1958), p. 858.

subsidies for Prussia, Russia, Sweden and in part also for Austria were all made through Hamburg.*

The classical exposition of these matters is the *Bullion Report* of 1808 in which a Parliamentary select committee attempted to answer questions about the price of gold, money circulation and the state of the foreign exchange market.† When in the course of hostilities with France in 1797 the gold reserves of the Bank of England were seriously depleted, it was decreed on a Sunday, 26 February, in the style still familiar to us today, after consultation with the King and the board of the Bank under William Pitt, that: 'It is indispensably necessary for the public service that the Directors of the Bank of England should forbear issuing any cash in payment until the sense of Parliament can be taken on that subject and the proper measures adopted thereupon for maintaining the means of circulation.'‡ On Monday 27 February, an editorial in *The Times* called for the public to accommodate itself to the situation in the spirit of the Elizabethan age, and a gathering of leading bankers decided on the same day at the Mansion House to allow the pound note to be used as a fully valid means of payment.§ The 'provisional arrangement' lasted until 1819, although in 1810 a need was felt to investigate the discount of the pound note in relation to gold coins.

The report that resulted is of special interest for Hamburg, since foreign exchange relations between London and Hamburg and the usages of the Hamburg market are treated with much precision in the testimony of a Continental merchant.‖ Until about twenty-five years ago there were only very vague suppositions about the identity of this merchant. Then the editor of the English Ricardo edition, Piero Sraffa, concluded on the basis of a series of penetrating arguments that this witness must have been the Hamburg banker John Parish. This is confirmed in the study by Karl

* These additional functions of the money market were nothing new for Hamburg: during the Thirty Years' War, French subsidies to Sweden were paid through Hamburg. In the years after 1660 English and Dutch aid was forwarded through Manuel Texeira to the Northern states. H. Kellenbenz, *Sephardim an der unteren Elbe* (Wiesbaden, 1958), pp. 265 ff. and 291 ff.

† *Report together with Minutes of Evidence, and Accounts, from the Select Committee on the High Price of Gold Bullion*, House of Commons, 8 June 1810 (edition by Johnson and Ridgeway, London, 1810).

‡ A. E. Feaveryear, *The Pound Sterling: a History of English Money* (2nd ed., revised by E. V. Morgan. Oxford, 1963), pp. 182 ff.

§ Ibid., p. 170.

‖ *Bullion Report*, pp. 77 ff., 83 ff., 96 ff., 102 ff.

Sieveking, *Geschichte des Pfund Sterlings vom 25. Februar 1791 bis zum zweiten Frieden von Paris.**

Parish reports on the basis of parity, about a form of foreign exchange arbitrage, and says explicitly: '. . . the course from London upon Hamburgh is regulated in a great measure by that from Hamburgh upon London.' Moreover, he diagnoses the decisive factor causing the discount with the following statement, which even today is relevant to English circumstances: 'I conceive the cause of the present state of exchange to be entirely commercial, with the exception, I should add, of the payments which Government have had occasion to make upon the Continent, in the shapes of subsidies, the payment of troops, etc.'† Tables of such payments from 1804 until February 1810 are given in the appendix to the *Bullion Report*, in which among others the Viennese bankers Arnstein & Eskeles, Edward Thornton, the English Minister resident in Hamburg, and John Parish & Co. are mentioned. Perhaps typical of the necessary detours in the channel of money transfers is an entry of 1808 for £310,202 15s. 2d. to Edward Thornton, at that time Minister in Stockholm, for 'Swedish subsidy, service of Sir J. Moore's army and of the Spanish troops'. For amounts entered to the last penny, one often finds only the entry 'public services'; for the subsidies for Austria 'to His Most Christian Majesty'.‡ In connection with these payments, aside from John Parish & Co. and Martin Dorner in Hamburg, there were also listed in the year 1795 Fries & Co. in Vienna, Bethmann in Frankfurt on Main, Heath & Co. in Genoa, François d'Honoré Berte in Livorno, J. und C. G. de Halder in Augsburg, and Frage & Co. in Leipzig.§ An even

* The study is in the State Archive of Hamburg. Cf. 'Mr.—' of the *Bullion Report*, in *The Works and Correspondence of David Ricardo* (Cambridge, 1951), Vol. 3, pp. 427–34. A reference to John Parish is in Heinrich Sieveking, *Karl Sieveking, 1787–1847. Lebensbild eines hamburgischen Diplomaten aus dem Zeitalter der Romantik* (Hamburg, 1923), Vol. 2, p. 229.

† *Bullion Report*, pp. 76 ff.

‡ A survey of the Continental payments from 1813 to 1815 is in the Public Record Office, London, Treasury Chambers. T. 56, No. 30. In his monograph *Das Haus Parish in Hamburg* (Jena, 1905), Richard Ehrenberg reports in a special chapter on the profitable transfer of English subsidies in the year 1794 and remarks explicitly that Parish was apparently much better informed about the technique of such transfers than his English customer 'whose limited knowledge in this field was sharply criticized a few years later by Busch as well' (pp. 62 and 66).

§ K. Holleiner, *The Imperial Loans* (Oxford, 1965), p. 47; from F.O. 7/40 in the Public Record Office, London.

greater expansion of banking connections was caused by England's support throughout the Napoleonic wars of a considerable number of agents and correspondents of every sort, who had to be supplied with the necessary financial means. In a passage that also emphasizes the significance of Heligoland, Buckland states: 'Hamburg, with its old commercial connections with England and its geographical situation, was the great clearing-house,' also for newspapers and letters for Russia.* Mentioned as well are the useful services furnished by 'the Anglo-German House of Parish, members of which, *bien vus* in Austria and Sweden as well as potentates in their own adopted town, did what they could'.†

Westphalen cites as another factor important for the special position of the Hamburg economy at the end of the 18th century the influx of emigrants and flight capital, which could not always be accompanied by its owners. The turning-points of recent history have brought new immigrants to many entrepôts. In a brief survey Bernd Lüthje writes: 'The typical present-day Hamburger is inconceivable without the influences of refugee Walloons, Flemish, Dutch, Spaniards, Portuguese, Italians, Huguenots, South Germans, Lutherans, Catholics, Jews, Calvinists and Baptists.'‡ Even before the dissolution of the Hanseatic League, Hamburg had maintained a very liberal settlement policy, which after 1792 also benefited refugees from France.§ The history of these migrations can to this day often be traced in Hamburg family names.

With regard to the French immigration, many observers emphasize more its influence on literature and art, while others, rather more moralistic, stress the increase of luxurious consumption in bourgeois life, which had already been observed around the middle of the eighteenth century.‖

* C. S. Buckland, *Metternich and the British Government from 1809 to 1813* (London, 1932), p. 130.

† Ibid., p. 131, especially worth noting Chapter III: 'Agents and Intermediaries', pp. 53–107, as well as Chapter IV: 'Communications', pp. 108–59. Further substantiation is provided by the letters of the English Consul in Hamburg (later Heligoland) from September 1812 and February 1813 to the Foreign Office in London: '... qui montre que la maison Parish était la banque du réseau de renseignements dirigé par Nicholas'. F. Crouzet, op. cit., p. 440, Annexe 43.

‡ B. Lüthje, 'Eine neue Heimat in Hamburg' in *Mitteilungen der Handelskammer Hamburg* (Hamburg, 1966), pp. 419 ff.

§ Ibid.; for the immigration of the Sephardic Jews, see H. Kellenbenz, *Sephardim an der unteren Elbe*, a good presentation.

‖ R. Ehrenberg, loc. cit., pp. 132 ff; V. Nolte, *Fünfzig Jahre in beiden Hemisphären* (Hamburg, 1853), Vol. 1, pp. 27 ff.

We do, however, also have a number of reports on the economic importance of the influx of new capital. In January 1798 the English Consul Charles Henry Fraser reported to Lord Granville of the Foreign Office in London that a French Commissioner had arrived, who, in addition to his general financial mission, had an additional mission which sounds familiar to us: '... as considerable sums of Money had been transmitted here during Robespierre's Reign, by Persons who afterwards fell a victim to the cruelty of the Monster, it is believed, that M. Bourdon is also instructed to endeavour to ascertain to whom this Money was transmitted, or at least to obtain some account of it, since no account whatever had as yet been given thereof by the Person who had received it.'* The Consul doubted the Commissioner would succeed, since it was assumed that some of the recipients had abused the confidence reposed in them, and used the money for themselves.† Although by the very nature of the matter it was difficult to arrive at conclusive evidence for these allegations, it does seem to be a general assumption that such lapses did indeed occur. In any case, this view is shared by Aby S. Warburg, who says in an unpublished draft of the firm's history that in this regard 'quite a good deal of misconduct had occurred', and that many a French nobleman's son, surviving the Revolution, inquired in vain as to the remains of the family fortune, 'and then disappeared into the Hamburg slums, sinking finally into some honest proletarian family'.‡ The wise Senator Westphalen may well have been thinking of just such effects when, writing for the church tower, he questioned 'whether the citizens of Hamburg are really happier with the increased standard of living ... whether the refinement of their manners had really contributed to the improvement of their morality', and whether

* Public Record Office, F.O. 33, No. 14, Hamburg, 19 January 1798.

† Maurice Lévy-Leboyer describes the flight of capital which was caused by the revolutionary exactions of the Montagnards. The banker Hottinguer travels in April 1783 to the United States via Zürich. His visit to Hamburg, which along with London and Basel is one of the refuges for flight capital, is announced for March 1786. 'La Révolution n'a pas simplement chassé les capitaux hors du pays ... elle a bouleversé le crédit sur tout le Continent et rendu nécessaire, avant toute reprise industrielle, la reconstitution des divers marchés financiers.' *Les banques européenes et l'industrialisation internationale dans la première moitié du XIXe siècle* (Paris, 1964), pp. 423 ff. Of Daniel Dollfus-Mieg, probably a partner of Schlumpeter, Dollfus & Cie. in Paris, Lévy-Leboyer writes: '... pendant la révolution, il critiqua ses cousins mulhousiens qui exportaient leur capitaux à Hambourg, mais il a dû faire de même en 1794.' Op. cit., p. 449, note 18.

‡ Unpublished Diaries of Aby S. Warburg.

the proverbial old 'Hamburg honesty had not somewhat been eclipsed'.* Let us, like Westphalen, leave the answer open and now try with the aid of some figures to shed further light on the economic situation around 1800.

Although finance and trade bills in circulation were accepted through the Bank of Hamburg only to an extent not readily demonstrable, we may still grant the turnover figures of that Bank special significance. A somewhat summary picture of the bank's activities is given by the number of ledgers used, a figure which was known exactly since a ledger fee was computed for each page. These numbers were:

1786	10,295
1792	12,177
1794	13,144
1795	16,918
1796	20,067
1799	24,151
1805	27,784
1806	27,094
1808	19,111†

The Bank's assets rose from 13 million Mark Banco in 1792 to 38·5 million in 1799, and the turnover, which had been kept completely secret, rose from approximately 343 million in 1781 to around 1·5 billion in 1799. At the time of its expropriation by the French (1813–14), the Bank's assets amounted to about 7·5 million; on 20 March 1800, the highest previous point, the assets were 41,298,026.‡

The number of those who had bank accounts was always small, since they were limited to citizens and those foreigners with special privileges, among whom were the Portuguese and German Jews who had settled in Hamburg. However, foreign funds and the property of immigrants could be administered and dealt in through these accounts.

According to contemporary opinions, completely confirmed by later research, Hamburg became the centre of north German trade in bills of exchange, and also, as Karl Sieveking emphasizes in his *Geschichte des £ Sterling*, the leading market for silver. We can dispense here with

* Westphalen, loc. cit., pp. 4 ff.

† H. Sieveking, 'Die Hamburger Bank 1619–1875' in *Festschrift für Werner von Melle* (Hamburg, 1933), pp. 82 ff.

‡ A. Soetbeer, *Beiträge*, loc. cit. p. 31.

figures on the volume of trade in Hamburg; it should be mentioned, however, as some indication of that volume, and because of the importance of the Sterling exchange rate, that imports from England rose from £2·4 million in 1793 to £8 million in 1795, and reached a temporary high point in 1800 of £12 million.* In addition, there was the trade with France, Spain and Portugal, and after 1781 with the United States and the West Indies. In the other direction, Hamburg was by the end of the eighteenth century the main export centre for a vast mid- and East European hinterland, with grain, Silesian linen, and Bohemian glass as important wares. Hamburg also occupied a vital position as intermediary in the distribution of foodstuffs such as coffee and sugar, as well as French wines to Scandinavia and Russia; this trade was linked with the extension of numerous credit facilities, and thus the volume of trade bills and banking business generally increased.† This was all the more so because until well into the nineteenth century, the inland merchant or factory owner did not try to establish his own import and export links to foreign countries: 'That was too risky, business developed more surely if it went through the mediation of the port city'; in addition, the Hamburg trader took care of the payments and necessary credit.‡

And finally, in order to gain a clear picture of the economic forces into which a firm founded around 1800 was thrust, we must refer once again to the blockade and the Continental embargo. The disruption of traffic by sea in the years from 1804 to 1814 cannot be disputed. And yet detours by way of Heligoland and ports in Holstein remained possible although costly, and payments were substantially less hampered than the trade in goods. The fact that England could finance the war in Spain under Wellington with the help of the Rothschild brothers by way of Paris, under the very eyes of the French, shows clearly enough that the couriers of the state and of finance were not as easily caught as goods, which were after all always visible. According to Crouzet, trade between Britain and Hamburg, via intermediate posts in Heligoland and Tönningen was approximately normal after the Spring of 1807, as was trade in 1808, with

* A. D. Gayer (ed.), *The Growth and Fluctuation of the British Economy, 1790–1850* (Oxford, 1953), Vol. 1, pp. 32 ff.

† For a more recent presentation, cf. H. Kellenbenz, 'Der deutsche Aussenhandel gegen Ausgang des 18. Jahrhundert', pp. 24 ff., in *Die wirtschaftliche Situation in Deutschland und Oesterreich um die Wende vom 18. zum 19. Jahrhundert* (Stuttgart, 1964).

‡ H. Kellenbenz, loc. cit., pp. 57 ff.

a cost increase of about 25 per cent due to the detour; in 1809, gold could be shipped to Hamburg at a cost of between 5·5 and 7 per cent, and was cheaper than payment through bills of exchange. Only in 1810, under the command of Davout, was an intensified watch mounted on the Elbe, Weser and Jade estuaries, and in January of 1811 a businessman paid £150 for the crossing from Heligoland to the coast of Holstein, where, according to the testimony of the British agent Nicholas, goods worth £4 million were stored, 'which were impossible to return to the Allied side'.*

Crouzet, whose penetrating investigation will hardly be surpassed by any future researcher, concludes that even in the war years England succeeded in expanding its economy, in modernizing and developing, and thus dominating the world for a century with its capitalist economy.†

One does not of course need to take this conclusion of Crouzet's quite literally. Granted, the development of the railways, of gas and water works was largely completed with British participation, and Napoleon's aim to free the Continent of maritime dependence on England was never realized. Yet despite all this, the Continental embargo had the effect 'largely of a protective tariff based on careful calculation of advantage'.‡ And if we want to retain the questionable but impressive concept of the 'industrial revolution', then we might – in agreement with Cunningham, Clapham, Spiethoff and Schumpeter – approve the verdict of Tugan-Baranowsky, that it came, especially on the Continent, in the second quarter of the nineteenth century rather than at the end of the eighteenth century.§ Of course, the men who founded firms around 1800 could not perceive that great Atlantic swell which would carry them into the future. But they could recognize, from their own practical experience, that war brings 'an increased activity in all branches of production that supply war requirements', and that, precisely through the disturbance of the economy, war creates 'that inequality in the prices of things which nourishes and fosters trade'. It is no coincidence that this observation was made by the shrewd Baden statesman, Nebenius, who was credited by Roscher as

* F. Crouzet, loc. cit., pp. 222, 439 ff., 529 ff., 664.

† Ibid., p. 872.

‡ A. Wohlwill, *Neuere Geschichte der Freien und Hansestadt Hamburg, insbesondere von 1789 bis 1815* (Gotha, 1914), p. 353.

§ J. A. Schumpeter, *Business Cycles* (New York, 1939), Vol. 1, p. 254.

having been the actual architect of the Prussian-German Zollverein.* And thus we indicate the specifically German factors, in addition to general European developments, that arose from Hamburg's hinterland and were gradually to create a constantly expanding field of operation.

* C. F. Nebenius, *Der öffentliche Credit* (Karlsruhe, 1820), pp. 420 ff.

2

M. M. WARBURG & CO. FROM ITS FOUNDING TO THE MIDDLE OF THE NINETEENTH CENTURY

The first of January 1798 is assumed to be the day of the firm's foundation, although the actual act of establishment, for which we have no documentation, perhaps took place the previous year. Several researchers into the family history point out, however, that 1725 may be considered the beginning since Samuel Warburg, the grandfather of the founders of 1798, and his son Gumprich Marcus Samuel Warburg were money changers. There exists, therefore, a tradition extending back for many years, from which we need not necessarily conclude that the talent required for banking business was consistently inherited. It will suffice to speak of frequent transmission and imitation in the family circle; for there are many in this prolific family who turned to completely different, albeit always commercial occupations, and some who distinguished themselves as men of learning.

But even without concerning ourselves with biological problems of heredity, we may assume that the family lived for more than two centuries in a certain bourgeois affluence, and, according to Jewish custom, maintained their attachment to the religious life of their people. We can now go briefly into this ancestral chain, which included two rabbis in the seventeenth century. The first authenticated ancestor, whose name was Simon von Cassel after his original place of residence, sealed a protection agreement* on 3 January 1559 with the city of Warburg for himself, his

* *Schutzvertrag.* Free cities or territorial princes and other noblemen issued letters of protection for a regular fee to the Jews living within their domains. The letter of protection *(Schutzbrief)* or protection agreement *(Schutzvertrag)* included clauses

family and his domestic servants. He lived until about 1566, and his occupation was listed as money changing and making loans on pledges of goods and grain. His grandson, Jacob Simon Warburg, resident in Warburg from 1596 and similarly employed as a money changer, was for twenty years the head of the Jewish community in the Prince-Bishopric of Paderborn, and the synagogue was located in his house. He died in 1636. The transition to North Germany begins with his son, Juspa-Joseph Warburg. He remained at first in Warburg as a money changer, paid the highest protection tax* there in 1649, and was from 1651 the Elder of the community and tax collector of the Jews in Warburg. He moved in 1668 to Altona, while his two sons remained in Warburg, and he died around 1678. His son Jacob Samuel had preceded him to Altona, but had also previously established residence in Hamburg, where he married in 1647 and died in 1668. With Jacob's grandson, Samuel Moses Warburg, who married in Hamburg in 1722 and worked there as a money changer from 1725, we approach the generation which gave birth to the firm. Samuel's son, Gumprich Marcus Warburg, born in 1727, initially conducted a money-changing and pawn broking business in Altona, but then moved around 1759 to Hamburg after marrying the daughter of the Hamburg banker Marcus Ruben Heckscher. He lived until 1801, but transferred his enterprise, now called M. M. Warburg & Co., to his sons Moses Marcus and Gerson Warburg in 1797 or 1798.

It may seem curious that in the foregoing survey Hamburg and Altona are on numerous occasions mentioned as places of residence. This arises from the fact that while Hamburg was the larger market from the economic point of view, the legal position of the Jews under the Counts von Schaumburg and later under the Kings of Denmark offered wider privileges earlier than in Hamburg. These privileges also permitted trade in Holstein and, above all, did not restrict the religious life of the Jews and the formation of a Jewish community and its institutions. Thus a rabbinical court was established in Altona; and, under Altona's leadership, Hamburg, Altona and Wandsbek were joined in 1671 to make up the

concerning commercial privileges, religious rights, freedom of movement and taxation, and had regularly to be renewed. Jews living under such a regime were known as 'protected Jews' *(Schutzjuden)* and were a feature of German Jewry until full emancipation was granted to the Jews early in the nineteenth century.

* *Schutzgeld*, the protection tax payable by Jews as a condition of their residence within a jurisdiction.

largest Jewish community in Germany.* Within the so-called *Dreigemeinde* there was a certain freedom of movement, which also extended to burials, since the cemeteries in Danish territory were assured to the community in perpetuity.

In 1811, 6,300 North German and 130 Portuguese Jews lived in Hamburg, out of a total population of 107,000 inhabitants.† This group of Portuguese Jews, although numerically small, was of considerable economic importance for Hamburg. They had been settled in Hamburg since the beginning of the seventeenth century and benefited from the special protection of the Senate, based on an agreement that had been concluded in 1612 and constantly renewed. Their trade with the Iberian peninsula and connections with Holland contributed significantly to the volume of Hamburg's trade in goods and money.‡ At the same time, this colony of the 'Portuguese' had the right since 1617 of admission to the limited number of brokers. In contrast, the German Jews were granted this right only in 1784, because the Portuguese Jews were concerned with the maintenance of their privileged position. In 1740 there were 180 Christian and twenty Portuguese-Jewish brokers, and after 1792 the number of brokers was regulated by the authorities.§ When in 1784 the number of Portuguese brokers had declined to ten, the *Commercium*, later the Chamber of Commerce, proposed a motion 'to fill out the number with North German Jews, in case there should be a lack of qualified candidates among the Portuguese nation'. The Council found the reasons for the motion 'quite compelling', but did not want to reduce the right of the Portuguese to twenty positions, and proposed 'to accept in addition yet another fifteen North German Jews as brokers, in due course, depending on the circumstances'. The *Commercium* also pointed out in its reply that the objection that business would thereby be taken away from Christian brokers could be dismissed by reference to the well-founded truth 'that in an independent and trading state the merchant looks neither to privileges

* H. Krohn, *Die Juden in Hamburg 1800–1850* (Frankfurt a.M., 1967), pp. 9 ff.

† Ibid., p. 9 and p. 88.

‡ For a fundamental treatment of these questions: H. Kellenbenz, *Sephardim an der unteren Elbe*, pp. 33, 265 ff., 291 ff., 316 ff.

§ G. Klein, *400 Jahre Hamburger Börse* (Hamburg, 1958), p. 8. According to the broker ordinance of 1697, those persons were to be given preference who 'had lost their property through some misfortune and without fault', who were settled in Hamburg for a long time and who had conducted themselves 'honestly and without reproach'.

nor to religion, but to his advantage; where he finds such, he pursues it.'* This rational, cool observation confirms the view that the merchant class had no use for economic restrictions against the Jews, in contrast to retail trade and handicrafts, which asserted the claim of protecting their livelihood so as to exclude Jewish competition.†

Legal restrictions on residence rights and property were hardly enforced any longer against the Jews in the eighteenth century. Here too the 'Portuguese' had already paved the way. The acquisition of property was expressly forbidden to them in the renewal of their agreement in 1617; but this prohibition was circumvented, in cases where a variance could not be obtained from the Senate, by the assistance of Christian trustees, mostly merchants who had business dealings with the Portuguese.‡ In the same way the German Jews also acquired property in the quarter of the new town that had been assigned to them. It is correct to emphasize that this demarcation of living areas did not constitute a ghetto: it was, as Haarbleicher stated, more a matter of custom than of legal compulsion. Even without such regulations, Jews almost always preferred to maintain their communal life in particular areas in order to live – because of the prohibition against Sabbath and holy day travel – in close proximity to their synagogue, as well as in the vicinity of kosher provision shops. With increasing emancipation, these motives certainly changed; but the Warburg firm moved outside the district only after 1853, and its partners moved their private residences only after 1863.

For the first decades of the firm, tangible evidence of its business activities is very sparse. It can be concluded, however, on the basis of some data, that the business was cautiously conducted, and that the firm enjoyed a certain respect. Connections with the Rothschild houses in London, Paris and Frankfurt on Main existed quite early. A folder with letters from Mayer Amschel Rothschild, which Dr. Fritz Warburg mentioned in his notes in 1950, was not to be found in the Hamburg archives of the firm. But early Rothschild connections are probable on other grounds as well, since Mayer Amschel Rothschild was often in Hamburg

* See M. M. Haarbleicher, *Zwei Epochen aus der Geschichte der Deutsch-Israelitischen Gemeinde in Hamburg* (Hamburg, 1867), pp. 31 ff. Compare also the very positive evaluation of the Jewish bill brokers, who had made themselves increasingly indispensable with the increase of trade bill business, in J. G. Büsch, *Versuch einer Geschichte der Hamburgischen Handlung* (Hamburg, 1797), p. 81.

† H. Krohn, loc. cit., p. 10.

‡ H. Kellenbenz, *Sephardim*, loc. cit., p. 37 and p. 273.

as the court agent of the Prince-Elector Wilhelm I of Hesse, especially in 1807 and 1808. 'In order to be in the proximity of the Prince-Elector, he established in the summer of 1807 an exchange office, i.e. a kind of branch establishment, in Hamburg, and from here he frequently visited the Prince-Elector in Itzehoe.'*

In a letter of 4 August 1815 to Rothschild in London, the Hamburg firm refers to an earlier letter of 28 July, discusses a bill of exchange, and offers a certain amount of gold or louis d'or for speedy delivery. The letter closes with an assurance to Rothschild that the firm is capable of handling similar transactions quite as well as any other firm on the Hamburg stock exchange.

There is no doubt that other Hamburg banking firms also, above all Salomon Heine, were in close contact with the Rothschild houses, and that this was understandably a much sought-after connection. In a letter of 17 March 1815 addressed to N. M. Rothschild, London, there is a postscript by James M. Rothschild (1792–1868) of Paris to his brother in London in which he states that at the moment there is not much business in Hamburg, that envy rules among the bankers, and that none likes to see that one also works with others: Hamburg is, he continues, a 'dandified "Grevinkel"' (which is apparently a somewhat arbitrary rendering of *Krähwinkel*).†

All the evidence indicates that the links with the Rothschild houses in Frankfurt, London and Paris were strengthened quite early on by personal connections. Thus, to anticipate matters we shall deal with later, there is a letter from Meier Carl Rothschild of Frankfurt dated 15 December 1838, in which he commissions Elias Warburg, partner of the firm until 1837,

* Ch. W. Berghoeffer, *Meyer Amschel Rothschild, der Gründer des Rothschildschen Bankhauses* (Frankfurt a.M., 1922), p. 80; also p. 179, note 121.

† The letter, of which only a photocopy of the original exists, is written by a firm in Hamburg which James Rothschild of the Paris house had visited. He covered the major part of the letter with his signature, so that the name of the firm which sent it cannot be ascertained. A comparison of the writing with letters of the same vintage to Rothschilds in London from M. M. Warburg & Co. and the Altona banking firm Warburg & Leidersdorf permits no sure conclusion: the Rothschilds worked with both firms, and we know that S. M. Warburg of the firm Warburg & Leidersdorf was in London at the end of June 1815, and that he personally delivered to Nathan Rothschild a packet of bills of exchange. The derisive characterization 'Krähwinkel' was an eighteenth-century term for 'small town narrow-mindedness' (Grimm) and was popularized by Kotzebue's *Deutsche Kleinstädter* (1803), which takes place in 'Krähwinkel'.

with the task of purchasing a silver salver Rothschild had seen on his visit to Hamburg. And in 1845 Willy S. Rothschild from Frankfurt lived with the Warburgs in Marktstrasse, since he could not have obtained kosher food in any of the Hamburg hotels. In his discussion on the crisis of 1825, Bertrand Gille writes about the firms that worked with the Rothschilds in Paris: 'il ne s'agit que de maisons de tout premier ordre.' There was an unpleasant surprise only with one French firm: 'les maisons allemandes (Beyfus à Francfort, Heine et Warburg de Hambourg) tiennent le haut du pavé.'*

If we try now to go back and describe more fully the experience of the firm in its first decades, it seems particularly appropriate for the history of a banking house in which the element of personal confidence was a factor of prime business significance, to say a few words about the partners themselves. We are thus required to investigate what has been preserved in the tradition of the descendants and in individual memoirs and other accounts.†

In 1950 a great-grandson writes the following about Moses Marcus Warburg (1763–1831) and Gerson M. Warburg (died 1825): 'In his will Gumprich Marcus Samuel Warburg earnestly exhorted his two sons to maintain brotherly peace, solidarity and cooperation. Moses Marcus and Gerson did in fact remain together until the death of Gerson Warburg (1825), although they had very different views and very often clashed energetically. Moses Marcus Warburg was according to tradition a very quiet and peaceable person and a very religious man, while Gerson Warburg was a rather cheerful bachelor.'‡ Another great-grandson wrote in a biography compiled in 1914 of his father Siegmund Warburg (1835–89): 'There is a half-length portrait of Moses M. Warburg, the study of which is rewarding. The features are strongly pensive, but absolutely down to earth, the gestures suggest the decisive man of action. At that time Hamburg was, as far as business was concerned, an army camp.' The brother Gerson is not mentioned at all in this account, but

* B. Gille, *Histoire de la Maison Rothschild*, Vol. 1: *Des origines à 1848* (Geneva, Droz, 1965), p. 164. We thank Prof. Gille for the kind information that there are 103 folders of correspondence with M. M. Warburg & Co. in Hamburg for the period 1838–1914 in the files of the Paris house. These files had to be removed because of the reconstruction of the Paris banking house (1967) and were stored without access in the archives of the Bibliothèque historique de la Ville de Paris.

† A discussion of these sources will be found on pages 175–8.

‡ Memoirs of Fritz M. Warburg.

we shall hear more of him in another connection. He also says: 'The fortune of Moses Marcus W. was supposed to have amounted to 250,000 Mark Banco, a quite extraordinary sum for those times.'* We lack evidence to document this supposition; the amount, perhaps equivalent to about 125,000 Prussian Taler, corresponds approximately to the figures mentioned in connection with the foundation of other private banks at that time.† The size of this fortune was not however maintained in the succeeding two generations, and only after about 1865 did a larger capital fund begin to grow. We shall discuss the business situation at a later point.

A comprehensive and balanced evaluation of the firm's founder was written 100 years after his death by the Altona Rabbi Dukasz, who also translated the inscriptions on the family's gravestones in Altona. He reports of Moses M. Warburg that he took an active part in Jewish community life, but that he had to decline for health reasons an offer of the Presidency of the community. He was an enthusiastic proponent of Jewish sacred writings, and in many works of this kind he not only underwrote the costs but also assumed the responsibility of co-publisher. On his tombstone, which confirms his generosity towards the poor and orphans, it says: 'He respected those who busied themselves with holy learning, and allowed them to share in the blessings that had been granted to him. In his leadership of the study house, he exerted a fruitful influence, and his example inspired many to foster and maintain the academy.'‡

If we wish to reconstruct a picture of his fortune – of the 'blessing

* Diaries of Aby S. Warburg.

† Thus C. O. Heuser writes: 'C. G. Jaeger's nephew Christian Gottfried Trinkaus inherited his fortune of almost 150,000 Prussian Taler, a considerable sum for the conditions of those times.' *175 Jahre C. G. Trinkaus*, p. 18.

See R. Tilly, loc. cit., pp. 50 ff., on the fortunes of private banking firms. For Wichelhaus, Elberfeld, 1801, he cites a capital of 53,000 Taler; for Herstatt in Cologne around 1796 more than 100,000 Taler; for Schaffhausen around 1810 more than 140,000 Taler; for Sal. Oppenheim jun., & Co., Cologne, around 1810 a capital of 250,000 Taler, with which, of course, navigation and a still rather important trade in goods were financed; only after 1830 did they call themselves bankers. The combined fortune of Meyer Amschel Rothschild and his two older sons was calculated at 800,000 Gulden, about 900,000 Mark Banco, for the year 1810.

Berghoeffer, loc. cit., pp. 32 and 172 ff.

‡ See documents in the firm's archive. One might recall here Kellenbenz's words from his depiction of the Marranos: 'Out of all this there speaks the expansive baroque sense of the world and that multifaceted life that could be found within the realm of trade, and, from the very beginning, in the field of talmudic learning.' Kellenbenz, loc. cit., p. 35.

which had been granted to him' – then the tax rolls of the Jewish community offer a certain point of reference. On the basis of the Senate decision of 5 July 1815 that established the tax rates for the community, a member could claim relief if his yearly contribution amounted to more than $\frac{1}{4}$ per cent of his assets or 3 per cent of his income. As Haarbleicher remarks on this point, the tax rate thus established was to be considered a maximum, but should not be applied to every taxpayer, since the needs of the community did not require such high taxes. Thus the maximum was reduced in 1855 to 2 per cent of income.*

Since the assessments in each case make only an approximate calculation possible, it should suffice to give the taxes for only a few years:

	Moses Marcus Warburg	*Gerson M. Warburg*
1814–15	300 Mark Banco	200 Mark Banco
1816–17	250 Mark Banco	166.8 Mark Banco
1818–19	280 Mark Banco	186.12 Mark Banco
1820–26	—	300 Mark Banco (died 1826)
1820–31	400 Mark Banco (widow of M.M.W.)	

If we take the figures of the last decade for Moses M. Warburg, the result – assuming that the tax liability was not assessed in full – would be a fortune that was greater than 160,000 Mark Banco, and a yearly income of at least 13,300 Mark Banco, amounts which probably come very close to the real state of affairs.†

With these figures, which reflect a certain comfortable standard of living, the Warburg brothers belonged to a broad middle class, but were not amongst the highest taxed members of the community. For the year 1815–16, for example, the taxes of W. E. von Halle amounted to 2,000 Mark Banco, of Salomon Heine 2,500 Mark Banco, David Moses Hertz 1,000 Mark Banco, Elias Ruben 1,000 Mark Banco, Lazarus Gumpel 1,100 Mark Banco, and Jacob Oppenheimer 1,250 Mark Banco. Correspondingly, no Warburg appears on the lists of the (forty) richest taxpayers of Hamburg, which were drawn up in 1813 for the forced war subsidy raised by the French.‡

* M. M. Haarbleicher, loc. cit., pp. 222 ff.

† The excerpts from the tax rolls of the community and further materials were placed at our disposal by Dr. Helga Krohn, Assistant of the Hamburg Institut für die Geschichte der deutschen Juden.

‡ *Mitteilungen des Vereins für Hamburgische Geschichte*, Vol. 12 (Hamburg, 1917), pp. 15 ff. This valuable information, which we acknowledge with gratitude, also comes from Dr. Helga Krohn.

It was perhaps the disturbed conditions of this temporary foreign occupation that led the dissimilar brothers, after a twelve-year partnership, to conclude a formal corporate agreement for the first time in the firm's history. The agreement was drawn up in Hebrew (see facsimile, facing page 98), signed before the duly qualified officers of the Jewish community and certified by these officers. The date is the 20th Sivan of the year 5570 after the creation of the world, or Friday, 22 June 1810.

Two technical terms might be explained here. '*Kinjan*' is the act of acquisition, valid according to Jewish law, by means of which the transfer of property takes place. The '*ketuba*' (literally, that which is written) is the marriage contract, in which the dowry of the wife must be cited. The wife has a claim only upon this dowry, likewise called '*ketuba*', upon the death of her husband, and not to his whole fortune; along with an additional '*ketuba*' according to her then circumstances. This supplement amounted in those years to 33⅓ per cent of the original dowry in Altona, and 50 per cent in the Hamburg community.* However, it appears from the text of the agreement that the father Gumprich Warburg could not leave the full amount of such a supplement, which is yet another confirmation of the fact that only the sons succeeded in forming a larger fortune.

The following version of the text of the contract is based on the translation made in Jerusalem in 1967:

Before the officers of the Jewish community in Hamburg duly appeared the brothers Moses and Gerson Warburg, in order to conclude a partnership agreement before witnesses and according to the requirements of the law; this agreement shall have absolute validity between them and for their heirs, and shall be irrevocable.

In accordance with the last will and testament of our father Gumprich Warburg, his fortune was left to his wife, our mother, Frau Mehla, as a substitute, albeit insufficient, for her dowry, with the stipulation that she be relieved from furnishing any bond or other security and that no oath shall be required of her. Our father instructed her to leave the legacy to us, Moses and Gerson, in due course, so that we might carry on trade and, as he did, provide sustenance for the members of the house, likewise without furnishing any bond. Thus our mother Mehla gave us all her property as an irrevocable gift,

* M. M. Haarbleicher, loc. cit., pp. 45 ff. Cf. the tale of the forgotten *ketuba* in A. Feilchenfeld (ed.), *Denkwürdigkeiten der Glückel von Hameln* (4th ed., Berlin, 1923), pp. 119 ff.

forswearing any other claims of inheritance, since this fortune is less than her dowry with the supplement therefor provided.

AND THUS WE have joined together in full partnership, and in this wise, that all expenditures for sustenance and livelihood are to be defrayed from the common earnings, even if one partner should consume more than the other. And so long as our partnership shall exist, the remaining profit shall be equally divided only after deduction of the aforementioned expenditures. Moreover, we brothers wish to take one another at his word, and demand no form of oath one from the other.

AND SINCE WE are but men and the day on which we shall be called unto God is hidden from mortals, so, if one of us shall die, no rabbinical court, no community and no executor shall intervene to investigate and disturb the normal course of business, but the surviving brother shall be the sole heir, and the learned Herr Seckel Kranich, who was in his day the confidant of our father, shall be the executor of the estate, and arbitrator of all claims. No one may raise objections against him, or demand inspection of the books, or an accounting of the funds or of inventory. He shall be authorized in his sole discretion to make distributions with the simple formula; "This money shall pass to this heir," and he, too, need not swear any kind of oath.

MOSES WARBURG makes provision for the case that Gerson shall survive him concerning pecuniary arrangements for his wife and daughter, and names his brother Gerson as guardian of his children.

THE SIGNATURE of the brothers is certified by two duly authorized officers of the community.*

With this partnership agreement the quite dissimilar brothers ran the firm jointly for fifteen years, until the death of the younger, Gerson, in 1825. Some years after the signing of the agreement, however, the bond between the brothers was put to a certain test, which is reported in family tradition, not without a certain irony at the family's expense.

At the 'time of the French', Hamburg was not only occupied territory under martial law, but was incorporated into the French state as the 'Département des Bouches de l'Elbe' by a decree of 10 December 1810.

* The exclusion of the regular courts provided for in the agreement was not uncommon. Such an exclusion can be found, for example, in particularly strong wording in the first partnership agreement that Meyer Amschel Rothschild concluded with his sons Salomon and Carl on 27 September 1810. C. Berghoeffer, loc. cit., pp. 219 ff.; the same can be found in the first corporate agreement of the firm J. H. Stein, Cologne, of 1820, on which Eckert reports in the jubilee volume of 1940. Ch. Eckert, *J. H. Stein: Werden und Wachsen eines Kölner Bankhauses in 150 Jahren* (1940), p. 43. Notwithstanding the kind assistance of experts on Hamburg, no information on the executor, the 'learned' Seckel Kranich, has been found.

For the French régime, even if it should consider itself short-lived, the constitutional advantage of this arrangement was that financial exactions were no longer requisitions under martial law, but were, at least in form, taxes duly levied on citizens, for the collection of which methods were used, of the sort familiar to us today, that envisaged the cooperation of those liable. Thus the Chamber of Commerce, before and afterwards called the 'Commerce Deputation' (*Commerzdeputation*), was compelled in July 1813 after the 'reconquest' of Hamburg, which lasted until May 1814, to address letters to the individual firms of the city, informing them how many francs each was required to contribute to the 'forced loan in aid of the extraordinary contribution' to the French of 6 million francs. A '*nota bene*' in the margin of each letter said: 'In case the above demand is not complied with by the appointed deadline, compliance will be compelled by all possible means, and even by martial law: your real and personal property will be sequestered as security for payment of assessed amounts, without prejudice to further personal penalties.' It is clear that this was not precisely the language of the Commerce Deputation. It appears that M. M. Warburg & Co. refused initially to pay the amount, the size of which we do not know, assessed against the firm, at which point the unmarried younger partner, Gerson Warburg, was arrested by the French and brought to Hamburg or Rothenburg, where, according to his own later testimony, he was well enough treated. Family tradition has it that Moses M. Warburg at first refused to ransom his brother, and only after representations from rabbinical authorities declared his willingness to pay an amount, admittedly smaller than had originally been demanded. This is probably a true enough version. We may assume that this form of distraint was not unwelcome to the older brother, since he could use it to bolster his objections to the size of the assessment.* It might also be mentioned that the citizenry of Hamburg nominated seven commissioners to determine and administer the forced contribution; Jacob Oppenheimer, at that time a partner of Salomon Heine in the firm Heckscher and Co., was one of the commissioners.

It is impossible to ascertain how the Warburg firm developed in the years between 1806 and 1814 because no business papers of any kind for

* See facsimile of the Chamber of Commerce letter in '*Dokumente zur Geschichte der Handelskammer*', loc. cit., p. 76. Compare also *Mémoire de M. Le Maréchal Davout Prince d'Eckmühl Au Roi* (Paris, 1814), p. 7. See also a later defence of the Marshal in *Davout in Hamburg. Ein Beitrag zur Geschichte der Jahre 1813–1814. Von einem Freunde historischer Wahrheit* (Mülheim, 1892), pp. 65, 67 and 72.

that period survived. There is however no evidence in the later diaries and memoirs kept by the Warburgs that would suggest any particular difficulties in those business years. From the account of C. Mönckeberg* we may conclude that in the autumn and winter of 1813, when Hamburg was refortified by the order of Napoleon, it was particularly the 'poor' who suffered by reason of the forced expulsion of all those who could not provide for their own livelihood and were required to live for extended periods on thin food rations. Haarbleicher describes in detail, and with a completeness that illuminates the tension between rich and poor in an era that knew nothing of 'social welfare' in our sense, the reception of the expellees in Altona and arrangements for public relief of Protestants and Catholics: '... Trade came to a complete standstill, and the poor suffered and starved even more than usual, for even the last wretched expedient of recent years, smuggling, was no longer available.' †

Despite all this, as Mönckeberg himself testifies, the homeless of both religions were taken care of, since expectations of aid were not directed toward the state but toward the religious communities, which were thoroughly conscious of their obligations. Providing for the Jewish poor and unemployed was an important task of the community, which was transferred to the state of Hamburg only in a law of 7 November 1864. Coinciding with this law, the previously existing requirement for Jews to be inscribed and to remain in either the German-Jewish or the Portuguese-Jewish communities was lifted. Until that time the communities had considered caring for the indigent not merely a duty but also a privilege, had established an orderly financial structure for this purpose and were assisted in this task by many endowments and gifts from the well-to-do. With the expropriation of the capital of the Bank of Hamburg, the community suffered an additional loss of 9,818 Mark Banco, held in S. H. Oppenheimer's account on its behalf.

It would be risky to attempt with the meagre figures available to us calculating the total income of Jewish business circles. However, the yield from community taxes, which amounted in 1816 for example to

* C. Mönckeberg, *Hamburg unter dem Druck der Franzosen, 1806–1814* (Hamburg, 1864).

† M. M. Haarbleicher, loc. cit., pp. 106 ff. Haarbleicher himself was secretary of the aid commission, to which two members of the Altona branch of the Warburg family also belonged. Cf. also Helga Krohn, *Die Juden in Hamburg 1800–1850*, loc. cit. pp. 17 ff., which cites the cooperation of Jews and Christians in providing for the refugees.

66,358 M. Courant, collected from 535 paying members of the community; and similar statistics for the years up to 1848, allow us to conclude that the wealth of the Jewish community members, whose economic activities were still limited by existing legislation almost entirely to commercial occupations, exceeded the average income of the rest of the population. Moreover, currency trading, especially in the time of the French, had a particularly important position among trade and commercial occupations. For while trade in goods declined sharply between 1806 and 1814 due to the Continental embargo and the English counter-blockade, the traffic in capital, which is so much more difficult to block, was able to escape the attempted controls almost completely.* This phenomenon has also been confirmed by recent research. Carl Mönckeberg reports that there was considerable liquidity in 1811 so that sizeable sums could be had at low interest rates. Adolph Wohlwill confirms as early as 1805 that despite considerable losses in the trade in goods, 'Hamburg's importance as the centre of the European money and bill markets was not affected.'† Adolph Soetbeer, writing in 1855 on the disruption of trade between 1806 and 1818, mentioned that it had occurred 'without any liquidity shortage throughout this period, or any need of special precautionary measures'.‡

The assumption that M. M. Warburg & Co. was able to proceed with business as usual is confirmed by the fact that the firm, together with Warburg & Leidersdorff and R. D. Warburg & Co., was among the first after the reopening of the Bank of Hamburg on 4 June 1814 to deposit silver coins in bags, such as piasters and Albertstaler, for the Bank's silver account. The same transaction demonstrates that the firm was only of medium size: of the total 1,311 fine silver bars deposited by 122 depositors, with a value of 4,283,182 Mark Banco, half the bars belonged to three firms: M. R. Beit, H. A. Jonas and S. Jacob Wwe. The major portion of the 455 bars worth 1,516,615 Mark Banco that had been deposited in July belonged to them. At the end of 1814 the Bank's capital amounted once again to about 8½ million Mark Banco, which is more than the 7,506,956 Mark Banco that had been confiscated by the French on 4 November 1813.§

For the next three decades, we must content ourselves with referring to the few cases in which the name of the firm is mentioned for any

* C. Mönckeberg, loc. cit., p. 37.

† A. Wohlwill, *Hamburg im Todesjahr Schillers* (Hamburg, 1905), p. 38.

‡ A. Soetbeer, *Beiträge*, loc. cit., p. 65.

§ H. Sieveking, *Die Hamburger Bank*, loc. cit., p. 91 and pp. 93 ff.

reason – as in most monographs about individual firms. Of particular interest is a letter dated 16 April 1830 addressed to N. M. Rothschild, London, which announces the shipment of 100,000 louis d'or in ten chests from 'your Baron von Rothschild in Berlin'. One sentence should be quoted in its entirety, since it considers the relative costs of shipment by sailing vessel and the newfangled steamboat:

'We could have cheaper freight costs with a schooner, but if one considers the possibility of bad weather and contrary winds, you could receive the gold 8 days later, which represents a considerable loss of interest on such a large sum; we have therefore decided not to take freight costs into consideration, and to ship it by steamer, especially since you called upon us to do so.'* The shipment also included £253.15 of Prussian and Danish coupons due for payment, £300 in sovereigns and £51 in notes for which Warburgs were to be credited. Moreover, the packet contained in addition five prime bills, with a total value of £1,048, on London firms with the request 'to have them accepted for the endorsers and to excuse the bother'. Some data about money market rates and the prime interest rate follow at the end.

Another bill of lading from the same era, dated 7 May 1830, refers to five chests containing dollars with a value of £7,500 from N. M. Rothschild to M. M. Warburg & Co. in Hamburg. The shipping costs amounted to £9 7s. 6d., 'being One Eighth p. Cent'. The shipping costs from Hamburg to London for the aforementioned shipment with a value of about £80,000 amounted to £40, 'which is very cheap', as the letter mentions rightly, since these shipping costs came to only one-twentieth per cent of the total value.

It cannot be ascertained to what extent the firm engaged in loan transactions throughout the early years up to and including 1862 in which it described itself in the Hamburg directory as merely 'money changer'. In relation to the many forced loans which Hamburg, like Prussia and Saxony, was compelled to raise at the beginning of the nineteenth century, the firm was primarily a passive taxpayer, to be sure 'like all distinguished tradesmen who trade wholesale and have the reputation and the credit of wealthy merchants'.† However, Hamburg was able to finance itself again from 1818 by voluntary loans, which with a 4 per cent coupon traded at

* The author possesses a photocopy of the original.

† 'For the forced loans of 1804 and 1806, recourse was had to class divisions as defined by the socially and historically informative per capita tax regulations of 1770, whose nine classes comprised an odd amalgam of the wealthy and those who considered

102, while the five per cent Saxon or Bavarian bonds only reached par or 99. All signs pointed to adequate liquidity, but in about 1819, under the influence of a crisis in London, Paris and Amsterdam, the volume of trade fell so sharply that money was offered at a rate of 2½ per cent, and as Soetbeer observes, one could conclude 'that a low interest rate is in and of itself no proof of a thriving state of trade'.* With the lack of bills of exchange, there was a danger, to which some succumbed, that liquid funds would be invested in goods in the hope of price increases; such investments often showed losses because of the uncertain market situation.† With the crisis of 1825, which mainly affected England, there were substantial silver transfers to England, and prime rates in Hamburg rose in November and December from 6 per cent to 10 per cent; the annual average remained nonetheless at only 4½ per cent, as compared with 3 per cent for 1826, 2 per cent for 1827 and only 1¾ per cent for 1828. For currency dealers there must have been sufficient business opportunities in these times as well.‡ In any event, the Warburg firm, as earlier confirmed by the Rothschild files, was throughout these crisis years spared from any perceptible dangers. Moreover, the general development of the economy, and the growth of German industry, in part stimulated by the Continental embargo, released energies that were conducive to the development of Hamburg's markets. The first stage in the establishment of the Prussian-German tariff union *(Zollverein)* came in this period (1819–44), and caused political uneasiness for the Free City, which rightly feared the Prussian encroachments that made stiff demands on the City Council concerning the age old art of navigation.

However the firm was in no way so important at this stage that it could have been endangered or advanced by the political tides of the time. In this era too the firm's name does not appear in the records of the State

a horse and carriage a luxury, to maids, nannies, lackies, and those rich, who notoriously do not live on alms.' See the dissertation by Egon Singer, *Die Entstehung der hamburgischen Staatsanleihen von 1801 bis 1857* (Hamburg, 1916), pp. 9 ff.

* A. Soetbeer, loc. cit., p. 66.

† Ibid., pp. 66 ff.

‡ A survey of twenty-two different computation units in the Taler currency area before the foundation of the Zollverein (1835) and the slow reorganization of currencies that came with it shows the opportunities that presented themselves to currency dealers in the first half of the nineteenth century; compare P. Martin, 'Rahmenordnung und Geldverfassung der Frühindustrialisierung' in H. Kellenbenz, *Öffentliche Finanzen und privates Kapital* (Stuttgart, 1971).

Archives on loans, and it is not among the 999 'contributors' who subscribed for the construction of the new Stock Exchange, inaugurated on 2 December 1841, with a voluntary loan.

It is therefore not external factors which we must consider here, but the internal circumstances of the firm itself. The somewhat precarious harmony between Moses and his brother Gerson was nonetheless maintained for a quarter-century, perhaps under the influence of the warnings in their father's will. Gerson died a bachelor in 1825, and his brother admitted his nephew Aby Samuel Warburg into the firm as his new partner and 'gave him in matrimony his daughter Sara, a very pretty girl of extraordinary piety, and much more energetic than her somewhat mild and later also sickly husband'.*

Abraham S., called Aby, Warburg was born on 30 April 1798; in 1828 he was sworn as a broker and in 1829 was accepted as a partner in the firm. The marriage with Sara took place on 11 February 1829 in Hamburg. According to family tradition, cousin Elias Warburg, a partner of the firm from 1831 until 1837, was also among Sara's suitors. Nevertheless, her mother decided on the other cousin with that determination over marriage arrangements which we know from the diaries of Glückel von Hameln. It would however be a mistake to consider this way of choosing a spouse peculiarly Jewish: it is widely known that marriages of ruling houses and so-called persons of rank were concluded on the basis of practical considerations that did not necessarily require the exclusion of personal preference. But in the more modest middle class as well there were often economic reasons arising from the requirements of the guild laws that brought apprentices and masters' daughters together. Even Hegel assures us in 1820 in his *Grundlinien der Philosophie des Rechts*,† it is objective fact that 'the arrangements of well-meaning parents constitute the beginning, and attraction arises in the persons who are chosen for the love union, from the fact of their recognition that they have been destined for this'. This procedure seems to Hegel more proper, in contrast to the 'subjective principle of the modern world', in accordance with which being in love is the only important consideration. It is not our task to weigh the motives of this alliance or of other marriages in the course of this account. But experience seems to teach us that such 'marriages of convenience', which were quite usual in the haute bourgeoisie and officer classes in the

* Memoirs of Fritz M. Warburg.

† G. W. F. Hegel, *Grundlinien der Philosophie des Rechts*, 1820, pp. 162 ff.

nineteenth century, were no more fragile than those which arose through that 'heat of passion' viewed by Hegel with distrust.*

Moses Marcus Warburg was able to manage the business jointly with his son-in-law for only a few years. He died on 14 November 1831 and left a substantial fortune, considering the type of enterprise that Warburgs was; as mentioned earlier, the estate was valued at 250,000 Mark Banco. Aby S. Warburg took over the firm and chose as partner his cousin Elias Warburg who, however, left as early as 1837 for reasons of which we have no record and founded his own firm, a business in currencies and bills of exchange that also enjoyed a good reputation. He appears among the middle-sized depositors of the Bank of Hamburg and was named administrator in 1857 of a firm that had got into difficulties. The second Aby S. Warburg (1864–1933)† writes of this period: 'Elias Warburg was an intelligent man with a Jewish study-room face, that is with more sensitivity than strength. In contrast, Aby Warburg, who took over as sole proprietor in 1837 must have been a notable personality. His rather conventionally painted portrait shows marked, dreamily thoughtful features with a consequently evident need for restful contemplation. His is a Southern, heavier type, more akin to Portuguese Jews than to the German, particularly North German Jews.' He had that talent for figures often encountered in the family, and even as a young man was praised by older colleagues when he solved difficult computations without apparent effort.

Based on this gift, Aby Warburg made arbitrage his speciality, and through that business was in touch with all the Rothschild houses. The business in bills of exchange was similarly expanded throughout Europe, and in the bank's still very simple books which we have from 1844, all the good names known from the history of private banking appear. We see in 1845 S. Bleichröder in Berlin; still-existing business links with the incomparably larger Salomon Heine, with whom there were also friendly personal relations; and throughout also Bischoffsheim & Goldschmidt in

* On the religious and family-political reasons for the frequent intrafamily marriages in the Rothschild house, see the informative comments of Lady Battersea (Constance de Rothschild, daughter of Sir Anthony, born 1847) in her *Reminiscences* (London, 1922), pp. 67 ff. For the second generation, Bertrand Gille, loc. cit., II, pp. 591, establishes that only four out of eighteen marriages had partners outside of the family. Heinrich Heine, in his Lutezia Letter of May 5, 1843, attributes the harmony of the family to the fact that they always married amongst themselves. H. Heine, *Werke* (Oskar Walzel, ed., Leipzig, 1910), Vol. 9, p. 516.

† See genealogy, pp. 172–3.

Antwerp, Paris and London.* The capital of the firm amounted to 180,000 Mark Banco at the end of 1844; net profit for 1845 was 23,000 Mark Banco, for 1846 only 4,800 Mark Banco, and in 1847 there was a loss of about 21,000 Mark Banco. Out of earnings of the succeeding years, the capital account was raised in December 1852 to 279,000 Mark Banco, but after three years of losses had declined by 31 December 1854 to 190,000. We do not know the precise reasons for this. We do find, however, that in 1848, when the firm had a capital of 186,480 Mark Banco, it had extended credit to one firm in the amount of 57,300 Mark Banco; moreover, in connection with the same firm a loss of 62,400 Mark Banco had to be written off in 1853 and 1854. And in 1850, with an initially modest credit of 16,000 Mark Banco, a certain firm known as M.B. makes its appearance, later to develop into a real skeleton in the cupboard, since its owner was practised, even without engaging in outright misrepresentation, in the art of always obtaining new assistance. M. M. Warburg & Co. finally found itself an unwilling partner, and a debit balance was built up that was only liquidated after two generations, with heavy losses. Such cases, which may also be found at other private banks, demonstrate in any event that banking business too is not conducted with the calculating hard-heartedness that theorists from Carlyle to Sombart consider defines the capitalist 'cash nexus'.

When Aby Warburg died on 8 July 1856 at the age of fifty-eight, the firm was in solid condition, with a capital of 227,000 Mark Banco at year-end 1856; although that figure represented no progress in the firm's development if we are correct to assume that the founder, Moses Marcus Warburg, left an estate of 250,000 Mark Banco at his death in 1831. The family too must have had the impression that the firm had experienced something of a setback. The grandson, Aby Warburg, writes that his grandfather's last years were shadowed not only by illness but also by grave worries. As far as business was concerned, these worries centred on the fact that he had been outflanked by L. Behrens & Söhne in Hamburg in relationships with the Rothschild banks. Another, and far more

* For summary information on this firm and others in the banking world, see as a thoroughly reliable reference: Paul H. Emden, *Money Powers of Europe in the Nineteenth and Twentieth Centuries* (London, 1937). A survey, similar in style, of Jewish bankers, their origins and family links, may be found in Frederick H. Brunner, 'Juden als Bankiers – ihre völkerverbindende Tätigkeit' in *In zwei Welten. Siegfried Moses zum fünfundsiebzigsten Geburtstag* (Tel Aviv, 1962), pp. 509–35. The author of this article was a partner of S. Bleichröder, Berlin.

oppressive preoccupation for the father was that his eldest daughter, who was very close to him, had been married in London on 18 August 1825 apparently to a swindler. There was a separation, and the daughter returned to Hamburg, but the divorce entailed heavy costs and only became final after the father's death, in May 1859. For all that, this private event would not belong in the history of a banking firm if it were not reflected in the balance sheet of 1858 in the name of the culprit, with a loss of 68,796 Mark Banco, which represented more than a quarter of the firm's capital at the time.

At the crucial point of July 1856, however, it became apparent that the widow Sara Warburg, born in 1805 and daughter of the firm's founder, was not only an exemplary mother to her children, but also, in accordance with the practical character of Jewish family life, had such insight into business matters that she was able to take over and manage the firm. On 23 July 1856 therefore a deed was drawn up in the presence of the commissioner for oaths J. D. H. Stockfleth and two civil witnesses, pursuant to which she as proprietor of the firm and 'with the counsel of Herr August Sanders, merchant, resident at Admiralitätstrasse 79 of this city, family guardian confirmed by higher authority on 10th July, declares: that she herewith appoints her son Herr Siegmund Warburg as holder of General Power of Attorney in her proposed firm, to conduct its business and represent her in all matters.'* There follows a conscientious listing of business transactions, from which we cite at least the beginning, since it gives a good survey of the activities of such a firm. He was thus authorized 'to buy and sell goods and government securities, to seal bills of exchange, to draw, accept, pay, call in and endorse as well as protest bills, to transfer registered government securities, to demand payment of trade debts, to receive monies or other securities, to acknowledge their receipt and to carry out all other transactions usual in the course of trade and among merchants, in case of need to conclude and enforce agreements with debtors, to appear before the courts, appoint attorneys and pursue claims to final judgment, to lodge appeals, to swear out oaths and to swear for his co-venturers . . .'†

The list continues with assignments, due dates and similar powers. For Siegmund Warburg, just twenty-one years old (born 4 April 1835), these were in any event sufficient tasks and duties. It is worthy of note

* Deed in archive of Aby S. Warburg.

† Ibid.

in this connection that he no longer required a guardian, since he had already been declared of age on 20 June 1856, due to his father's illness. In contrast, under the laws of that time, his mother, as a woman, required an administrator for running the business although she herself was empowered on 30 July 1856 to become guardian for her minor son Moritz (born 8 March 1838), jointly with Salomon Wolff and Sally von Halle as 'assistant guardians'. August Sanders was an old friend of the family, and his duties were made easier since the firm itself, after about two years at Neuer Wall 36, moved its offices to Admiralitätstrasse 59.* He lived for several years in the same house with the Warburgs, at second Markstrasse 22.† Aby S. Warburg wrote of his father Siegmund Warburg: 'Only his unusually early maturity could have made it possible for a twenty-year-old to assume such burdens, which he was able to handle not merely by reason of his keen business acumen, but also his firm strength of will.... He had inherited from his father that extraordinary mathematical gift which enabled him to plunge immediately into arbitrage, at that time the foundation of regular currency and bill business.'‡ Had it not been for the death of his father, Siegmund Warburg would have wished and sought an education that went far beyond the scope of his father's teachings. He was thus able, only from June 1853, to spend about a year with a smaller London firm, and apparently went back to London in July and August 1855.§

A number of letters from this year have been preserved, from which we see to what extent Aby Warburg already included his son in all

* August Sanders was from 10 December 1848 to 10 June 1855 one of the elders of the German–Jewish community; see M. M. Haarbleicher, op. cit., p. 177. On his business and community activities, see H. Böhme, 'Wirtschaftskrise, Merchant Bankers und Verfassungsreform' in *Zeitschrift des Vereins für Hamburgische Geschichte*, Vol. 54, 1968, p. 96. See also, H. Krohn, *Die Juden in Hamburg* (Hamburg, 1974), pp. 28, 90, 93.

† One year after the transfer of the business, on 30 June 1857, a notice appeared in No. 179 of the *Hamburgischer Unpartheiischen Correspondent* containing a proclamation of the District Court of 2 July 1857 in which all those having claims against the estate of Abraham Samuel Warburg were requested to file them 'by 20 November 1857, as sole and final filing date, in this Court; and to justify claims upon demand, on pain of exclusion and forfeiture without further recourse'.

‡ Memoirs of Aby S. Warburg.

§ Among the family papers is a certificate of the Bewaffnungs-Commission (Military Board) of 23 May 1853 authorizing the sojourn abroad until further notice of the young man liable to conscription.

business matters. The son also was active in the attempt to resolve satisfactorily the unfortunate affair of his sister (five years older than himself), who was again living in Hamburg with her parents. Since apparently the planned judicial proceeding proved too difficult, he was unable to prevent the final costs of this matter from far exceeding the loss of his sister's dowry. In one letter, there is a postscript from Siegmund's younger brother Moritz, which is reproduced here because it is not atypical of Moritz's temperament: 'You appear to have made some very nice connections there [London] which pleases me a lot, because I am a great enthusiast for commission business, even if the brokerage is only $\frac{1}{8}$%, because I reckon that this is always the *most solid* sort of business.' And then he excuses himself as the junior for offering advice to his brother. The father, on the other hand, writes more seriously on 1 August 1855: 'If you have the honour of seeing R. [Rothschild], you may tell him that we very much regret having to dispense entirely with his orders.'*

Thus when Siegmund Warburg in July 1856 took over management of the firm jointly with his mother, he faced an uphill task: the bank's capital had shrunk, the credit standing of the firm had correspondingly suffered and relationships with the Rothschild banks had been undermined. Moreover, only one year later the firm, along with many others, found itself caught up in the dangers of the world financial crisis of 1857.

* Letters from the papers of Aby S. Warburg.

3

THE CRISIS OF 1857 AND THE FIRST YEARS OF THE THIRD GENERATION

In his memoirs, which give an excellent picture of Senatorial Hamburg around 1870, Julius von Eckardt writes that three themes bound up with memorable events repeatedly came up in the course of conversations in society. Elderly ladies spoke of the French occupation and the 'vexations they and their parents had to endure from "Eckmühl" and company'. Somewhat younger people spoke of the 'ominous Ascension Day of '42' on which the great Hamburg fire began. 'A further theme, that never failed, was the "great crisis" of 1857, especially since it afforded opportunities to compare Austrian and Prussian loyalties as allies, in which the latter definitely suffered by the comparison.'*

This crisis (or panic as it would be described in English), which hit the entire Hamburg market, would not belong in the history of an individual firm of medium size were it not in a quite special way bound up with its fate and indeed its very existence, as will be described in due course. As is the case with most such disturbances in the economy, the crisis had more than one cause. Aby Warburg mentions especially the business boom that followed the conclusion of the peace treaty of Paris in April 1856, which ended the Crimean War, a boom that very rapidly led to speculation in commodities and a dangerous expansion of credit facilities. With the

* J. von Eckardt, *Lebenserinnerungen* (Leipzig, 1910), Vol. 1, p. 195. On pp. 202 ff. there is a valuable observation also on the position of the Jews in public affairs. 'Many of my dearest and most loyal friends came from among the Hamburg Jews, baptized and unbaptized, and I found in their circles, despite multiple differences of opinion on political and religious matters, an understanding for moral and intellectual idealism that is only rarely met with elsewhere. It was clear to me and other observers that the Hamburg Jews made a very important contribution to the integration of Hamburg into the conditions and arrangements of the new Germany.'

benefit of hindsight we, unlike those of the time who took the opposite view, can see that the crisis was feared long before the autumn of 1857, at least in England and Austria, where it gave rise to anticyclical measures. The English discount rate for three-month bills rose between October 1855 and May 1856 to 7 per cent, fell during the summer to $4\frac{1}{2}$ per cent and was again raised to 7 per cent at the beginning of October 1856. The Rothschild banks in Paris and London reduced their outstanding credits, particularly to Austria, where in 1857 there was a one-year moratorium on the formation of new companies.* But the decisive shock 'could come even then, in 1857, from America, the giant empire of raw materials', as Aby Warburg justly observes. On 25 August 1857 the Ohio Life and Trust Company suspended payments. But this was just the initial explosion of the ample fuel for a crisis that had accumulated in all countries and was sufficient in itself to set off a panic.† By 17 October, 150 United States banks had suspended payments, and in that connection there was an extraordinarily steep drop in railroad shares, almost half of which were at that time in English hands. The effects were felt in England by the end of September; one-fifth of all England's exports went to the United States. The complex structure of trade and finance bills depended partly on funds that the discount houses had borrowed short-term from banks, which in their turn called these loans. The first bankruptcies of cotton firms, discount houses and banks began in October; Bank Rate was raised to 9 per cent on 5 November 1857; on 11 November the Bank Act of 1844 was suspended, an increased note issue was thereby permitted, and the discount rate was set at 10 per cent. Guarantees in the amount of £2 million were given to the issue department and a corresponding sum

* See B. Gille, op. cit., Vol. 2, pp. 202 ff., 237. In France, an official announcement was published on 9 March 1856 in the *Moniteur* stating that the Government would not grant permission for new projects that 'would lead to the issue of new securities'. Cf. Hans Rosenberg, *Die Weltwirtschaftskrise von 1857–1859* (Stuttgart, 1934), pp. 106 ff., Vol. 30 of VSWG. This monograph gives in Marxist terms a very good survey of the world ramifications of the crisis. See also L. Muret de Bort, *Crise monétaire* (Paris, 1856). This work, which appeared in January 1856, calls on the Banque de France to curtail credit, and points to the dangers of speculation on the stock exchange.

† Cf. J. Schumpeter's precise formulation in *Business Cycles* (New York and London, 1939), Vol. 1, p. 331: 'To begin with, the crisis was an international one, commercial and financial relations between our countries (and others) being strong enough to synchronize events remarkably and to play a large role in shaping the surface. But it is nonetheless a fact that fundamental explanation could run for each country in terms of its own development.'

in notes was placed at the disposal of the Banking Department. These measures overcame the acute crisis so successfully that it was possible for the discount rate to be lowered on 7 January 1858 to 6 per cent and on 11 February to 3 per cent. This rate remained unchanged until December 1858, but the entire year was affected by the repercussions of German and Scandinavian bankruptcies.*

Hamburg's situation in the subsequent period is described with special clarity in Adolph Wagner's early classic *Die Geld- und Credittheorie der Peel'schen Bankacte* (Vienna, 1862). The position of Hamburg as intermediary in North European trade and money markets is so exhaustively described that the key sentences are here reproduced, since they are as authoritative now as they were when written: 'Generally speaking, it [Hamburg] has to pay its multiple debts to England and the rest of Europe with the proceeds from its claims against Germany, Northeast Europe and countries overseas. Moreover, its creditors are principally the wealthy and important traders, the British, while its debtors are for the most part inhabitants of Northeast European and many transatlantic states, notably from South and Western America, who are poor, credit-starved, geographically remote, and from every point of view less able to offer security and guarantees than others. The Hamburg market is thus the crossroads for debtor-creditor relationships of quite varied kind and quality.'†

In this last sentence we see the core of the problem. By 1857 Hamburg had accepted and discounted an excessive number of bills that were to a considerable extent based not on trade in merchandise, but were purely finance bills issued to maintain inventories against falling prices. Rumours spread that these obligations amounted to 1,200 million Mark Banco for Hamburg banks and merchants. Much later it transpired that the total had in fact only been 340 million Mark Banco. But in times of panic rumours sweep away all attempts to ascertain the real facts and use them as a basis for decisions.

Emergency measures, the effectiveness of which was limited by the fact that the Hamburger Bank was not a credit institution in any sense but a clearing house based on silver deposits, were confined under the con-

* See A. E. Feavearyear, *The Pound Sterling: a History of English Money* (2nd ed., revised by E. V. Morgan, Oxford, 1963), pp. 219 ff., and J. W. Gilbart, *The History,*

† A. Wagner, op. cit., p. 283.

Principles and Practice of English Banking (London, 1907), Vol. 1, pp. 100–6, for discount rates from 1694–1892, and Vol. 2, pp. 302 ff. for a description of the crisis.

servative, hesitant leadership of the Senate essentially to two measures: the 'Garantie-Disconto-Verein von 1857' was created, on the model of the 'Darlehen-Compagnie' of the less severe crisis of 1842, and its capital of 5 million Mark Banco paid in partly by deposits of the Senate, and partly by subscriptions of Hamburg firms. We may obtain from documents preserved in the Staatsarchiv, as we did from ledgers of the Bank of Hamburg, an approximate notion of the financial standing of individual firms. The following were the bank's subscribers:

	Mark Banco
Elias Warburg	5,000
M. M. Warburg & Co.	15,000
R. D. Warburg & Co.	15,000
W. S. Warburg	20,000
S. S. Warburg	20,000
Berenberg, Gossler & Co.	100,000
L. Behrens & Söhne	100,000
Conr. H. Donner	200,000
Salomon Heine	500,000*

The Senate sought a silver loan to strengthen the market further, and above all to make it possible through such a loan for the endangered larger firms to increase their deposits in the Hamburger Bank. The Senate turned first to Berlin with a request for a loan of 3 million Taler. Minister Manteuffel not only refused, but added to his refusal a sermon designed to teach the 'heavily indebted' Hamburg merchant class elementary lessons in business. And all this was called forth by a request for an advance in which the richest city on the European continent asked for no more than 3 million Taler.† After soundings had been taken through various intermediaries in London and Paris as well, and the prospects for credit were deemed hopeless, the Senate finally turned to Vienna. Hamburg's difficulties had already been observed with disquiet and sympathy in Vienna, because the firm belonging to the Austrian Consul-General in Hamburg, Ernst Freiherr von Merck, was among the larger houses particularly at risk because of its commitments in Scandinavia. The Hamburg Minister resident in Vienna, Heckscher, did his best to inform the Government of developments, and his efforts were crowned

* Further data in H. Böhme, 'Wirtschaftskrise, Merchant Bankers und Verfassungsreform', op. cit., p. 88, n. 35.

† J. von Eckardt, *Lebenserinnerungen*, op. cit., Vol. 1, p. 196.

with success: by the end of November, the Austrian Finance Minister Bruck 'sent Director Schiff of the Kreditanstalt to his home city Hamburg, in order to investigate the crisis there.'*

With the appointment of Paul Schiff, a brother-in-law of the young Siegmund Warburg, as Vienna's emissary to Hamburg we reach the point where the previously mentioned special relationship of the crisis to the history of the Warburg bank becomes evident. But first we shall describe the further unfolding of events. On 8 December, at 3 p.m., Heckscher was implored by the Hamburg Senate to lodge an immediate appeal for help with Bruck. That same evening Bruck reported to the Emperor, whose consent made it possible for the Governor of the Austrian National Bank to announce on 10 December 1857 'that with the consent of the Finance Minister he was prepared in the name of the National Bank to place the sum required at the disposal of the City of Hamburg, in return for which the Senate of the City of Hamburg undertook to repay the loan, also in silver bars, within a half year, at 6 per cent interest.'† By 13 December the famous silver train, with free passage through the states of the Prussian-German *Zollverein*, departed for Hamburg, arriving on 15 December; and on 19 June 1858 the silver bars, still in their original packing, were returned with interest to Vienna. The fact that this loan was primarily used to support the big Hamburg firms, among them H. J. Merck & Co., on the practical grounds that their collapse would have dragged down many smaller firms, led to many attacks, and cast something of a chill over that perhaps too-often evoked 'feeling of gratitude.'‡ That on the contrary the effective intervention of

* Annual Report, Österreichische Kreditanstalt, 1857, cited in Gustav Weiss-Wellenstein, 'Ein altes Beispiel mitteleuropäischer Interessengemeinschaft' in *Mitteleuropäische Wirtschaft* (Wien, December 1927), p. 18.

† S. Pressburger, *Österreichische Notenbank 1816–1966. Geschichte des Österreichischen Noteninstituts* (Wien, 1966), p. 91. Ernst Baasch published a description of the negotiations based on the files: 'Zur Geschichte der Handelskrisis von 1857', *Zeitschrift des Vereins für Hamburgische Geschichte*, Bd. 30, pp. 81–105. Paul Schiff's rôle as intermediary, not apparent in the documents, is overlooked in the Baasch study, as are the efforts of David Hansemann, who went to Hamburg on 1 December 1857 and endeavoured in vain to instruct the Senate in modern methods of dealing with the crisis through credit banks. Cf. Alexander Bergengrün, *David Hansemann* (Berlin, 1901), pp. 683 ff.

‡ G. Jantzen, 'Hamburg und Wien. Zur Geschichte hamburgischer Beziehungen zu Österreich im 19. Jahrhundert', *Mitteilungen der Handelskammer Hamburg* (Hamburg, 1967), pp. 641 ff.

Paul Schiff in securing this loan is no piously preserved family legend is proved by a letter which he received from Freiherr von Merck on 15 July 1858, which says: 'Now that it is all over, I hope that the old confidence in us will gradually return. In any event, I declare once more, and shall not forget till my dying day, that you were the man who saved me and all of us.'*

Paul Schiff was however also the saviour of M. M. Warburg & Co. and that leads us back to the experience of the firm in the crisis year 1857. Paul Schiff was born in Frankfurt on the Oder in January 1829. He came to Hamburg in 1845 to learn the banking business, and was by 1853 with the firm L. Behrens & Söhne, where he became the closest collaborator of Wilhelm Leopold Behrens (1838–1928), when Behrens began to convert the Hamburg firm principally to a banking business, while trade in Manchester goods was retained in the branch in that city. In the course of this transformation into banking a close relationship with the Rothschilds, soon to be further strengthened, was forged: Nathan Meyer Rothschild, the founder of the London house of Rothschild, who himself had started his career in Manchester, sent his son Nathan to Behrens in Manchester as a trainee. This relationship makes it understandable that Behrens, which by 1844 had a capital of 10 million Marks, was favoured by Rothschilds in London with short-term deposits and substantial participations in each issue.† It was probably also this same cooperation that led to the nomination in September 1856 of Paul Schiff, who married Rosa Warburg, the sister of Siegmund and Moritz, the same year to the Board of the K. K. privilegierte Kreditanstalt für Handel und Gewerbe (Imperial and Royal Credit Bank for Trade and Industry) in Vienna, which had been founded in 1855.

This bank, which was founded by the Vienna and Paris branches of the Rothschild family with the London house remaining distinctly aloof, was a daring enterprise that with the support of Emperor Franz Joseph and

* G. Weiss-Wellenstein, *Mitteleuropäische Wirtschaft* (Wien, 1927), No. 215. The minutes of the Commerzdeputation of Hamburg for 3 December 1857, under the heading 'Trade Crisis', indicate among those present: 'Herr Direktor Schiff from Vienna, Herr Pornies and Herr Königswarter from Frankfurt a.M. and Herr Lieben from here.' On Marcus Königswarter, see Erich Achterberg, *Der Bankplatz Frankfurt am Main, Eine Chronik* (Frankfurt a. M., 1955), pp. 23 and 99. From Baron Testa's report to Vienna of 2 December 1857 it emerges that Paul Schiff's mission to Hamburg especially concerned support for the firm H. J. Merck. Böhme, op. cit., p. 112.

† Based on *175 Jahre L. Behrens & Söhne* (Hamburg, 1955), pp. 14 ff.

Finance Minister Bruck blocked the proposed establishment in Vienna of a branch of Pereire's Crédit Mobilier. This represented the first participation of Rothschilds in a modern credit bank, administered by a member of the third generation, Anselm, thus accommodating themselves to one feature of the age, as Bertrand Gille describes:

La contagion des Crédits mobilier gagnait tous les Etats, même s'il n'avait pas lutté entre les deux puissants groupes financiers. Partout on en espérait des miracles: l'expansion économique assuré, la création d'une industrie, en un mot le début d'une croissance que n'avaient encore connue que les nations de l'extrême occident européen.*

In the two years 1855 and 1856, thirteen such credit bank corporations were founded in Germany alone with a total capital of 156 million Taler, of which two, the Vereinsbank and the Norddeutsche Bank, each with a capital of 20 million Taler, were established in Hamburg.† These newly-founded banks, initially opposed by the distrustful Senate, and in which the Warburg firm had no participation, were not yet sufficiently integrated into the Hamburg economy to play a decisive role in the crisis of 1857. Their subsequent rapidly increasing business was however seen as further proof of the inadequacy of a pure silver-deposit or clearing bank. 'The prestige that they [silver-deposit and clearing banks] had enjoyed since 1790 and retained in 1813 and 1842 was lost in the crisis of 1857.'‡

A more flexible form of extending credit could have helped just those middle-sized and smaller firms that were far more the victims than the practitioners of over-speculation. Discount rates from September 1857 may serve to chart the course of the crisis, which has often enough been described:

* B. Gille, op. cit., Vol. 2, p. 219. On the Rothschild-Pereire conflict in Vienna, see also, Kurt Grunwald, 'Railways and Jewish Enterprise', *Year Book XII*, Leo Baeck Institute (London, 1967), pp. 181 ff.

† For a list, including private banks, see B. Gille, op. cit., p. 221.

‡ H. Sieveking, *Die Hamburger Bank*, op. cit., p. 104. A. Wagner agreed with this criticism, writing that Hamburg 'had forcibly prevented the development of institutions that could ... have rendered the best service [in the crisis].' Wagner, op. cit., p. 299. James Wilson, respected member of the staff of the London *Economist*, wrote as early as 1859 that the Hamburger Bank could have used one-third of its silver resources for extending credit facilities. *Capital, Currency and Banking* (2nd ed., London, 1859), p. 160.

Discount Rate on	*Hamburg**	*London*
	%	%
1 September 1857	6	$5\frac{1}{2}$
15 September 1857	$5\frac{3}{4}$	$5\frac{1}{2}$
22 September 1857	6	$5\frac{1}{2}$
6 October 1857	7	$5\frac{1}{2}$
13 October 1857	8	6
16 October 1857	9	7 (17 Oct. 1857)
10 November 1857	$9\frac{1}{2}$–10	9
24 November 1857	9–$9\frac{1}{2}$	10
4 and 8 December 'no business and no quotations due to the crisis'		
11 December 1857	$10\frac{1}{2}$	10
15 December 1857	$9\frac{1}{2}$	10
18 December 1857	6	10
22 December 1857	4	10
29 December 1857	4	8†

The sharp drop in the discount rate between 15 and 18 December can clearly be ascribed to the favourable effects of the silver shipment. Uncertainty still persisted nonetheless, and to calm the markets further yet another loan of 5 million Mark Banco was arranged on 29 December 1857 with the Österreichische Nationalbank; this loan took a somewhat complicated form, and ultimately consisted of foreign currencies on London and Hamburg. This support was not required, however, and after two months the loan was repaid.‡

If we mention at this point moreover that only 145 out of 4,000 firms went into receivership during the crisis, we have sufficiently described the milieu in which an individual firm such as M. M. Warburg & Co. maintained its existence.

* Rates from the handwritten collection of money and bill rates from 1710–1913 in the Commerzbibliothek of the Chamber of Commerce in Hamburg, furnished to us in photocopy. *The Economist* of London wrote on 26 December 1857, p. 1433: 'At Hamburg the crisis has past away, and the rate of discount has fallen to 4 to 5 per cent.'

† The London discount rate declined on 9 January 1858 to 6 per cent, on 16 January to 5 per cent, on 30 January to 4 per cent, on 6 February to $3\frac{1}{2}$ per cent and 13 February to 3 per cent; and remained from 11 December 1858 till 30 April 1859 at $2\frac{1}{2}$ per cent, which indicated liquidity rather than general economic recovery.

‡ See E. Baasch, op. cit., pp. 94 ff.

The firm ended the year 1856 with a net profit of about 18,000 Mark Banco, and began 1857 with a capital of 227,603 Mark Banco. The bill of exchange accounts, which in 1852–6 fluctuated between 150,000 and 250,000 Mark Banco, suggest cautious management of the business. The bill account stood at 200,411 Mark Banco on 31 December 1856. When however at the height of the crisis an increasing number of bills with its endorsement were protested and came back to the firm, it found itself in very great difficulties, for which the rigid structure of the Hamburg money market afforded few opportunities for relief. When the twenty-one-year-old Siegmund Warburg could hardly see a solution, his brother-in-law Paul Schiff, who was only six years older, helped him by placing his entire savings at his disposal, and – as is demonstrated by one of the few letters that survive – by arranging for further facilities in the form of credits.

Paul Schiff appears in the balance sheet for 1857 with an account receivable of 101,813 Mark Banco; but in a letter of 18 January 1858, written in very affectionate terms, he expresses to his brother-in-law, whom he calls 'my good son', his satisfaction that everything has gone so well, and that 'money is so plentiful there [in Hamburg]' that an extension of credit facilities can be assured.* We do not know exactly how Paul Schiff was ultimately repaid. At the 1858 year-end his account receivable had been reduced to 4,251 Mark Banco, and there was an account payable to the Österreichische Kreditanstalt in the amount of 5,621 Mark Banco, but the few remaining letters suggest that Schiff continued to maintain some assets in Hamburg. It was most helpful to the Hamburg market as a whole when in February 1858 Salomon Heine, jointly with the Norddeutsche Bank, arranged a loan of 9 million Mark Banco for the support of the Stockholm Garantie-Kreditverein; in that transaction the many Hamburg holders of protested Swedish bills also benefited.† In contrast, conditions in Austria throughout 1858 remained difficult. Paul Schiff writes to his brother-in-law on 10 January 1859 about substantial personal and general losses, hopes for a moderate improvement, and adds '. . . a recovery cannot be expected meanwhile; everyone is fearful as long as Napoleon is in France. I do not see the dark side of things and, in contrast to you, am a natural optimist, but nonetheless I have become anxious and am limiting my speculations. Do the same yourself; one must be able to look into the future with some

* Letter from collection of Aby S. Warburg.

† E. Baasch, op. cit., p. 99.

equanimity, and that one cannot do under the present circumstances in France.' *

In the already mentioned year-end balance sheet of 1857 the bill of exchange account is 79,670 Mark Banco; the credit balance with the Hamburger Bank 48,764 Mark Banco, and cash on hand 15,059 Mark Banco; but unfortunately the precarious claim on the textile firm already mentioned comes to 73,138 Mark Banco. Net profit for 1858 is 9,197 Mark Banco, and the firm's capital at 1 January 1859 amounted to 237,201 Mark Banco.

The year 1858 was one of consolidation and reordering of all business relationships, and significant for the firm because it showed Sara Warburg, as sole proprietor, the extent to which she could rely on the prudence and talents of her eldest son. She thus decided at the end of that year to admit him as a partner of the firm. The partnership agreement, the second in the firm's history, has been preserved: it is a manuscript of eight folio pages, and its precisely formulated details are best characterized by the introductory words which describe it as having been 'carefully thought out and discussed'.

The firm is now described as a 'Banking and Currency-Exchange Business' in which Siegmund Warburg is a full partner [*firmierender Compagnon*]. He is authorized to assume the 'sole and exclusive conduct of business'. Then however comes the following addition: 'Although Herr Siegmund Warburg is empowered ordinarily to act according to his own judgement, he must nonetheless seek the opinion of Madame Warburg in matters of special importance, and to act in agreement with the latter. In particular, Herr Siegmund Warburg may not grant Power of Attorney to anyone without the consent of Madame Warburg, while in all other respects the employment of staff is his responsibility.'

The general stipulations regarding property are of no further interest for the history of the firm, unlike the origins of the new partner's own capital in the firm. He was assured an allowance of 15,000 Mark Banco for the three years 1856 to 1859, and this constituted the first tranche of his investment in the firm. In the same paragraphs, in accordance with the usage of that time, the following was added: 'If he [Siegmund Warburg] should receive a dowry on the occasion of his eventual marriage, he is obliged to invest at least two-thirds of the marriage settlement in the business; he is similarly under obligation to pay in to the firm the same proportion of assets that may come his way from other sources.' The real

* Letter from collection of Aby S. Warburg.

property of Sara Warburg does not constitute part of the firm's capital, but in the event of possible mortgages being foreclosed, the firm is obliged to put at her disposal any necessary bridging finance. Withdrawals for personal use are limited to 10,000 Mark Banco per annum for Madame Warburg and, for Siegmund Warburg, to 5,000 Mark Banco, raised to 12,000 after an eventual marriage. Madame Warburg is entitled to three-fifths of the annual profits, and Siegmund Warburg to two-fifths; losses are shared in the same proportion. There are very careful stipulations regarding the possible dissolution of the contractual relationship by consent or through the death of one of the partners. 'The partnership is to last for five years, i.e. until 31 December 1863.' The position of the younger brother Moritz is governed by a special paragraph.* If he remains active in the business, he is to receive an annual salary of 2,500 Mark Banco; upon his majority he is to be admitted as a partner, and to participate with a one-fifth share in profits and losses, whereby Madame Warburg's share diminishes to two-fifths. As long as they are living in their mother's house, Moritz Warburg is obliged to pay her 800 Mark Banco annually for room and board, and his older brother 15,00 Mark Banco for the same purposes. On 9 May 1861 Moritz Warburg confirms that he attained his majority on 28 March 1861 upon completion of his twenty-second year; that he has been admitted as a partner; and that he 'approves all the provisions of the foregoing contract'.

Since we find in this agreement certain data on the personal expenditure of the contracting parties, it may be useful to ascertain what they reveal about the standard of living of the Warburgs. In 1858, according to her own account book, the annual expenditures of the widow A. S. [Sara] Warburg were 13,616 Mark Banco. In that year, the salary of the First *Bürgermeister* of Hamburg was 13,000 Mark Banco; the 5,000 Mark Banco per year of Siegmund Warburg corresponds to the salary of a junior *Senatssekretär*. And we might compare the 2,500 Mark Banco of brother Moritz with the annual salary of the Steward of the Hamburg Stock Exchange, who received 800 Mark Banco per annum, to be sure 'in addition to free lodging, heat and light'. The senior porters of the Stock Exchange, doubtless fathers of families, received a total of only 600 Mark Banco per year.†

* Moritz M. Warburg was born on 8 March 1838.

† Data based on the kind communication of Dr. Günther Jantzen, *Syndikus* of the Handelskammer, Hamburg, from the draft State Budget of 1860 and a memorandum of the Commerzdeputation, October 1857.

Those inclined to consider personal expenditures for this generation excessive, and to share with later generations susceptibility to the influence of Veblen's concept of 'conspicuous consumption', should not overlook the fact that for a private banking house, which is not required to publish financial statements, the standard of living of the partners is determined according to the usages of their social class, and excessive parsimony might have unfortunate repercussions on the credit standing of the firm.

It might be helpful here, although the figures belong chronologically in the next section, to reproduce the statistics from the ledger books of the Hamburger Bank (see facing page) which show how many pages each firm required annually for its dealings with the bank. This is, as Heinrich Sieveking also admits, a crude measure of a firm's standing. But it is the only one left for the years from 1851 onwards: 'At the dissolution of the Bank (on 31 December 1875) the Bank's books, in which "each individual's Banco worth" was inscribed, appear unfortunately to have been destroyed.'* We have thus only this series of comparative figures, available in the always doubtful company of index statistics.

The allusion to an eventual marriage of Siegmund Warburg contained in the partnership agreement of 1859 was soon to become reality. The business developed favourably under his energetic and prudent direction. There was a surplus of 62,500 Mark Banco in 1860, which declined in 1861 to only 12,860, but was again 53,200 Mark Banco in 1862. The firm was thus sufficiently strengthened for the young partner to think of an appropriate matrimonial alliance. He married on 2 April 1862 in Wiesbaden Theophilie Rosenberg, from Zhitomir in Russia. From memoirs preserved by the family it is apparent that the engaged couple first met after Siegmund had reached an agreement with the parents. The marriage contract, executed in the presence of the municipal executive of Wiesbaden† and confirmed by two witnesses, declares that the bride shall receive, from a marriage settlement appropriate to her standing, a dowry in the amount of 40,000 Prussian Taler, or about 80,000 Mark Banco. The deed contains the usual stipulations about the dowry in the event that one of the spouses should die, and what provisions should be made in various cases for the remainder or a possible refund of the dowry.

The addition to the firm's capital was indeed welcome. Much more important, however, was the fact that through this marriage the economic

* H. Sieveking, *Die Hamburger Bank*, op. cit., pp. 107 ff.

† *Landoberschultheisserei des Amtes Wiesbaden.*

HAMBURGER BANK, LEDGERS IN THE STAATSARCHIV HAMBURG
(from 1851)

	1851	*1853*	*1854*	*1859*	*1860*	*1861*	*1862*	*1863*	*1864*	*1865*	*1866*	*1867*	*1868*
Total Ledgers	30,103	33,129	35,584	31,159	31,368	31,204	30,342	30,541	29,960	30,458	29,639	29,402	28,970
L. Behrens & Söhne	180	275	204	5	3	4	3						
Salomon Heine & Co.	416	495	500	539	583	583	662	Salomon & Carl Heine 660	650	315 224 (in Liqu.)	in Liqu. 46	in Liqu. 2	in Liqu. 2
Münchmeyer	36	26											
Nottebohm	108	119	110	108	104	107	113	109			114	115	108
M. M. Warburg & Co.	295	281	256	169	163	181	191	225	190	188	231	247	242
Elias Warburg	200	190	226	173	185	177	164	160	153	162	175	179	167
Norddeutsche Bank			3,017	2,886	2,607	2,886	3,017		3,266	3,364	3,767		3,702
Vereinsbank			4,629	4,634	4,494	4,634	4,610	4,675	4,620	4,456	4,784	4,758	4,840

and cultural dynamics of the firm decisively changed. The bride's father, who had married a sister of Josef Günzburg, was a respected businessman in South Russia, where he played a leading role in the sugar industry near Kiev. One of the bride's sisters, Anna, married her cousin Horace, Baron de Günzburg. He was the proprietor of the banking firm J. E. Günzburg in St. Petersburg, which had been founded in 1859 by his very wealthy father. But far beyond his business activities, Baron Horace de Günzburg was concerned with the legal and cultural position of the Jews in Russia, and, following in his father's footsteps, played in this area a role similar to that which Sir Moses Montefiore, allied by marriage to the Rothschilds, played in Russia, North Africa and the Near East. Siegmund Warburg was almost the same age as his Russian brother-in-law. Another sister of Theophilie Warburg married L. E. Aschkinasi, the founder of the banking firm E. Aschkinasi in Odessa; her sister Rosa married Baron Joseph von Hirsch-Gereuth, and thus arose a personal relationship to the banking firm of Bischoffsheim & Goldschmidt.* We shall indicate later to what extent these links with Eastern Europe, further strengthened by inter-marriages in the next generation, contributed to an expansion of the firm's business. The biographer of Horace de Günzburg writes of the Rosenberg daughters: 'Tous les membres de la famille Rosenberg se distinguaient par leur beauté, et tous les filles reçurent une éducation européenne.' †

One important consequence of this marriage was that it led the Rothschild houses to a reappraisal of the firm's standing. Even in the first few years of Siegmund Warburg's leadership of the firm, relations with the Rothschilds had to some extent revived, doubtless influenced also by the link with Paul Schiff and the Österreichische Kreditanstalt.

By the end of 1862 the younger brother, Moritz, was also to be admitted as a partner of the firm. Doubtless as a preparation for his increased responsibilities, he made a business trip to France and Italy in the autumn of 1862, about which he reported to his mother in a number of detailed letters. The reception accorded this twenty-four-year-old young man at leading banking firms reflects the respect and excellent reputation enjoyed by the firm. At the bank of Achille Fould, to whom he presumably had a

* See S. Adler-Rudel, 'Moritz Baron Hirsch', Leo Baeck Institute, *Year Book VIII*, (London, 1963), p. 35.

† Henri Sliosberg, *Baron Horace O. de Gunzbourg, sa vie et son oeuvre* (Paris, 1933), p. 33.

letter of introduction from Fould's son-in-law Carl Heine, he was introduced to Prince Torlonia, who immediately invited him to the theatre. The next day, at the offices of the Crédit Mobilier, he called on Eugène Pereire, who drove with him to the Pereire residence, where he also '... met the intelligent father (Emile) Pereire, also very friendly, but a typical Spanish Jew.' He reports further: '... The residence is truly palatial, I have never seen anything like it; he promised me to establish business links with us, but since other people have most of his day-to-day business, there seem to be few opportunities for that.' These doubts are typical of Moritz Warburg who, despite his youth, was not dazzled by splendour and the princely style of life. He closes this part of his letter with these words: 'That money *compels* deference in this world seems incongruous; but one cannot eat with philosophical phrases alone.' *

In the accompanying letters from Italy there is occasional mention of a marriage prospect, but the writer is on his guard against regarding this winter journey, in which he also visited and fully described artistic sites, as a bridal search.†

Two years later the firm's field of operations was auspiciously enlarged in the direction of Western Europe through Moritz Warburg's marriage on 12 June 1864 to Charlotte Oppenheim from Frankfurt am Main.‡ Through this marriage links were forged with leading Frankfurt banking houses, especially with the firm of Moritz B. Goldschmidt.

But that is not the most decisive factor. With Charlotte Oppenheim the family gained once more a very considerable woman of cultivation and character, who, like Sara Warburg before her, was not only concerned with the carefully guided education of her children, but also showed strong signs of that creative talent that was later to characterize several of her sons.§ She left in manuscript a memoir of her Frankfurt youth in which her father's occupation of goldsmith and jeweller is described in

* Letter from the collection of Aby S. Warburg.

† *Brautschau:* the formal series of calls on eligible families that often preceded the conclusion of marriage arrangements.

‡ The marriage contract for this union has not survived.

§ Another example of the importance of the matriarchal factor in the development of a firm may be found in Ludwig Bamberger's description of his grandmother Bischoffsheim. Her strictly brought up sons, 'two real financial geniuses', were the founders of the important firms Bischoffsheim and Goldschmidt, which had many business links with Warburgs. Ludwig Bamberger, *Lebenserinnerungen*, ed. by Paul Nathan (Berlin, 1899), pp. 224 ff.

valuable socio-historical detail. And in her advanced years, in the winter of 1903–4, she wrote for her husband, to commemorate their fortieth wedding anniversary, a description of the Hamburg years from which may be gleaned a notion of the firm's business in those early years. We cite a portion from her chapter 'The Office' to give some idea of conditions at the time:

> In 1864 the offices of M. M. Warburg & Co. were still in the first floor of the building at Hermannstrasse 47, where even the cashier Simon had most uncomfortable quarters. In 1867 the Eggers building at Ferdinandstrasse 75 was acquired, and the banking rooms were installed in the ground floor, while Siegmund moved from his previous residence at Alsterdamm 3 to take up residence in the first and second floors of the building. The time-table of both partners was as follows at that time: my husband took his main meal at 4, came back to the office at 5.30 and relieved Siegmund, who went home at 6 while the junior partner remained until 9 or 9.30.*

When younger brother Moritz came in as partner on 31 December 1862, Siegmund was not disinclined, in accordance with his more domineering temperament, to confine Moritz to running the back office of the firm – something that Moritz with some justification refused to permit. Siegmund very soon realized that there were business matters the handling of which was better left to the more courteous manners and milder temperament of his brother. According to family memoirs, he may well have received a nudge in this direction when Carl Heine, Salomon's son, said to him one day at the Stock Exchange: 'You are supposed to have such a very pleasant brother, do send him round to me some time.'

In other respects as well it would be quite unrealistic to assume that the relationship between elder and younger brothers or cousins always went smoothly. In the first generation, Marcus and Gerson got on quite badly; in the second Aby parted from his cousin Elias after a few years; in the third generation, strong temperamental differences were described unforgettably by Max M. Warburg, the son of Moritz:

> Of the two brothers, Siegmund was the enterprising spirit. Without any doubt it was primarily he who built up the firm and brought it to its present importance. My father was far more conservative, hesitant and careful; he successfully represented the firm on the outside.

* Manuscript memoirs of Charlotte Warburg, née Oppenheim, 1904. Reproduced in several copies for family use.

Siegmund was a family man. . . . In the year of his mother's death he arranged a synagogue in the house so that he could recite memorial prayers every day. He himself was the cantor, and stood at the pulpit dressed in his prayer shawl, riding boots and spurs; he had hardly finished his prayers before he was already out of the door and mounted on his horse. The brothers loved one another, but disputes were a daily occurrence. Regularly, once or twice a week, there were quarrels which echoed down the whole Ferdinandstrasse.*

Even in the fourth generation, tensions between older and younger brothers were not unknown. But reconciliations were low-keyed, often moreover in writing, with humour and irony. Aside from natural family feeling, strengthened by upbringing, there was the decisive factor of the need to maintain the unity and good name of the firm.

The firm's business in the first half of the 1860s was entirely satisfactory. Net profit for 1862 was about 53,000 Mark Banco, according to that year's financial statements; in 1863 it was 81,000 Mark Banco, and in 1864 33,000 Mark Banco. At the end of that year, Frau Sara Warburg, who had been born in 1805, decided that from 1 January 1865 she would withdraw from the firm and leave its management to her two sons. Again, a detailed contract was drawn up, from which we shall cite the essential points.

The proprietors of the firm, Siegmund and Moritz Warburg, left their total capital, in addition to later possible increments, in the business, and calculated interest on this amount, before determination of net profit, at 3 per cent. Aside from the unlimited amounts that may be withdrawn from the firm for personal use, capital sums may be withdrawn only for the purchase of property for the residence of one of the partners, and on that amount interest is also charged at 3 per cent. The capital share of Frau Sara Warburg was determined by the regular balance sheet of 31 December 1864. If losses should occur on account of debts appearing in this balance sheet and deemed collectable at the time it was drawn up, such losses would only affect the new partners. These partners might however indicate which of those accounts receivable they considered doubtful, and 'of which they do not wish to bear the risk alone'. If a loss should occur on one of the accounts thus designated, then Frau Sara Warburg would share in the loss proportionately. If on the other hand debts written off as doubtful or non-collectable should be repaid up to

* Max M. Warburg, *Aus meinen Aufzeichnungen* (New York, privately printed, 1952), p. 3.

1864, Frau Sara Warburg was to participate in the repayments. Frau Sara Warburg left her capital in the firm, and received in return 'without regard to the size of her participation and the results of future business activities 10,000 Mark Banco in quarterly instalments *praenumerando*'. The new partners pledge 'their entire property, real and personal', to the fulfillment of all obligations in respect of capital and yearly income payments. After deduction of all costs of doing business, interest payable and the yearly pension for Frau Sara Warburg, the net profit remaining was divided among the partners so that in the first four years, 1865 to 1868, Siegmund Warburg would receive three-fifths and Moritz Warburg two-fifths. If however net profit exceeded 40,000 Mark Banco in this period, each partner would share in the surplus equally. From 1 January 1869 each partner would receive 'one half of the entire net profit'. The same stipulations also governed the division of possible losses.

The contract was drawn originally to be valid for eleven years, until 31 December 1875, but was to continue in effect thereafter unless notice of termination should be given a half-year before the proposed termination date. There were precise stipulations regarding a possible liquidation of the firm, as well as the consequences of death of the partners, in which connection the possible remarriage of a widow was not overlooked.* If Frau Sara Warburg wished to withdraw her capital from the firm, she was to declare that intention no later than 31 March 1875. On page 21 of this contract, which does honour to the well-known quality of Hamburg notaries, it is prescribed that if differences should arise between the partners or their heirs concerning the content or dissolution of the contract, 'these should then be brought to the attention of Herr Paul Schiff in Vienna for his final decision.' If his decision is not accepted, then each partner must appoint an arbitrator, and the arbitrators must choose an umpire, or alternatively one could be appointed by the President of the Commercial Court. 'The decision of the arbitral tribunal so constituted is binding, without appeal or a new cause of action.' Here we see also, as in the agreement of 1810, the exclusion of legal remedies pursued in the public courts.

In a letter of 29 December 1864, preserved with the contract deed, Siegmund Warburg set out for his mother's information how her income

* This provision contains the archaic formula: 'The firm is moreover dissolved in and of itself when the widow forsakes her widowhood [*die Wittwe den Wittwenstuhl verrückt*], and at the expiration of the year in which her remarriage takes place.'

was made up from various fixed accounts, and explained that after all special expenses, she would have at her disposal for the regular household a monthly sum of 550 Mark Banco.* For two more decades Frau Sara Warburg was able to enjoy her new life, throughout which she never lost her inclination for duty and hard work. In the introduction he wrote to the family genealogy, S. Fürst wrote of her: 'She lived after her husband's death at "Beim Rothenbaum" No. 45, and there ran a hospitable house. As the chairman of many charitable associations, she did much good work among the poor and the sick, and died one month after her seventy-ninth birthday, on 10 October 1884.'

In her memoirs, Charlotte Warburg dedicates to this mother-in-law a most perceptive portrait in writing, valuable also for what it reveals of middle-class culture. In the memoirs of Max M. Warburg also, she figures as a formidable matriarch to the lively young man. These matters do not perhaps belong to the depiction of a bank; but from the point of view of social history, we should not forget what importance, particularly for a family enterprise, women of such gifts and strength of character had as preservers of tradition and educators of the succeeding generations.

* One of the mother's fixed expenses was a payment of 800 Mark Banco interest to Paul Schiff. Since Sara Warburg had participated from 1862 as to two-fifths in profits and losses, we may assume an interest obligation of 2,000 Mark Banco. Assuming 5 per cent interest, we may take it that Paul Schiff still retained, or had again made, a capital investment in the Hamburg firm of 40,000 Mark Banco.

4

THE FIRM UNDER SIEGMUND AND MORITZ WARBURG: 1865–1889

Before we continue the history of the firm, we should once again give some attention to the economic and political milieu in which it functioned. A business enterprise must be very important in terms of its capital, business purpose and number of employees before it can itself exert some formative influence on economic and political circumstances. But even the very smallest enterprise is dependent within its own sphere of activity on these external factors.

Our first survey from the beginning of the century showed how very favourable the general trend of the economy was for a banking enterprise; the same can definitely be said for further developments. The Napoleonic wars brought about a quite extraordinary simplification of economic territories. In 1790 there were some 1,800 tariff boundaries within the territory of the later German Reich. Trade moved along routes bristling with fiscal obstacles through a maze of petty states, and even for the time around 1830 Werner Sombart could write of the 'impossibility of finding a unified German economic territory'.* But the evolution to states of a larger area had already begun. In 1828 tariff unions are established in middle, North and South Germany, and in 1833 under Prussia's leadership they are combined in the *Deutscher Zollverein*; at midnight between 31 December 1833 and 1 January 1834 that lifting of tariff barriers occurred which later historians saw as the most important step leading towards the foundation of the German Reich in 1871. To be sure, Prussian policy, which led with logic and consistency to the wars of 1864 and 1866 against Denmark and Austria-Hungary respectively and the exclusion of the latter from the Reich, was more concerned with state power than with

* W. Sombart, *Die deutsche Volkswirtschaft im 19. Jahrhundert* (Berlin, edition of 1925).

unifying territory. Precisely for that reason, having Prussia as a neighbour was not without its dangers for Hamburg, in its capacity as a free port and Free City – as the fate of Frankfurt am Main demonstrated; these dangers were only overcome by a most circumspect policy. A compromise satisfactory to both parties was finally reached in the tariff accession treaty of 25 May 1881. This treaty was the most important one for Hamburg of perhaps 150 state treaties which were required between 1815 and 1900 to create German economic unity. Hamburg had joined the North German Confederation by the decision of its citizens on 15 May 1867, but it remained outside the tariff zone until 1888.

More important however than the constitutional changes since 1815 were the transformations of fundamental economic factors, and thereby of the way of life that was classically described in the first edition of Werner Sombart's great work, *Der Moderne Kapitalismus.**

This development should not be conceived as sudden or, as we would say today, explosive. It was rather a constant expansion of old boundaries, coupled with extraordinary technological changes. With growing industrialization, population increased and cities became the focal points for new labour- and capital-intensive enterprises. In a nutshell, all this was the transition from timber to steel as the most important construction material; from wood to coal as fuel; the competition of the new railroad with the old road system; the slow displacement of sail by the steam engine, and the gradual blossoming of an entire new chemical industry. In addition, there was for many agricultural products a lessening of seasonal demand fluctuations, since at any given moment there was a harvest somewhere in the world, and enough shipping capacity to take advantage of these possibilities for import and therefore also for export. But even this development, which was particularly important for Hamburg, took place much more slowly than hindsight would suggest. The first English steamship, *Lady of the Lake*, appeared as early as June 1816 in Hamburg harbour; but it was only in 1853 that the Hamburg–America Line, which was founded in 1847, decided to go over to steamers, which were initially built in England. The first iron steamship built in

* W. Sombart, *Der Moderne Kapitalismus*, Bd. 2: *Die Theorie der kapitalistischen Entwicklung* (Leipzig, 1902): especially see the Introduction and first book on 'the propelling forces' and 'the new style of economic life'. Further similar descriptions in Sombart's later book, *Die deutsche Volkswirtschaft im 19. Jahrhundert*, first Berlin, 1912, then in later editions with the supplement '*und im Anfang des 20. Jahrhunderts*', revised to 1925.

Hamburg for Hapag, the *Deutschland*, was launched in 1857, while iron sailing-ships were built in Hamburg as late as 1849.*

However, neither maritime nor railroad problems were of immediate importance for the firm's business activities in the period of time dealt with in this chapter. In complete contrast to the Rothschild houses in Paris and Vienna, the firm initially avoided participation in new railroad ventures, and dealt in railway securities only to a limited extent as part of its brokerage business. It may be sufficient to recall in this context that the railroad network within the area of the German customs union totalled 469 km. in 1840, 7,800 km. in 1855 and some 18,450 km. in 1870.†

On the other hand, there were two developments that proved of decisive importance for the particular kind of business transacted by M. M. Warburg & Co. The first was the technical invention of the telegraph, and the second a slow evolution in state banking policy that made trade bills more important than ever.

The development of the long-distance telegraph began about 1850. The methods of telegraphic payment that thereby became possible led to the creation of a world market for currencies and securities, in which through all kinds of arbitrage business accounts could be settled in a much shorter time than before; and at any given moment not merely two countries, but all those linked to the world telegraph network could participate as partners: 'Thus the world money market has become an agency, at once firmly unified and highly specialised.'‡ The development of the telephone that followed some thirty years later only further compressed the time element in these transactions. Television viewers of today are familiar with the picture of currency dealers with their batteries of telephones and mysterious computers.§

* Otto Mathies, *Hamburgs Reederei 1814–1914* (Hamburg, 1924), pp. 75 ff. This monograph is fundamental, and will be cited again in this discussion.

† It was to a large extent the banks and banking firms of Frankfurt, Cologne and Berlin that backed railway enterprises. A good survey on participating firms under Jewish management may be found in Kurt Grunwald, 'Railways and Jewish Enterprise', *Year Book XII*, Leo Baeck Institute (London, 1967), pp. 177 ff. This study makes clear the speculative element in such business, which suited neither the then capital resources nor the more traditional style of the Warburg firm.

‡ A. Marshall, *Money, Credit and Commerce* (London, 1924), pp. 141 ff. Cf. also Ludwig Bamberger's lively description, in his *Lebenserinnerungen*, of securities arbitrage after the carrier pigeons maintained by the larger firms were replaced by public telegraph.

§ For non-expert readers, an explanation of 'arbitrage' may be in order. The literal

The change in the position of the trade bill that has already been mentioned occurred at almost the same pace as these purely technological innovations. At this point, at least a glance at banking theory is unavoidable; and is all the more justified since two of the firm's partners in the next generation, Max M. Warburg and Paul M. Warburg, were both leading theorists on these questions.

Looking at the development from the point of view of banking theory, it represents, in capsule form, the supplanting of the 'currency school' by the 'banking school'. The essential element of the currency school is to back the note issue of a central bank, perhaps up to one-third, by a currency metal; while the banking school considers 'short-term trade bills' a sufficient backing for note issue. In the Banking Law of 1875 the Reichsbank was for the first time permitted to cover two-thirds of its notes in circulation by such bills; the remaining third still had to be backed by gold. Laymen too will see not only that this new regulation gave trade bills a new and strengthened legitimacy, but also that the demand from central banks for first-class bills necessarily increased. For through these bill purchases a new policy emerged, not at first entirely clear to the participants, under the external protection of the gold standard: '. . . the conscious and planned influencing of fluctuations in the prices for foreign trade bills; or more precisely, cross-currency rates, by purchases and sales of foreign trade bills and foreign obligations by the central bank'.*

At this point, we might supplement our earlier explanation of arbitrage by saying something about trade bills; we give here a somewhat shortened version of G. F. Knapp's statement in his *Staatliche Theorie des Geldes*. The bill of exchange is defined by commercial law: it is a specially privileged promissory note expressed in the legal tender of the country of origin. It places on someone the obligation to pay a certain amount at a particular time to the drawer. The drawee indicates his agreement on the bill itself: he 'accepts' it and sends it back to the drawer. The latter usually

meaning may be rendered as 'settlement' or 'decision'. In trading of securities, trade bills and other obligations in domestic or foreign currencies, quotations for the same security may often differ on various markets. The arbitrageur buys such securities on the market at the lowest price and sells them immediately by telephone or telex on a market at the highest price, often to a friendly firm with which the profit on the transaction is divided for joint account. For these and other technical details, see Wolfgang Compter, *Bankbetriebslehre* (Darmstadt, 1967).

* With this quotation from Kurt Singer's epilogue to G. F. Knapp and F. Bendixen,

wishes to receive the sum owing to him before the maturity date on the bill, and he therefore offers the bill to a bank, which pays him the face value with a certain deduction for its services; the bill of exchange is thereby 'discounted'. The bank can circulate the bill further, with its acceptance and against another discount, and this transaction can be repeated indefinitely. Each new holder of the bill of exchange endorses it and thereby assumes the obligation to pay the drawer if the original drawee, or endorsers prior to him, should prove unable to meet their commitments. Knapp summarizes thus: 'It is difficult to understand how this extraordinarily important and consistently reliable branch of business, the honourable conducting of which is the pride of all civilized countries, seems to be so mysterious: perhaps because its technical terms are unfamiliar to the public and its operation with large amounts confuses the laity. Basically, these are pledge transactions and credit transactions with analogues on a smaller scale, and no mystical clouds should accumulate about the matter.'*

A fundamental change in the character of the money market came about through a highly dynamic factor, namely the establishment of numerous new banks throughout Europe inspired by the incorporation in 1852 of the Société Générale du Crédit Mobilier by the brothers Emile and Isaac Pereire.† The express purpose of these newly-founded banks was less

---

Zur staatlichen Theorie des Geldes. Briefwechsel von 1905–1920 (Basel, 1958), p. 228, we somewhat anticipate chronological developments. Friedrich Bendixen, a director of the Hamburg Hypothekenbank, developed out of this transformation – which had been in the making at least since 1875 – a new theory of money creation based on the market economy (1908), which on the economic side should be seen as a supplement to Knapp's work. J. A. Schumpeter criticized this development in his *History of Economic Analysis* (New York, 1954), p. 695: 'The theory of central banking that links the bank note to the trade bill proved an extremely hardy plant: its influence dominated banking legislation on the Continent beyond the nineteenth century; it asserted itself strongly in the Federal Reserve Act of 1913.' The real author of the Federal Reserve Act was Paul M. Warburg, schooled in the tradition of the Hamburg firm. An earlier German criticism of the Currency School may be found in A. Wagner's work, cited above in connection with the crisis of 1857.

* G. F. Knapp, *Staatliche Theorie des Geldes* (München, 1905), p. 118.

† E. C. Palgrave, *Dictionary of Political Economy* (London, 1901), says of the founding of the Crédit Mobilier that it 'gave a wonderful impulse to great financial and industrial enterprise both in France and elsewhere', p. 94. Of the voluminous bank history literature which can be consulted in standard bibliographical guides, we cite only the monograph by Plenge, *Gründung und Geschichte des Crédit Mobilier* (Tübingen, 1903).

deposit business linked with note issue, than conscious sponsorship, in the spirit of Saint-Simon (whose thought inspired the Pereire brothers), of existing and new economic enterprises. In accordance with these aims, Gustave Mevissen declared in 1854 at the first general meeting of the Darmstädter Bank that the bank had been established 'to promote substantial and large-scale new enterprises through its own participation and the investment of other funds; and so far as possible, taking advantage of that clear insight into the totality of German industry conferred by an overall point of view, to make certain that entrepreneurial spirit and capital should be led into appropriate paths that correspond to contemporary needs';* in the event, a high ideal which expressed the fundamental Saint-Simon notion of the organizing importance in economic life of the individual managing entrepreneur. To be sure, 'clear insight', 'substantial' enterprises, 'appropriate paths', 'contemporary needs' – all these formulae pose problems whose *réalités terrestres* cannot be surmounted, even in part, without much legislative assistance. But the basic thought which underlies the banker's professional ideology is the spiritual legacy of the early nineteenth century. And we might add in this context that despite the heightened competition represented by the new joint stock banks, there were, in the practical achievement of these wide-ranging definitions, tasks for the completion of which the private banker, even as an appendage of the big banks, was often better equipped than the more impersonal large enterprises.

Bertrand Gille's history of the Paris Rothschild bank gives a good survey of the German '*Crédits Mobiliers*', since the new banks founded by the Pereires, in which the brothers Benoit and Achille Fould had a decisive rôle, aimed to break the alleged Rothschild monopoly, or more accurately the hegemony of the Rothschild house. Achille Fould (1800–67), who was several times Finance Minister after 1848, and who at the end of his career again occupied that office under Napoleon III in 1861–2, is supposed to have remarked to Napoleon when he was still Prince-President: 'Il faut absolument que vous vous affranchissiez de la tutelle des Rothschild, qui règnent malgré vous.'†

* H. Schumacher, 'Geschichte der deutschen Bankliteratur im 19. Jahrhundert', in *Festschrift für Schmoller*, Bd. 1 (Leipzig, 1908), p. 27.

† B. Gille, op. cit., Bd. 2 (1848–1870), p. 98; for table of German bank incorporations see p. 221. A contemporary source described as follows the temperamental difference between Rothschilds and the Pereire brothers: the Pereires had 'le défaut immense en affaires de vouloir tout dominer, tout embrasser, tout envahir, par la

In view of the close cooperation of M. M. Warburg & Co. with all the Rothschild banks, these various alliances and conflicts have a certain interest, to the extent that their repercussions were felt as far away as Hamburg. For Achille Fould was the father-in-law of Carl Heine, the son of Salomon Heine, who belonged to Sara Warburg's circle of friends. During the crisis of 1867 there was a vain attempt on the part of Hamburg interests to utilize the Heine-Fould connection for the credit requirements of the Hamburg market.

Of the many new German banks founded on the model of the Crédit Mobilier, the Vereinsbank (July 1856) and the Norddeutsche Bank (October 1856) were significant for Hamburg, as was the Berliner Handelsgesellschaft (July 1856), which was geographically and in business terms the closest to Hamburg. The Disconto-Gesellschaft, founded in 1851 by David Hansemann who came from Finkenwärder, also had close connections with Hamburg from its inception.

In our third chapter the history of the firm itself was described until the beginning of 1865, when the brothers Siegmund and Moritz, thirty and twenty-seven years old respectively, began jointly to manage the enterprise as sole partners. Both were married and well-settled in both private and public life.

Through their origins, and by virtue of their new family connections, the brothers belonged now to that 'vaste famille de banquiers qui offre partout comme garantie sa responsabilité morale', as Capefigue has it, adding 'une fois admis dans cette haute famille il en résulte une sorte de solidarité: si on ne peut empêcher tous les accidents, prévenir les crises individuelles, on les évite, tant qu'on peut, on les répare avec un dévouement incomparable.'* Siegmund learned something of this solidarity in the crisis of 1857, and it became manifest under less dramatic circumstances for Moritz when he visited France and Italy in 1862 in order to greet fellow-members of his guild.

But in their native city of Hamburg as well, the process of settling in was beginning, at least for Siegmund. In February 1862 he had been

conviction sincère de leur perfectibilité illimitée et le désir de tout primer par leurs idées.' J. Capefigue, *Histoire des grandes opérations financières*, tome 4 (Paris, 1860), pp. 236 ff. For Fould's relationship with Napoleon III see Ludwig Bamberger, *Charakteristiken* (Berlin, 1894), pp. 76 and 83.

* J. Capefigue, op. cit., p. 245. Many years later, L. M. Jenks made the same observation on the propensity of the private banks, mostly of Jewish origin, such as

sworn in as a Hamburg citizen,* and he served as a musician in the citizens' militia from 16 January 1862 to 30 July 1868 when it was dissolved; we may assume that he took sufficient advantage of his right to hire a substitute for active service. His preference was far more for work in the Jewish community, which in 1867 elected him to membership of its governing body; his principal task here was to help in the transfer of the community's taxing powers to the state.

A few years later, Siegmund Warburg was elected with effect from 1 June 1869 to membership of the association of securities dealers. The official letter of the Chamber of Commerce is signed by the famous secretary Ad. Soetbeer, as is the renewal letter of 19 December 1870. A similar letter of December 1874 bears the signature of the secretary, Dr. G. Embden, a nephew of the poet Heinrich Heine.

Also in 1870, on 24 December, Siegmund Warburg was appointed by the Senate to the Deputation for Indirect Taxes and Fees. The official letter to that effect, signed by the later Mayor Versmann, contains the sentence: 'The prospect of having official business with you is most gratifying to me, and I trust that you too have been pleased by your election.' On 7 December 1871 this appointment was renewed with the supplementary stipulation that Siegmund Warburg was to undertake the supervision of stamp-duty offices jointly with Herr Henri Louis Des Arts; this letter was signed by G. Mönckeberg, later to become Mayor of Hamburg.†

We have a few indications of the way the firm's partners lived in these years from the description which Aby S. Warburg (1864–1933) wrote and dedicated to his father. He makes it clear that both brothers were characterized by strong family feeling; and that despite all their enthusiasm for the business interests of the firm, they were far from defining their lives in terms of those interests alone. Although he emphasizes that the years following 1865 were years of real capital growth and a strengthening of the firm's general standing, a retrospective consideration of these developments must conclude that modern notions linking capitalism with ascetic-

---

the Rothschilds, Oppenheims, Sterns, Erlangers, Raphaels, Bambergers, Bischoffsheims, Seligmanns and Speyers, to extend their business areas by founding branches: 'Their branches were linked by family loyalty, pride in the possession of a common name, and in some cases by the community in profits.' L. H. Jenks, *The Migration of British Capital to 1875* (London, 1927), pp. 268 ff.

* '*Grossbürger*'.

† Letter of appointment in collection of Aby S. Warburg.

puritan values are not applicable to this case. All evidence indicates that even in the earlier generations, there was a certain comfortable ease in the Warburg family style, and that good fellowship, art and literature were valued and cultivated. We cannot observe any inordinate desire to increase capital by abstemiousness or self-denial; and the chronicler who finds traces of neither greed nor stinginess may perhaps be inclined to observe somewhat critically the connection between standard of living and capital reserves. Perhaps we have the explanation in the fact that, well into the third generation, the firm's business consisted overwhelmingly of brokerage, with income from commissions and discounts, and thus the desire to strengthen the firm's own capital was not yet so imperious.* The following sentences from Aby S. Warburg's memoirs are quite characteristic: 'Once the Rothschilds had again strengthened their links with the Warburgs, the latter reaped the advantages that came from the most varied market opportunities, as reflected in daily orders from Paris and London. These houses [Rothschilds] had meanwhile become incomparably more important in the acceptance business, so that their demand for three-month bills increased enormously. In addition, there were very large-scale transactions in Italian government loans, American securities and secured Lombardy bonds, which latter Baron James never tired of offering to all European investors.' Even the 'constantly calculating Siegmund Warburg, who was almost passionately attached to notions of expansion, confined himself nonetheless to certain definite limits.'† This sense of moderation, the son asserts, preserved the firm from impatience and participation in risky ventures, because the partners were not driven from the domestic hearth by boredom.

Matters were not, however, quite so simple. The firm had its warning example of dependence on an almost blackmailing debtor, the firm M. B. mentioned in Chapter 2, whose account stood at 84,000 Mark Banco in 1862; and it was also more timely than the fourth generation surmised in becoming interested in moving out of pure commission business into the

* In his study of the crisis of 1857, Helmut Böhme correctly points out the dangers incurred by firms which were under-capitalized in relation to their acceptance obligations, and thus unable to withstand reverses. H. Böhme, op. cit., pp. 84 ff. Thus, even for firms primarily engaged in commission business, there was a greater interest in strengthening capital; and based on a larger capital, the desire to participate in new-issue business.

† Memoirs of Aby S. Warburg.

new-issue business that implied the need for growing capital in order to carry underwriting and selling group commitments.

Extensive business records do not survive from these years, but certain conclusions may nevertheless be drawn from the few remaining documents that we have.

To begin with, here – as an approximate guide to general developments – is a list of the balance-sheet assets for the period 1865–72, the first period of expansion. Net profits – still in Mark Banco, approximately equivalent to Mark 1.20 – were as follows:

	Mark Banco
1866	88,764
1867	40,685
1868	79,797
1869 January–June	104,162
1869 July–December	15,751
1870 January–June	13,977
1870 July–December	106,310
1871 January–June	118,799
1871 July–December	360,795
1872 January–June	348,659
1872 July–December	155,167

The capital account on 1 January 1870 showed 278,221 Mark Banco for Siegmund's participation, and 246,521 for Moritz's share in the firm.

We see from the accounts remaining from those years that the firm did business not only with the Rothschild houses, but with almost every one of the larger banking firms on the Continent mentioned in Paul H. Emden's valuable and often entertaining guide, *Money Powers of Europe*. From the statements of 1871–2 we cite J. Allard & Co., Paris; Stern Bros., London, with branches in Frankfurt and Paris; Bischoffsheim & Goldschmidt in London, Paris and Brussels; S. Bleichröder in Berlin; L. Behrens Söhne and Lieben in Hamburg.

In the decade after 1860, one can hardly speak of an actual 'organization' of the firm's office. We know from one memoir that in 1868 the firm had ten employees and one counting-house messenger. Among these employees however was Adolf Dorner, the first staff member who was later to be given single Power of Attorney. Dorner had moved to Dresden on 1 October 1864, with the Hamburg straw-hat manufacturing firm of H. J. Quast & Co., but in January 1866 he applied for a position in the Warburg bank, since he had always been attracted by banking, and had in any event to return to Hamburg in order to support his widowed mother. In response to his application, an annual salary of 1,000 Mark Courant was offered, but he wished to have 1,250 Mark Courant for the first two years, with prospects of a later increase to 1,500 Marks. He was nonetheless so eager to enter the banking business in Hamburg that he was prepared to start at 1,000 Marks per annum, without a contract; '. . . and am prepared after three or six months, when you have come to know me and my capabilities, to conclude a contract: I am quite convinced that you will at that point grant me a salary corresponding to my abilities and agreeable to me.' The quiet self-assurance of this letter proved fully justified, as the later story will demonstrate; and a salary of 1,500 Marks appears entirely appropriate for the income and net profit figures of that time: in 1866, net profit was some 90,000 Mark Banco.

In these years, the external standing of the firm also improved markedly through several changes of office premises. In 1860, the bank moved from Admiralitätstrasse to Hermannstrasse 44, and in 1863 to Hermannstrasse 47; in 1868, the building at Ferdinandstrasse 75 was bought and Siegmund Warburg took up residence there on the first floor, above the bank offices. From 1863 the firm is listed in the Hamburg directory as 'Bankers' rather than 'Money Changers'.

Aside from the rather summary balance-sheets, we have no surviving business documents from the decade 1860–70. By sheer chance, however, we do have a copy of a letter dated 18 July 1865 addressed to N. M. Rothschild & Sons in London, which we reproduce in part because of its rarity and contents:

> We last had the pleasure of receiving your valued order of the 10th March this year, and you have not since then had occasion to favour us with orders for your worthy account. . . . As you doubtless know, the banking house of Heine had to be liquidated following the untimely death of Herr Carl Heine, and thus our premier banking firm is no more. We are aware that you were for many years in close business relations with the Salomon Heine banking firm, and it would give us most particular pleasure if you were to transfer to us the business that you transacted with the above-mentioned house. We need hardly add that we are able to serve you as advantageously as any other firm here, and you may be assured that we shall protect your interests in every way.*

At the close there are quotations for bills on London, Paris and St. Petersburg. We no longer have the reply to this letter, but all indications

* Copy in possession of E. Rosenbaum.

are that business with London soon became as active as with the Rothschild houses on the Continent.

It is certainly true that after the crisis of 1857 those firms that were still doing an extensive trade in goods along with their banking business were far more careful in limiting their credit commitments, and that for a time Hamburg acceptances lost some of their market standing.* For the 1850s the average short-term credit claims of England on Germany have been estimated at approximately 250 million Marks.† A portion of these credits was extended to finance the rapidly growing trade, especially with Silesia and Saxony, that went through Hamburg, and this assumption will be borne out by figures to be cited hereafter.

Since the books of the firm are unavailable for the 1860s as well, we must be content with an 'indication' from the memoirs that Aby S. Warburg wrote in 1915, in which there is also an undertone of that antipathy often felt by Hamburgers towards 'Prussian Berlin'. He writes: 'Since these days bank directors in Berlin are as unaware as they are contemptuous of Germany's former business relationships, and go so far as to assert that Bismarck was the first to achieve our mercantile greatness, it would be advisable sometime to cite just the daily volume figures for foreign-exchange transactions that M. M. W. & Co. was transacting as far back as the middle of the 1860s. They would be quite amazed there [Berlin] at the very large amounts involved.'‡ Of these transactions, a significant proportion was done with the Paris Rothschilds, with whom there were particularly close personal relations. When Baron James de Rothschild died on 15 November 1868, Siegmund Warburg went to Paris for the funeral. That later the expenses for his coach to the cemetery were debited to the Warburg current account amused him for many years as proof of the care with which the Paris Rothschilds kept their books. The outbreak of war with France came as a surprise to Siegmund Warburg, and as with many others – on the French side as well – it decisively altered his notion of Europe. The year 1870 can therefore justifiably be regarded as a turning point for the firm as well.

In the following years, the magnitude of profits, but also of losses, changed; and documents that remain give us a rather more precise insight

* See H. Böhme, *Wirtschaftskrise*, op. cit., pp. 103 ff.

† Richard Hugh Tilly, 'Los von England. Probleme des Nationalismus in der deutschen Wirtschaftsgeschichte', *Zeitschrift für die gesamte Staatswissenschaft*, Bd. 124, Heft. 1, pp. 192 ff.

‡ Memoirs of Aby S. Warburg.

into the evolution from bill discounting and foreign-currency arbitrage to a true securities brokerage business.

We have a number of letters to Siegmund Warburg for the period from January 1869 to the end of April 1870, written by a friend in Paris who signs his letters only with the initials 'TZE', and presumably was one of the staff members of the Rothschild bank. These letters reveal that Siegmund Warburg was engaged in securities trading, evidently not just for his own account, but also on behalf of clients. Proof for this assumption is offered by a letter dated 24 January 1870 to the London Rothschild firm:*

We heard today by telegraph from London that according to an announcement in *The Times* an issue of Russian Government bonds sponsored by your most honoured firms is to be made within the next several days. Referring to this report, we took the liberty of sending you a telegraphic request kindly to reserve us a firm participation of 40,000 pounds sterling, and we fervently hope that you will be so kind as to grant our request. The aforementioned loan will doubtless meet with a favourable reception under your sponsorship, so that we shall hardly be able through the ordinary channel to receive any meaningful allotment unless you grant us priority as we requested, for which we send you our heartiest thanks in advance.

We still hope for your favourable response to our request that we be entrusted with the issue of the loan here, and send our compliments.

Yours most faithfully,
M. M. WARBURG & Co.

A comparison of handwriting indicates that this very carefully composed letter was written by Adolph Dorner, and concerned most probably the Consolidated Russian Railways loan of £12 million, with a 5 per cent coupon, that was issued at 80.† Since this loan was issued jointly with the Paris Rothschilds, we find in a letter from Paris by 'TZE' dated 26 January 1870 a report on the negative results of the effort from Hamburg. This letter gives such an entertaining glimpse of the seamy side of such affairs that we cannot refrain from citing verbatim the most important sentences:

You can well imagine that I should gladly have furthered your interests, and made all sorts of efforts to obtain permission for you to accept subscriptions

* Copy in M. M. Warburg & Co. files, Hamburg.

† Cf. the instructive list of Rothschild issues from 1804 to 1904 printed in E. Achterberg, *Der Bankplatz Frankfurt am Main, Eine Chronik* (Frankfurt a.M., 1955), p. 160.

there on our behalf to the new loan, but the jealousy of the gentlemen in Frankfurt and in London put all sorts of obstacles in the path of your market, and I was not even in a position to arrange a firm participation for you, since such participations, neither here nor anywhere, were conceded to anyone. *Sub rosa*, Schwabach of Bleichroeder himself was here, and despite all his efforts achieved exactly as much in this connection as you did. You must therefore ascertain how you may otherwise profit from this *évènement*. Meanwhile, the 'good friends' of the house were today engaged in efforts to alarm the Bourse through all sorts of sensational rumours, e.g. the death of the Pope and the illness of Victor Emmanuel, so that in consequence all Rothschild-sponsored securities, including Lombards, were depressed.*

These letters to London and from Paris reveal without any doubt that Warburgs were very much interested in participating more in the securities business. In a further letter dated 5 February, 'TZE' reports that the Russian loan was 'a tremendous success'; subscriptions had not yet been processed, but it could nonetheless be assumed 'that the large participations would amount to hardly 3 to 4 per cent'. The price had meanwhile already risen, since many who hoped for allotments had already sold on speculation, 'and are now forced to buy bonds at any price in order to be able to make delivery'. 'TZE' goes on to report that the price of Lombards has meanwhile recovered, and asks at the end 'what further profitable business can be done'.†

The last letter received in this series, dated 26 April 1870, is overshadowed by a death in the family, but contains a number of expressions that give a characteristic picture of the type of mutual business interests involved. The general impression is that the subject here is not only securities trading for the account of third parties, but also for the investment accounts of the correspondents themselves. 'TZE' initially reassures Siegmund Warburg about a company not mentioned in the letter, the precarious situation of which is about to improve substantially as a result of steps taken by new management. There follows material which again we reproduce word for word because it represents a typical example of the reflections of 'TZE':

* For the origins of these 'Lombards' see B. Gille, op. cit., p. 321. Cf. Achterberg, op. cit., p. 159, who lists in 1856 'Imperial Lombardy-Venetia and Central Italian Railway, jointly issued by all Rothschild firms, 6 million shares at £20 each nominal, par, 3%, 3·13 million at 500 Francs, 3%, issue price 270 Francs.'

† Letter in collection of Aby S. Warburg.

The next sad drama about to enfold is that of the State Railway shares, for which a competitive struggle is developing that will hit you hard. I draw your attention to this matter early, because I may be wrong for a period of months, but certainly not in the matter itself. I believe that anyone who has the staying power to sell Staatsbahn shares today, and buy Austrian Nord Westbahn, will double his capital within two years. Business at the moment is otherwise very uninspiring. The plebiscite is a dangerous swindle, and fraudulently affects the price of fixed-income securities, which a host of bullish optimists see rising a few percentage points. May these good people not be wrong. I myself don't believe in any rise.

After a few critical remarks on American securities, he goes on:

I have a favourable view of Spanish securities despite all opposing opinions; the reason therefor will be explained to you in due course by our information office.

He closes with:

Too bad that the Commerzbank does not make good progress. I cannot interest the gentlemen in the affair; they have a firm antipathy to all enterprises launched by their competitors.

To explain this letter, into which we should not surely read too much, the following information may be of use. Österreichische Staatsbahn shares and mortage bonds are listed in Achterberg's book for 1855–61 among the securities introduced at Frankfurt am Main, as are the 5 per cent Austrian Nordwestbahn mortgage bonds of 1869 and 1870. The Spanish securities that 'TZE' mentions obliquely in this letter may be the Spanish quicksilver 5 per cent mortgage bonds issued at 80, of which Rothschilds in London and Paris issued £2.32 million. This loan secured to Rothschilds sole rights for an initial period of thirty years to the total production of the mercury mines of Almaden.* The plebiscite referred to so sceptically was one that was meant to decide on a 'liberal' amendment to the Constitution of 20 April 1870 transforming the Senate into an upper chamber, but depriving it of any right to amend the Constitution

* This assumption appears to be justified by a letter of Warburgs to Rothschilds in London, dated 31 May 1870, in which there is a postscript by Siegmund Warburg stating that if it is intended to issue the new Spanish 5 per cent loan in Germany as well, the Hamburg market would doubtless participate substantially in the subscription, since a 'strong demand' for Spanish securities had been evident recently there. We do not have the reply to this letter.

without approval by a popular vote. The poll of 8 May gave the Government 7·5 million votes, and the opposition 1·6 million. This victory for the Emperor, and the other speculations of this letter were doubtless quickly overtaken by events. The statement of 'TZE' in his letter of 21 January 1870 that '... the Government is consolidating its position steadily, since it has the undivided support of the propertied class and the intelligentsia' had not much time to be proved correct.

The Commerz- und Disconto Bank mentioned in the letter of 26 April, for which Warburgs apparently tried to awaken some interest in Paris, was referred to as early as 26 February 1870 in a letter to Baron Lionel de Rothschild in London, enclosing the prospectus and statutes of the proposed bank. Although there was apparently no positive response from London as well, we cite a few significant sentences from the letter, since initially Siegmund Warburg, and then from 1889 Moritz Warburg, were members of the Board of this bank which played an important role in the Hamburg market. Introducing the prospectus and bank statutes, the letter says:

If you give these documents a favourable examination, you will rapidly come to the conclusion that this is not an enterprise designed to assure advantages to its founding shareholders, or to achieve a premium over the issue price for its shares, but that it aims in an unexceptionable way to facilitate and support the trade of our city.

After some time, when it transpired that the Norddeutsche Bank and the Vereinsbank were not satisfying demands for commercial credit, it seemed appropriate to establish an institution that should be primarily devoted to the interests of trade. . . .

Until now we had made it a principle not to participate in the founding or management of such enterprises. In view of the truly patriotic purposes that underlie this enterprise, we have nevertheless felt compelled to modify our rule, and have agreed to the request made of us, joining the founding committee and the Board of the Commerz & Disconto Bank.*

The firm expresses the hope that although the new bank will not be international, Baron Lionel will decide to acquire some shares, as certain other foreign houses have already done. If Rothschilds in London turned down this invitation to participate, we need not assume, with the writer of the 'TZE' letter, that their position was determined solely or indeed at all by fear of the competition. The somewhat overblown rhetoric of the

* Letter from collection of Aby S. Warburg.

argument that the new bank had 'truly patriotic purposes' was certainly not destined to make a good impression in London; moreover, perhaps the London Rothschilds considered that such participations, if they were to be indulged in at all, were an affair for the Frankfurt house.

In a few further letters still extant addressed to N. M. Rothschild & Sons in London, we hear in a few words the echoes of events in world history. A letter of 13 July 1870, after announcing a debit of £16,347 11s. for the account of the Vienna Rothschild firm, says: 'Trading on the Exchange was very subdued, with lower prices. The stubborn resistance being shown by the French is unsettling the markets.'*

The next letter, dated 28 October 1870, again containing orders executed for the account of the Vienna house, comments as follows on political matters: 'Upon news of the surrender of Metz, yesterday evening's markets were very firm.† The Exchange opened firm today as well, but that could not be maintained, and the close was somewhat lower.'

The last of these letters preserved by chance looks ahead in quite typical fashion to the end of the Franco-Prussian war. It is dated 31 May 1871 and, after confirmation of a remittance to London, contains the following:

> It is being generally assumed here that the French loan will now be arranged through your worthy firm, and we should very much like to participate in a substantial amount.
>
> We took the liberty of telegraphing you today in this sense, and requested you to let us know if possible the terms and the amount which you would kindly be prepared to allot us.
>
> The Exchange staged a good rally today, with quite active trading.‡

We do not know what answer Hamburg received from London, but it was presumably negative, since it was a German syndicate that organized the first loan of 5 billion francs for payment of the war indemnity. Three weeks later, the *Hamburgische Correspondent* of 21 June 1871 reports:

* Cf. Bismarck's remark: 'I decided to depart on July 12th from Varzin to Ems in order to propose to His Majesty calling the Reichstag into session with a view toward mobilization.' Otto Fürst von Bismarck, *Gedanken und Erinnerungen* (Berlin, 1932), p. 305.

† On 27 October 1870, General Bazaine surrendered the fortress of Metz together with 173,000 surrounded troops.

‡ Letter from collection of Aby S. Warburg.

Telegram from Berlin. The Berliner Börsenzeitung reports: a syndicate was formed today under the leadership of the Berliner Disconto-Gesellschaft and the Bleichröder bank to place a new French loan on the market here. There is considerable interest in participating in the new issue. The issue price has not yet been set definitely.

There is further news about this loan from Berlin, Vienna and Paris in the *Hamburgische Correspondent* of 27 June 1871, and the same day the supplement contains a two-page advertisement of the French Government, written in German, inviting subscriptions to the loan; the advertisement was carried again on the following day. For Hamburg that advertisement was the prelude to one of the most astonishing financial transactions of modern times. The relatively civilized character of these events – the fact that hardly eight weeks after the conclusion of peace it was possible to advertise in the newspapers of the 'enemy country' for subscriptions to the loan designed to free France of occupying troops – will convince the modern reader that continental legal definitions of war still governed the Franco-Prussian War of 1870–1. Thus war was defined as a conflict between sovereign states, to be fought out by state agencies, but not at the same time a struggle between citizens as individuals. In consequence, trade with the enemy, so long as it did not consist of war matériel, was not by definition forbidden. And since there was no coastal blockade in this war, it was to a certain extent possible, especially through third countries, to continue trade. 'Enemy aliens' business winding-up orders and similar measures had not yet been invented. Private contractual relations could therefore be restored much more rapidly after being interrupted by war. Such restoration of normal relations was also furthered by the extraordinary speed with which the French government, under the leadership of Thiers, paid the war indemnity, so as to liberate the territories occupied as security for such payment as rapidly as possible from that heavy burden.*

* The technique of these financial events was not merely admired by a small circle of experts. Jakob Burckhardt twice commented quite categorically on the matter. On 6 March 1871 he wrote to his friend Friedrich von Preen: 'What do you think of the old Jew Crémieux, who stood at the head of the list with his 100,000 francs for a subscription that will make it possible to pay 5,000 millions immediately. If 50,000 people with his resources (and there may be such in France) were similarly inclined, the entire matter might be done. The affair impresses me deeply, and perhaps it will succeed.' *Briefe*, ed. by Fritz Kaphahn (Leipzig, 1935), p. 339. Burckhardt writes in his *Weltgeschichtliche Betrachtungen*: 'The entire financial world is astonished by the ability

Since the Hamburg market was involved in all sorts of ways in these events, a summary description seems to be required.*

The basis for the first issue was the law of 20 June 1871 which provided for a public offering of 2 billion francs of fixed-interest bonds. Subscriptions were invited from 27 June, and the lists were closed before the 30th. The Government ran no risks, since a syndicate led by Rothschilds guaranteed the availability of the issue amount. The issue price was 82.50 francs, and the underwriters' price for the Rothschild syndicate was 77.50 francs. The loan was over-subscribed, so that with an overall allotment of 45 per cent it was possible to obtain the sum of 2.226 billion francs for the French state.† The loan in July 1872 for the further 3 billion francs required turned out much more dramatically. The coupon remained 5 per cent, but the issue price was raised to 84.50 francs. With very strong demand, the loan was more than twelve times over-subscribed; of the buying demand, some 17.5 billions came from France and 26 billions from foreign countries. Berlin alone subscribed for 3 billion francs, and North Germany for 1.5 billion. After successful allotment of the loan, France realized 3.5 billion francs at a real interest cost of 7·88 per cent.

On the basis of these revenues a large-scale transfer operation was now undertaken, of which the completion pursuant to the very precise regulations of the peace treaty required the mobilization and remittance of vast quantities of coins, precious metals and trade bills. The French government had concluded agreements with more than fifty-five banks and financial groups entitling it to draw finance bills on these firms, against payment of commission.‡ Moreover, the government established special agencies in London, Brussels, Amsterdam, Hamburg, Frankfurt and Berlin for executing these transactions. In Hamburg these agents were the Norddeutsche Bank and L. Behrens & Söhne, but there can be

---

of the French to pay; France in defeat enjoys a credit standing that hardly any country in triumphant victory could claim.' *Gesamtausgabe*, Bd. 7 (Stuttgart, 1929), p. 157. Crémieux was a member of the provisional government of Gambetta after the fall of Napoleon III.

* The most important German source is the work of Knapp's student Franz Gutmann, *Das französiche Geldwesen im Kriege (1870–1878)* (Strassburg, 1913); see also Ernst Levy von Halle, *Die Hamburger Girobank und ihr Ausgang* (Berlin, 1891).

† Cf. Jean Bouvier, *Les Rothschild* (Paris, 1960), pp. 187 ff., with valuable details on profits of the placements made by the banks.

‡ Gutmann, op. cit., p. 290.

no doubt that M. M. Warburg & Co., which even at that time was a quite significant dealer in bills, participated in these matters.* Hamburg also had a quite special position, because the French government made a portion of its payments through the Hamburg Girobank – itself on the eve of liquidation – so that in a last burst of euphoria the bank's assets rose from 17.34 million Mark Banco on 20 June 1872 to 62.7 million Mark Banco on 17 October the same year. The difficulties that arose for the bank and its temporarily insufficient silver reserves are described by Gutmann.† There were similar tensions with temporarily high discount rates on the London money market as well.‡

We have some information on the proportion of bills denominated in Marks Banco thanks to the quite precise official statistics. In the first payment period from June to October 1871, 4,372 bills in the total amount of 718 million francs were presented for payment in Strasbourg. Among these were 418 bills drawn on Hamburg, of which the smallest was for 111 Mark Banco and the largest for 1.8 million. For the period from 13 January to April 1872, the comparable figures are: 1,013 Mark Banco bills, for amounts ranging from 181 to 2.95 million Mark Banco. In the next delivery from 29 August to 10 December 1872, there were 1,480 Mark Banco bills; the smallest amounted to 82 Mark Banco and the largest to 24.7 million. And finally, from 16 January to 13 September 1873, there were 2,093 bills in amounts from 108 Mark Banco to 3.12 million.§ Before the liquidation of the Hamburger Bank, which underwent conversion to Reich currency on 15 February 1873 (at 1 Mark Banco = 1.50 Reichsmark) and was closed on 31 December 1875, the French government took delivery of Hamburg silver ingots in the amount of 92 million francs, and had French talers coined from them.

Although from July 1872 no further silver had been coined in Berlin, there remained in Germany such a surplus of French five-franc coins (with which the war indemnity had been paid) that they were in unofficial circulation, especially in South Germany; and the Chamber of Commerce

* E. Rosenbaum, 'M. M. Warburg & Co., Merchant Bankers of Hamburg', p. 130.

† F. Gutmann, op. cit., p. 272; see also H. Sieveking, 'Die Hamburger Bank', op. cit., p. 109.

‡ J. W. Gilbart, *The History, Principles and Practice of English Banking*, Vol. 2, pp. 348 ff., report on payments made through London; see also Max J. Bonn, 'Die Vorgänge am Edelmetallmarkt in den Jahren 1870–1873', *Münchner volkswirtschaftliche Abhandlungen*, Nr. 40 (Stuttgart, 1900), pp. 118 ff.

§ F. Guttmann, op. cit., pp. 225 ff.

in Frankfurt am Main even proposed, without success, that they be temporarily accepted as legal tender.

In any event, the non-withdrawal of surplus German silver coins, later acknowledged as an inflationary mistake, and the French need for silver five-franc coins led to the return of some of these to France by way of silver arbitrage transactions. Max von Schinckel, who was on the Board of the Norddeutsche Bank from November 1872, gives a very perceptive account of such a reverse silver transportation in two freight cars, which he accompanied to Paris at the request of L. Behrens & Söhne, on a trip of several days in which he rode part of the way in the locomotive. He also mentions that the largest bill drawn by the Banque de Paris et des Pays Bas* on the Norddeutsche Bank amounted to 11,856,728.13 Mark Banco, or about 17.784 million Reichsmark.†

After this perhaps detailed yet necessary description of the general situation, we must now ask how M. M. Warburg & Co. fared in these years. Memoranda on individual business transactions no longer exist. But a glance at the balance sheets and capital accounts makes certain conclusions possible.

The 'Capital Account Book of Siegmund Warburg's Heirs'‡ sets forth as follows the respective capital shares of the partners Siegmund and Moritz Warburg:

		Mark Banco
1 January 1870	Siegmund W.	278,221
	Moritz W.	246,521
1 January 1873	Siegmund W.	677,336
	Moritz W.	675,380
1 July 1873	Siegmund W.	1,101,961
	(after loss of)	185,162
	Moritz W.	1,081,027
	(after loss of)	185,162
1 January 1874	Siegmund W.	904,515
	(after loss of)	147,283
	Moritz W.	862,088
	(after loss of)	147,283

* In connection with the founding in 1862 of this still-active bank by Bischoffsheim & Goldschmidt, see L. Bamberger, *Lebenserinnerungen*, op. cit., p. 539.

† M. von Schinckel, *Lebenserinnerungen* (Hamburg, 1927), p. 209. The description is also in Erich Achterberg, *Kleine Hamburger Bankgeschichte* (Hamburg-Altona, 1964), p. 53.

‡ Capital Account Book in collection of Aby S. Warburg.

Further losses were charged:

	Mark Banco
1 July 1875	89,820
1 July 1876	177,722

On 1 January 1878, the capital accounts were as follows:

	Reichsmark
Siegmund W.	2,075,041
Moritz W.	2,304,200

The further development of these accounts reflected the progress of the firm's business, which for 1879 again is described as 'in a slow upturn'.

Certain accounts in the financial statements for 1871 and 1872, which do not have any analogues in earlier statements, reflect active participation in the indemnity payments transactions, as we have earlier assumed from the standing of the firm in the bill market.

In the balance sheet of 1 July 1871 we find among the accounts receivable 227,593 Mark Banco from N. M. Rothschild in London, an account payable to the same house in the amount of 30,000 Mark Banco, and accounts payable also to Rothschild in Vienna in the amount of 42,751 and to Stern Bros. in London of 27,000 Mark Banco. Stern Bros. attained a special position because its Frankfurt branch was particularly favoured by the German government; Bismarck found the attitude of the Frankfurt Rothschild bank insufficiently 'German'.

The balance sheet of 1 January 1872 contains the following entries, which indicate participation in the indemnity payments. Among the accounts receivable: L. Behrens & Söhne, 50,000 Mark Banco; J. Allard & Co., Paris and Brussels, 48,000 Mark Banco; French Coupons, 62,675 Mark Banco. Among the accounts payable: Bischoffsheim & Goldschmidt, London, 45,300 Mark Banco; Allard in Paris, 94,118 Mark Banco; J. E. Oppenheimer in Brussels, 102,372 Mark Banco, and the bill of exchange account 760,603 Mark Banco. On 1 July 1872, among the accounts receivable are again L. Behrens & Söhne, 127,755 Mark Banco, and J. Allard in Paris, 226,478 Mark Banco. Among the accounts payable we find: Lieben Königswarter, Hamburg, 114,929 Mark Banco; Bischoffsheim & Goldschmidt, London, 75,509 Mark Banco; the Bischoffsheim firm in Paris, 43,424 Mark Banco. Rothschild Frères in Paris are debited for 1,347,928 Mark Banco, and the Banque de Paris et des Pays Bas, which was very much involved in the transfer of indemnity payments, is debited in the amount of 1,000,127 Mark Banco. The bill of exchange account stands at 1,435,194 Mark Banco.

On 1 January 1873, the balance sheet contains among the accounts receivable: bills on London, 1,291,292 Mark Banco; and among accounts payable, 338,355 Mark Banco to Banque de Paris et des Pays Bas, 365,176 Mark Banco to Rothschild Frères, 199,661 Mark Banco to Günzburg in Paris and 1,690,276 Mark Banco in the bills of exchange account. There is in addition a new entry, merely titled 'French paper' *(Franzosen)*, that amounts to 2,573,287 Mark Banco. Finally, a glance at the balance sheet of 1 July 1873: among the accounts receivable are 448,220 Reichsmark from Günzburg, Paris; 1,148,721 Reichsmark from Westminster Bank, London; 481,349 Reichsmark from the London and Hanseatic Bank, a branch of the new Commerz- und Disconto-Bank; and again 'French paper' in the amount of 78,120 Reichsmark. Among the accounts payable are Banque de Paris et des Pays Bas, 416,252 Reichsmark; Rothschild Frères 6,971,998 Reichsmark; Bleichröder in Berlin, 38,987 Reichsmark; and Samuel Montagu, London, 45,120 Reichsmark. The bills of exchange account stands at 1,446,931.

With that account, the series of loss-free balance sheets ends for some four years: on 8 May 1873, a few days after the opening of the great Paris Exposition, a panic began on the Vienna Stock Exchange that immediately had repercussions on the German money and securities markets.

The *Hamburgische Correspondent* of Sunday, 11 May, wrote in its political weekly report:

> There are no political reasons for the events on the Vienna Stock Exchange.... The difficulties that appear, at least for the moment, to have caused financial circles in the Austrian capital to lose their heads, are entirely the consequence of the feverish speculation that has gone on since the end of the recent war—to be sure, not only in Vienna—and whose consequences are now coming home to roost.

The next day, Monday, 12 May, an ominous telegram from Berlin is quoted in the same newspaper: 'The crisis on the Vienna Stock Exchange is being followed here with even greater suspense, because there is reason to believe that conditions here are ripe for a spreading of the phenomenon.' And two days later, on 14 May 1873, there is an editorial in the newspaper about the coinage law, containing a criticism of the demonetization of gold and a warning about the immediate coining of silver 2-Mark coins:

The future will doubtless recognize the regrettable blunder committed by those in responsible positions who failed to take sufficiently into account the general economic effects of the sudden pouring into Germany of enormous sums on account of the French war indemnity. The very rapid expansion of the money supply in Germany, from 200 to 250 million Taler, which could have been prevented if from the beginning the issue of new Reich gold coins had been accompanied by withdrawal of silver-courants, paper money and small bank-notes, was certainly the chief cause of the excesses on the Stock Exchange, or at least of their duration and exaggerated dimensions. . . .

The article is not signed; but one may nevertheless assume that it is by the outstanding Secretary of the Chamber of Commerce, Dr. Adolf Soetbeer, who was working with Lasker and Bamberger on the structure of the German currency regulations. In 1874 he published a small monograph, *The Five Billion: Reflections on the Effects of the Great War Indemnity on the Economic Relations of France and Germany*.* In that monograph, following the theme of his editorial, Soetbeer mentions that at the beginning of 1870 the value of the entire money supply, including currency and bank deposits, at 480 million Taler would be 'estimated on the high side'.†

Before we go further into particular features of the '*Gründerzeit*', the new company boom, let us first examine the position of the Warburg firm in this context. The loss figures for 1873–6 have already been given. Aby S. Warburg writes about them in his unpublished memoir of his father Siegmund:

Then came the boom years with their wild frenzy, which a large firm could hardly escape. Siegmund W. was badly depressed by the crash that followed, because losses persisted for so long a time. In any event, thanks to its old principles, the firm was far less affected by losses than were many other firms of the same standing. The brothers did at that time make certain domestic economies. By the way, Siegmund W. remained detached enough to ask the

* 'Die fünf Milliarden. Betrachtungen über die Folgen der grossen Kriegsentschädigung für die Wirtschaftsverhältnisse Frankreichs und Deutschlands', in the series *Deutsche Zeit- und Streitfragen*, ed. by Fr. von Holtzendorff and W. Oncken, III, Nr. 33 (Berlin, 1874). An excellent modern account of the boom of 1871–3 may be found in H. Böhme, *Deutschlands Weg zur Grossmacht* (Köln, Berlin, 1966), pp. 320 ff.; on the collapse in Vienna, see pp. 341 ff.

† A. Soetbeer, op. cit., p. 8.

retrospective critics of the time where they had been when their warnings might have been of some use. Later years more than made up for the losses sustained in 1873 and 1874.

In order to fill out this picture, we cite another contemporary voice from the same milieu. Max von Schinckel writes in his memoirs:

The boom period that Germany went through at that time, often characterized as a wild spree of speculation, was in fact no more than the necessary consequence of the monetary surplus that so suddenly burst over Germany. The individual German states paid back all their loans, bondholders were compelled to seek out new investment opportunities, and the enormously strengthened German economy strove quite naturally for that expansion which before the war had been hindered by the disunity of money markets and communications, and by the artificial tariff and other barriers erected by the states which for so many years had limited and checked all such efforts.*

Since von Schinckel inclined more to sarcastic criticism than benevolent forbearance, this passage is notable. Perhaps we have the explanation in the fact that the Norddeutsche Bank in Hamburg came through the crisis unharmed, while its close correspondent in Berlin, the Disconto-Gesellschaft, had participated in many new companies and suffered accordingly. On this point von Schinckel comments:

The Norddeutsche Bank participated under the leadership of the Disconto-Gesellschaft in Berlin in the formation of the Gelsenkirchener Bergwerks-Gesellschaft. Jointly with the Berliner Handelsgesellschaft, the Norddeutsche Bank also financed a number of Strousberg's railway enterprises in Germany, which at first were highly profitable, but ultimately collapsed when Strousberg's star waned, in much trouble, strife and lawsuits. The initially very friendly relationship with the management of the Disconto-Gesellschaft was for a time clouded by these Strousberg lawsuits, and by the establishment by the Norddeutsche Bank of its own representation in Berlin in the form of the Hamburg-Berliner Bank.†

In the light of these admissions, the losses of the Warburg bank, which arose for the most part from bill commitments, do not seem excessive.

Before we go further in describing the firm's fortunes, a phenomenon must be discussed which was not without importance for the next genera-

* Max von Schinckel, *Lebenserinnerungen* (Hamburg, 1927), p. 211.

† Ibid., p. 213. On the conflict with the Disconto-Gesellschaft, see also *Dr. Strousberg und sein Wirken. Von ihm selbst geschildert* (Berlin, 1876), pp. 283 ff. We refrain from comment on the pathos and reliability of this account. Schinckel's judgement on this large-scale entrepreneur, often unjustly maligned as a swindler, is

tion as well: the rise of economic populist anti-Semitism. There were similar manifestations in France as early as the first half of the nineteenth century, aimed against Rothschild enterprises.

In Germany, contemporaneously, there was the still inchoate anti-Semitism of the lower middle class, which fought against equal civic rights for Jews out of jealousy of economic competition and anxiety for their guilds and mercantile associations.* For the new Germany, one of the first preludes to the campaign was represented by the work of 'Hilarius Bankberger', *Die sogenannte 'Deutsche Reichsbank', eine privilegierte Aktien-Gesellschaft von und für Juden. Nebst Betrachtungen über Laskerhafte und Bambergerliche Politik.*† The real name of the author was Franz Perrot, a financial journalist and staff member of such conservative newspapers as the *Nationalzeitung*, *Deutsche landwirtschaftliche Zeitung* and G. Hirth's *Annalen des Deutschen Reiches*. He published in 1872, under the title *Der Kampf gegen die Ausbeutung des Publikums durch den Banknotenschwindel und die Papierpest*, a collection of articles that had been published in these journals and newspapers in 1870 and 1871. This work, often shrill in tone and with distorted arguments, attacks with some justification the unregulated chaos of multiple issues of banknotes – a struggle that had to be waged in other countries as well until central banks were assured priority and regulatory rights in this matter.

Anti-Semitic charges appear first in the anonymous pamphlet of 1876, which in 1879 was published in a fourth edition and again pseudonymously, this time with the more pretentious title *Die Juden im deutschen Staats- und Volksleben*. One of the main themes of this work is that Jews are found in all occupations where the largest profits may be earned with the least effort, 'namely in the banking business and in wholesale trade'. A key sentence asserts: 'The general creditors of all present-day economic institutions, from the state down to the private individual, are

---

considered and judicious: '... People who rely on their luck and their superior knowledge, who undertake obligations far beyond their means, who want to conquer the entire world, – be they a Strousberg or a Stinnes – come one fine day to an abrupt end.' A very careful and intelligent view of Strousberg, in which he is compared with the somewhat luckier Pereire brothers, may be found in L. Bamberger, *Lebenserinnerungen*, op. cit., pp. 214, 525 ff.

* See Jacob Toury, *Die politischen Orientierungen der Juden in Deutschland. Von Jena bis Weimar* (Tübingen, 1966), pp. 90 ff. Ibid., pp. 171 ff., for discussion of the crisis of 1873 as the origin of a new, aggressive anti-Semitism.

† Berlin, 1876.

the big financial powers, and these financial powers are quite overwhelmingly Jewish. Here we see Jewish world domination already achieved.'*

Otto Glagau was the one who linked this theme with the panic of 1873 and its consequences; in 1876 and 1877 he published his voluminous reports on 'Stock Exchange and new-company swindles' in Berlin and Germany in book form, after extracts had already appeared in the German family newspaper *Gartenlaube*, where they were presented to a receptive lower middle class. Both volumes contain instructive facts on establishment of new companies in the years after 1871, the composition of their Boards, issue price of their shares, the subsequent boom and later collapse. It is noteworthy that among the approximately 1,750 company names listed, only about five are from Hamburg, and not one significant new company had its headquarters there.† The acceptable factual contents of the book are however distorted by a continuous defamation of Jews that is full of remarkable inconsistencies.‡ In the second volume on Germany we read: '. . . The Stock Exchange and new company swindles for which they are 90 per cent responsible, and which are really their achievement, have brought them millions and billions.'§ Influenced by Franz Perrot, the author writes a few sentences about the Seehandlung and the Reichsbank which encapsulate the basic theme of the later campaign:

> Without the Seehandlung, the Government could be completely foiled in a conflict with Parliament, could fall into the most oppressive and humiliating dependence on Bamberger's Reichsbank, which is really run by a Central Committee composed almost entirely of Jews and their friends, a sort of Sanhedrin or Supreme Council of the New Jerusalem. There is an enormous difference between the two institutions. The Seehandlung is a German, conservative state institution; the Reichsbank, on the other hand, is simply a Semitic-national-liberal joint-stock company that one fine day can also collapse and be liquidated.||

If after this lesson we continue studying the book, in which many aristocrats by birth and letters patent, men of landed families and senior

* *Die Juden im deutschen Staats- und Volksleben* (4th ed., 1879), p. 20.

† Max von Schinckel reports on the 'first overseas bank', the Deutsch-Brasilianische Bank in Rio de Janeiro, and its swift collapse: Schinckel, op. cit., pp. 212 ff.

‡ There is a particularly malicious treatment of Strousberg in the volume on Germany, pp. 57 ff.

§ O. Glagau, *Der Börsen- und Gründungsschwindel in Deutschland* (Leipzig, 1877), p.215.

|| Ibid., p. 350.

civil servants are listed among the incorporators and Board members, we come to the following statement about the partial list of founders and 'first signers' of incorporation papers:

But even incomplete as it is, this listing makes an appalling impression. Quite apart from the individuals listed without asterisks, most of whom are blameless, there is still quite a group of entrepreneurs and their henchmen, and among these we find the flower of the aristocracy, holders of the highest state honours, the most celebrated parliamentarians. The Duke of Ratibor, the present President of the House of nobles, and Herr von Bennigsen, now President of the lower House, are both company incorporators and both comrades of Baruch Hirsch Strousberg. . . .*

How is this assertion to be reconciled with that about the 90 per cent Jewish proportion in the founding of new enterprises? Obviously, we are not engaging here in any polemic; but it seems necessary to point out how early in this movement its leading spirits recognized that attracting the desired number of followers could only be achieved through massive lies. It is, moreover, noteworthy that even in the heroic beginnings of the movement there was an attempt to seek a scapegoat among a minority for the mistakes of broad classes among the general population. In the next generation, it was above all Max M. Warburg's painful task to protect the reputation of the firm in German courts against the persistent campaign of anti-Semitic slanders.

Turning now to our narrower subject, we find among the few documents for the years after 1870 a letter of April 1871 confirming that Warburgs saw their 'chief activity in the bill business' † but that they were prepared increasingly to participate in the securities business. We have already mentioned the 'Lombards' which were apparently among the most actively traded securities on the Stock Exchange.‡ In connection with these securities, there was a 'special relationship' between Warburgs

* Ibid., p. 519.

† M. M. Warburg & Co. Archive.

‡ Strousberg writes in his autobiography, p. 429: 'On the day that the candidacy of the Prince von Hohenzollern [for the Spanish throne] was withdrawn, and at the moment of rejoicing . . . I bought for settlement at the end of the month a large position in the two fungi that poison Continental markets: Lombards and French bonds.' Strousberg calls himself 'a sworn enemy of any Stock Exchange speculation'; he says he bought these securities only to demonstrate his good faith, and lost a great deal, since his banker 'in deadly fear' demanded payment in advance for this commitment. This incident too reflects something of the style and mood of the time.

and the Rothschild banks. In the letter mentioned above (page 70) from Warburgs to the London house, several securities and bill quotations are given, with the Lombards mentioned first:

13 July 1870, 360, relatively firm; 28 October 1870 349–347½ and on 31 May 1871 343–342, steady and dull, French bonds on the contrary in demand, 859–863.

On Sunday, 4 May 1873, the *Hamburgische Correspondent* contained the following announcement,* flanked by two archaic locomotives from the compositor's old type-box:

South Austrian-Lombard Railway. As agents for Rothschild Brothers in Paris, we announce that the final dividend due on 1 May for the shares of the above railway, of Fr. 12.50 per share will be payable at our offices. Dividend notices with serial numbers are presentable from 9–12 in the morning, and payment will be made until further notice in Reichsmark at the average spot exchange rate on Paris.

M. M. Warburg & Co.

The firm's records yield a few more examples of its growing interest in the securities business. On 30 March 1871 a number of letters appear in the firm's copy book addressed to several firms, informing them that according to a report from Paul Schiff in Vienna 'negotiations for the proposed Egyptian business have been terminated because of difficulties in assuring debt service, and the transaction is therefore off.' In the proposed loan, £5,000 had been reserved for Emile Nölting in Hamburg, £2,000 for Hesse, Newman & Co., Altona; and £1,000 for S. & J. Fränckel in Hamburg.

At the beginning of May 1871 the following telegram was sent to a trusted correspondent on the Berlin Stock Exchange, presumably a member of the S. Bleichröder firm:

Please telegraph if further information concerning 100 million francs 6-month Treasury bonds 6% coupon ½ to 1% commission therefore 7 to 8% per annum with quarterly interest. Strictly confidential.

In the next communication to the same party, dated 9 May 1871, the first French indemnity loan was discussed: 'This is to ask if, subject to the following proviso, you can entertain further expression of interest in the new French loan: aside from francs 500,000 already noted, a further francs 500,000...'

* *Hamburgische Correspondent*, 4 May 1873, p. 8; repeated on 6 May.

A few days later, on 8 June 1871, an interest in foreign business was shown. The Consul-General of Nicaragua in Hamburg reported:* 'Nicaragua wishes to issue a loan with very generous conditions;' the letter went on to request clarification from the Nicaraguan Consul in the addressee's city. The letter was addressed to 'Dear Sirs', without repeating the firm's name, which was doubtless on the envelope alone; this omission, which we find repeatedly in many of the copy books – themselves hardly legible – gives some notion of the very modest staff that ran the bank. We also note that the trainees, if any, or other employees who were charged with registering letters in some order, seldom did so although each copy book was provided with an index.

There remains however one source that offers a somewhat more precise notion of the securities business for those years. By chance three volumes have been preserved in which certain key employees noted the details of individual transactions, not for book-keeping purposes but to keep track of matters being handled by the firm. These books cover the years 1871–7, and we publish in the following section selected extracts. It cannot be ascertained with any certainty whether these books contain all the securities business transacted in those years.

* Letter from copy books of firm, Hamburg.

APPENDIX TO CHAPTER 4

SELECTION OF BUSINESS TRANSACTIONS 1871-1887

One of the last of Max M. Warburg's aphorisms from Kissingen, which we reported in the Preface, was the following:

> It should be made quite clear that our firm arose from bill-broking, and that the first fifty years were almost exclusively devoted to bill business. Until 1900, securities business played a subordinate role for the firm – only after that year were large issues and international financings on a grander scale undertaken. [Then, in a handwritten postscript . . .] One should not however say too much about the last 25 years and eclipse the old generations.

This assertion may be correct, if we look at the range of transactions. The existing files and letters, however, give the impression that the firm sought, at least after 1871, to participate more actively in new-issue business. The following extracts may serve to demonstrate this point.

1871	St. Gotthard Railway Shares. Fr. 400,000 subscribed for with Gebr. Sulzbach, Frankfurt am Main, received 16,000. Fr. 1,200,000 subscribed for with Moritz B. Goldschmidt, Frankfurt am Main, received 48,000.
1872	Participation in the establishment of the Italienisch-Deutsche Bank in Rome, through Anglo-Österreichische Bank in Vienna.
1872	50,000 Gulden shares of Rotterdam'sche Handels-Vereeniging, through Gebr. Sulzbach, Frankfurt am Main.
March 1872	£53,000 5 per cent Peruvian Loan, of which subscribed £25,000 with Stern Brothers, London £20,000 with Bischoffsheim & Goldschmidt, London £4,000 with B. Premsel, Hamburg £4,000 with Lieben Königswarter, Hamburg Of which £44,000 distributed to fourteen clients.

1873	M. Bco. 20,000 Hamburg-Berliner Bank, through Norddeutsche Bank, Hamburg.
March 1873	Incorporation of London and Hanseatic Bank through Commerz- und Disconto-Bank, Hamburg. Siegmund Warburg, 938 shares Moritz Warburg, 812 shares Total payment to 30 June 1874: RM 248,591.
1873–4	One-twenty-fifth share in a syndicate of the Österreichische Bank-Gesellschaft, Vienna, with 6,000 shares at 2,000 Gulden.
July 1874	4½ per cent Bremen State Loan of 1874. RM 150,000 subscribed through Norddeutsche Bank.
February 1874	Vienna Municipal 5 per cent Gold Loan. 25,000 Gulden nominal received through Österreichische Bank-Gesellschaft, Vienna. Syndicate dissolved on 16 March 1873, with 4·03 per cent profit, equalling 1,007.50 Gulden.
February 1874	Vienna Municipal Premium Loan. Subscribed for 75,000 Gulden nominal, to be paid in until January 1878. 40,967 Gulden, for which received 470 municipal lottery tickets, at price of 90¾ Gulden.
August 1874	Consortium for purchase of M. 2,700,000 shares of Breslauer Discontobank from Friedenthal & Co.: Two-ninths Wilh. Ledermann, Breslau One-ninth Gustav Friedmann, Breslau One-ninth Herm. Schweitzer, Breslau One-ninth M. M. Warburg & Co., Hamburg Two-ninths Meyer Jüdel, Berlin Two-ninths Gebr. Schiff, Berlin.
January 1875	Gulden 100,000 nominal Austrian Treasury Bills, participation through S. M. von Rothschild, Vienna. Of which distribute Gulden 60,000 to Commerz- und Disconto-Bank on original terms.
October 1875	Wiener Bankverein, 250 shares, nominal 100 Gulden, participation through Moritz B. Goldschmidt, Frankfurt am Main.
1879	4 per cent Austrian Gold Bonds. Participation through the Württembergische Vereinsbank in Stuttgart in a new consortium that took 60 million Gulden at 63·30 per cent gold, firm, with an option on further 40 million. M. M. Warburg & Co. take nominal Gulden 105,000. Further, Deutsche Bank, Berlin, transfers in March 1879 another Gulden 45,000 to M. M. Warburg & Co. From these holdings 80,000 Gulden sold to Gebr. Schiff, Berlin, 25,000 Gulden to Paul Schiff, Vienna, and 22,500 Gulden to H. Spitzer in Paris.

November 1879 — Atlantic and Great Western Railway Reorganisation. Participation through Kuhn, Loeb & Co., New York, for $50,000.

1880 — Königs- und Laurahütte Consortium. Participation of M 150,000 (of 60 million) through the sole manager of the consortium, S. Bleichröder, Berlin. S. Bleichröder will advance the money, without deducting commission, at discount rate of Reichsbank. Duration of syndicate until end of May, extended to September, dissolved on 15 December 1880.

1881 — Diamant Bultfontein Mine. Sale of two-thirds share of fifty-seven claims in Baltfont Mine. Participation through J. E. Günzburg in Paris per their letter of 29 June 1881. £2,000 of £100,650 total participation in Paris, on same terms as theirs. The participation was converted in March 1888 after lengthy negotiations and reorganization into the 'Spes Bona' Company to a holding of 2,450 shares of £1 nominal each.

1881 — New Texas and St. Louis Subscription. Participation through Kuhn, Loeb & Co., New York per letter of 17 June 1881 with

$50,000 General First Mortgage Bonds,
$25,000 Land Grant Bonds,
$25,000 in stock.

One-fifth of this allotment was sold on 2 June 1881 to J. E. Günzburg in Paris.

1884 — Russian 5 per cent Consolidated Bonds, Series VII.
Loan of £15 million, of which 10 million taken up by S. Bleichröder, Berlin, 5 million reserved for its own account by Russian Government. Bleichröder concedes to us on original terms a participation of £25,000 per letter of 12 April 1884. Further participation through J. E. Günzburg for joint account. Net profit through S. Bleichröder, 19 May 1884: RM 10,098. (Payment to H.S. for one-third subparticipation RM 3,336.10.) Profit through J. E. Günzburg of £100,000, RM 40,393.50, equivalent to 19,420 Roubles at 2.08.

1884 — Lemberg Czernowitz Jassy Railroad – Mortgage Loan Conversion. A syndicate consisting of Österr. Länderbank in Vienna, Berliner Handelsgesellschaft, Mendelssohn & Co., Rob. Warschauer & Co. in Berlin, von Erlanger & Söhne in Frankfurt a.M. took up from the Lemb. Czernow. Jassy Ry. Co. Austrian Gulden 52,755,000 4 per cent Silver Mortgage Bonds with the commitment to redeem a prior 5 per cent loan. Participations of Gulden 150,000 from Robert Warschauer, Berlin, per letter of 29 September 1884 and of Gulden 100,000 from Jacob Landau, Berlin. From both, total earnings of M 3,490.

1884 Norwegian Loan (Conversion). Subscription through Commerz- und Disconto-Bank Hamburg. Kronen 25,000,000 4 per cent Norwegian Government Loan, underwriters' price 98·05 per cent. Management, Commerz- und Disconto-Bank in Hamburg, Deutsche Bank in Berlin, Deutsche Effekten- und Wechselbank in Frankfurt a.M. Duration [of consortium] to 31 May 1885.

Participation through Commerz- und Disconto-Bank Kronen 850,000 on original terms. We laid off:

Kr. 170,000 to Veit L. Homberger, Karlsruhe,
Kr. 58,000 to J. E. Günzburg, Petersburg, jt. account,
Kr. 10,000 to H. Sp. [Paris].

Net profit for syndicate 0·87 per cent, besides 4 per cent interest on subscription paid in (2 March 1885). Commerz-Disc. Bk. credits on 850,000 Kr. M 7,395 profit and 5,172 interest, proportionately divided [among us, Günzburg, Homburger & H.Sp.].

October 1884 Serbian Railway Bonds.

A syndicate consisting of:

Comptoir d'Escompte in Paris
Österreichische Länderbank in Vienna,
Berliner Handelsgesellschaft in Berlin
Mendelssohn & Co. in Berlin
von Erlanger & Söhne in Frankfurt a.M.
and Norddeutsche Bank in Hamburg,

purchased from the Société d'exploitation des chemins de fer Serbes Fr. 32,000,000 5 per cent mortgage Serbian Railway Bonds at 500 Fr. = 20 T, partly firm, partly in options. ... Robert Warschauer & Co. in Berlin allot us per their letter of 1 October 1884 a participation on syndicate terms of nominal Fr. 50,000 firm and 80,000 in options. The syndicate calculates a commission of 1 per cent for management and settlement of this transaction; Warschauer charges us no commission.

Total earnings for M. M. Warburg & Co. per final accounting of 16 December 1884, M 13,479.65.

March 1885 Hamburg $3\frac{1}{2}$ per cent State Revenue Bonds Bid of 3 March 1885 for 25,000,000 M $3\frac{1}{2}$ per cent Hamburg State Revenue Bonds which awarded to S. Bleichröder in Berlin on their bid of 97·14 per cent. Participation through S. Bleichröder in Berlin nom. 1,500,000 M. Bleichröder informs us on 25 January 1886 that total profits amount to M 156,720.75 and net profit after deduction of expenses comes to M 12,022. On 25 January 1886 our share of the profits due, 7,741.30 M, was credited to us. [Text somewhat abbreviated.]

January 1886

St. Paul, Minneapolis and Manitoba Railway 4½ per cent Bonds. A consortium consisting of Kuhn, Loeb & Co., Brown Brothers & Co., J. Kennedy Tod & Co., New York, Brown, Shipley & Co., London, Berliner Handelsgesellschaft, Mendelssohn & Co., Warschauer & Co., Berlin purchased firm: $5,400,000 4½ per cent consolidated 1st mortgage bonds of above railway co. at price of 92½ per cent with option on further 2,700,000 at same price. The takedown may be made in installments.
Participation through Rob. Warschauer, Berlin, letter of 19 October 1886, $20,000 plus corresponding options.
Participation through Kuhn, Loeb & Co., New York, 20 October 1886, $50,000 incl. options.
Per letter from Kuhn, Loeb & Co., New York, of 28 January 1887 securities sold. Profit credited from Rob. Warschauer, M 5,544.25, from Kuhn, Loeb & Co., $2,074.58. [Text abbreviated.]

August 1886

3 per cent Hamburg State Loan of 1886 in amount of 40 million M nominal.
Participation through Commerz- und Disconto-Bank [Hamburg] per letter of 10 August 1886 in M 2,000,000 at purchase price of 94⅛ per cent. We allot to J. E. Günzburg, Petersburg, for joint account M 1,000,000 on original terms, and to Isaac Dreyfus Söhne in Basel M 250,000 and to Dr. Marc Rosenberg in Karlsruhe M 200,000, both on original terms. [Abbreviated; detailed final accounting in June 1888.]

August 1886

Kursk Kiev Mortgage Loan Conversion Consortium.
Consortium consisting of Berliner Handels-Gesellschaft, Directorate of Disconto Gesellschaft, Mendelssohn & Co., Robert Warschauer & Co. in Berlin, Petersburger Disconto Bank, Petersburg, re call and repayment of Thaler 19,605,600 nom. 5 per cent Mortgage Bonds, and new issue of same amount 4 per cent Mortgage Bonds. Participation through Robert Warschauer & Co. in Berlin, letter of 13 August 1866, for M 100,000 nominal. Wound up on 15 December 1887, net profit M 1,773.90. [Text abbreviated.]

October 1886

Gruson'sche Gewehrfabrik.
Conversion of H. Gruson'sche enterprise in Madgeburg into joint-stock company. Preliminary contract concluded with Berliner Handels-Gesellschaft, Robert Warschauer & Co., Meyer Cohn and Commerzienrath Meyer. Share capital 9,000,000 M in fully-paid shares. Hr. Commerzienrath Gruson undertakes to manage the company for five years.

Participation through Robert Warschauer & Co. in Berlin per their letter of 29 October 1886 with M 90,000 and options. Settlement on 11 December 1886 with profit for the firm (90,000 plus 30,000 [shares]) of M 28,850.25 net. [Text abbreviated.]

March 1886 Berliner Handels Gesellschaft Consortium.
A consortium under Born & Busse, Berlin, agreed with Berliner Handels Gesellschaft to take up those warrants for the 10 million new shares to be issued that are not taken up by holders of the old warrants, immediately after expiration of the subscription period; and to pay the 30 per cent premium as well as 25 per cent of the nominal amount plus 4 per cent interest, and the 75 per cent balance within four weeks. The consortium receives from Berl. Hand. Ges. 4 weeks after expiration of subscription period a commission of M 300,000 net. The consortium stands ready to purchase up to 1,500,000 nominal old Berlin Hand. Ges. warrants for joint consortium account to support [the market] until completion of this transaction. Born & Busse in Berlin allot us a participation of M 300,000 or 3 per cent of entire deal, per letter of 6 March 1886. [Verbatim; hereafter abbreviated.] Transaction completed 24 May 1886 with net profit of M 302,000, of which M 9,060 for Warburgs.

January 1887 5½ per cent Chinese Loan.
Underwriting of M 5,000,000 Chinese Loan, payable within fifteen years, sinking fund beginning after fifth year.
Participation through Robert Warschauer & Co., Berlin, per their letter of 22 January 1887, of M 100,000 with ¼ per cent commission. Rob. Warschauer & Co. credit us on 13 October 1887 with net profit of M 3,141.75. [Abbreviated.]

January 1887 Niederländisch Südafrikanische Eisenbahn Gesellschaft Bonds.
The Niederländisch Südafrikanische Eisenb. Ges., established with participation of Labouchère Oyens & Co., Amsterdam, Berliner Handels Gesellschaft and Rob. Warschauer & Co. in Berlin, for construction of a railway in the South African Republic (Transvaal) from the frontier to Pretoria, for whose first section a capital of

Holl. Fl. 2,000,000 (6 per cent) shares
Holl. Fl. 6,000,000 (5 per cent) mortgage bonds

is fixed. The Transvaal Government directly guarantees the payment of interest on shares and bonds in Dutch guilders and Reichsmarks. Robert Warschauer allot us participation of Holl. Fl. 30,000 bonds nominal at 85 per cent on January 1887.
Consortium dissolved on 14 December 1887 with net profit, after

deduction of all costs, of 8·10 per cent net profit on the bonds. Robert Warschauer transfer to us on 15 December 1887 our share in profit of M 4,093.30, thus closing the transaction. [Entry slightly abbreviated.]

5

THE DEBUT OF THE FOURTH GENERATION: 1890–1914

The transitional period following the death of Siegmund Warburg in May 1889 came to a close at the end of that year, when his widow and her children withdrew from the firm as joint partners, leaving her eldest son Aby S. Warburg as co-partner with his uncle Moritz M. Warburg.

The establishment whose destinies the two Warburgs now guided remained, in the best Hamburg and *haute banque* traditions, a modest one. A total of twenty-three employees conducted the bank's affairs in austerely furnished and rather cramped quarters, which were expanded only gradually and piecemeal by the acquisition of adjacent properties in Ferdinandstrasse and their incorporation into the central offices by means of improvised and occasionally awkward alterations. As the new decade began, the bank was still frugally lit by oil lamps, and linked to the outside world by a single telephone, used sparingly and with considerable caution by senior employees only.

The firm's business, too, continued along traditional lines. It consisted very largely of commission transactions in foreign exchange and commercial bills with large trading houses and banks, particularly outside Germany. New issue business, although slowly growing, still represented only a small part of the bank's activities, and by deliberate choice the Warburg partners did not strive for too rapid an expansion of their private or corporate clientele, preferring the careful cultivation of each individual client and the gradual accumulation of modest profits on a slowly increasing volume of steadily recurring transactions. Despite the preservation of an unpretentious façade and of a cautious conservatism in its business, M. M. Warburg & Co. had by the end of the year 1889 already attained a respectable size in the German private banking community, with a balance sheet total of 35,298,436 marks.

For German banks generally, Germany's high rate of industrial growth continued to ensure a strong domestic demand for capital; while the transition of the Reich from a capital-importing country to a capital exporter – a development favoured for political reasons by the Foreign Ministry – was leading to a rapid spread of German banking interests abroad. German private banks with well-established international links were in a particularly favourable position to participate in both these parallel developments. For M. M. Warburg & Co., the full integration, from 1888 onwards, of Hamburg, Germany's largest port, into the Reich and its burgeoning economy gave an added impetus to the development of its business.

The strength and independence of the German banking community were demonstrated at the end of 1890 by the comparative calm with which they weathered the crisis in London caused by the near-collapse of the mighty house of Baring Brothers & Co. Barings, which since 1884 had placed a vast sum in excess of £100 million in new issues, of which £19 million had been in Argentine loans of dubious soundness, suddenly found its liabilities far in excess of its liquid assets, and was rescued from a collapse – the consequences of which might have been disastrous for the international banking community – by an unprecedented rescue operation mounted by the Bank of England and the entire City financial fraternity. Writing to the Banque Nationale in Brussels,* Moritz Warburg reported in the wake of the crisis that the difficulties of Baring Brothers 'aient été loin de produire en Allemagne une impression aussi durable qu'en 1857, par exemple, époque à laquelle les grands industriels et le Haut Commerce allemands avaient leur crédits en blanc plus ou moins chez les Banquiers ou des Banques de Londres.' Indeed, he continued, there had been a considerable shift away from the London market by German seekers of credit, whose needs could now be met in Germany; the number of acceptances on Barings in circulation within Germany was in fact 'rélativement minime'.

Although the independence of the German financial community was thus growing apace, personal ties with banks abroad remained all-important, and it was in the traditional desire to strengthen those ties that Moritz M. Warburg arranged the banking training of those among his five sons who were destined to join him in the family firm. The eldest

* Moritz M. Warburg to M. Weber, Director of the Banque Nationale, 28 November 1890.

son, Aby M. Warburg,* had early renounced the traditional right of the first-born to enter the firm, and devoted himself entirely to the study of the humanities, especially to tracing the influence of the classical tradition in the history of art. The semi-serious childhood agreement in which his banking brothers undertook to supply Aby Warburg with all the books he might need for his studies was ultimately to result in the world-famous collection of the Kulturwissenschaftliche Bibliothek Warburg, now the Warburg Institute of London University.

Max M. Warburg, the second son, began his banking apprenticeship in 1887 with I. Dreyfus & Co. of Frankfurt am Main. He later recalled this experience without enthusiasm,† but it nevertheless gave him a valuable acquaintance with the Frankfurt *haute banque* and its methods. After a further half-year with Wertheim & Gompertz in Amsterdam, during which he achieved his first business success – the nomination of M. M. Warburg & Co. as correspondent of the Nederlandsche Bank – Max Warburg completed his military service with the 3rd Bavarian Light Cavalry Regiment in Munich, which led him to contemplate the possibility of a career as a cavalry officer. Such military notions were firmly suppressed, however, by the practical-minded Moritz Warburg, who sent Max in 1890 to the Banque Impériale Ottomane in Paris, where he completed a year's service as Secretary to the bank, and at the same time attended lectures at the Sorbonne. It was a wrench for the young man to part from the light-hearted Paris of the *belle époque* and proceed to the London stage in his training, but Max Warburg successfully if reluctantly made the transition, serving throughout 1891 with N. M. Rothschild & Sons in their offices, rich in banking tradition, at New Court.

Paul Warburg, one year Max's junior, completed an exacting training period with a Hamburg trading firm, went on to spend some time with Samuel Montagu & Co. in London, and then worked for two years in the Paris branch of the Banque Russe pour le Commerce Etranger. Paul and Max Warburg, close in age and linked throughout their lives in an intimate working relationship, were contrasting but happily complementary personalities. The personal motto which each brother chose early in his career epitomized his individual temperament: for Max, with

* Moritz M. Warburg had five sons; Aby M. Warburg, 1866–1929; Max M., 1867–1946; Paul M., 1868–1932; Felix M., 1871–1937; and Fritz M., 1879–1964.

† See Max M. Warburg, *Aufzeichnungen* (New York, 1952), p. 10.

his restless urge to break new ground, his occasional impetuosity and his great personal charm enlivened by a sense of humour, the motto was – with rare appropriateness – '*En avant*'. Paul, of an intellectual cast of mind more akin to that of his academic brother Aby, with a lofty sense of public duty and a certain reflective austerity of manner, chose as his device '*In serviendo consumor*'. So it was to be.

Of the two younger brothers, Felix settled in the United States in 1895, where he married Frieda Schiff, the only daughter of Jacob H. Schiff, senior partner in the renowned firm of Kuhn, Loeb & Co., then second only to J. P. Morgan & Co. in importance as a Wall Street issuing house for governments, railways and major industrial enterprises. The personal and business links with Kuhn, Loeb & Co., which conferred on the Hamburg firm uniquely important standing within the German banking fraternity, were further strengthened by Paul Warburg's marriage, also in 1895, to Nina Loeb, daughter of Solomon Loeb, one of the founding partners of Kuhn, Loeb & Co.

The youngest of the brothers, Dr. Fritz M. Warburg, completed his law training at Berlin and Rostock, and began a banking apprenticeship with the Disconto-Gesellschaft in Frankfurt. From there he went on to the London metals trading firm of Brandeis, Goldschmidt & Co., an experience that equipped him later to direct the metals trading department of Warburgs. Following his training period, Dr. Fritz Warburg joined the bank and was put in charge of the Credit Department, becoming a partner in 1907.

Max Warburg's apprenticeship was brought to an abrupt end: he was compelled to cancel his plans to stay beyond 1891 in London, and then undertake a world study tour, when his father summoned him back to Hamburg in order to join the firm as holder of Power of Attorney and help the bank over a difficult period occasioned by the sudden suspension of payments by the Günzburg bank in St. Petersburg. The Günzburg house, which had invested heavily and with excessive optimism in the Lena goldfields of Siberia,* was M. M. Warburg & Co.'s closest banking connection in Russia, and had drawn bills on Warburgs for 7 million marks.† There were in addition family connections to be considered:

* Cf. *L'Economiste Français*, 19 March 1892, describing the Günzburg house as 'une sorte de Baring russe, toutes proportions gardées'.

† For a description of the Günzburg bank's liquidity crisis, see Henri Sliosberg, *Baron Horace O. de Gunzbourg* (Paris, 1933), pp. 109–10.

Siegmund Warburg's daughter Rosa had married Baron Alexandre de Günzburg in June 1891. Despite the very substantial sums involved, M. M. Warburg & Co. protected all the Günzburg bills, thus earning the deep gratitude of the Günzburg house and in the event raising its own already high credit standing. The Günzburg bank was able some years later to repay all its outstanding loans and interest, and indeed did so in gold coin.*

The challenges of Max Warburg's first year in the bank were by no means over with the successful resolution of thc Günzburg crisis. The bank had in addition to contend with the difficulties of a large Hamburg export firm which was a substantial client; and then a severe cholera epidemic broke out in the city in the summer of 1892. While most of the bank staff stayed at home, and several died from the disease, Max Warburg and two volunteer employees worked throughout the epidemic from seven in the morning till midnight in order to transact the firm's business and maintain the continuity of its foreign correspondence. Characteristically, Warburg refused to consider that the cholera might represent a personal danger: 'I felt quite confident of my immunity', he was to write later.†

Early in 1893 the firm suffered a severe loss in the premature death of one of its key employees, Adolph Dorner, who had joined the bank in 1865, and had been its sole holder of a single Power of Attorney and chief clerk since 1889. Dorner's death caused Moritz Warburg to recall his son Paul to Hamburg from what had been planned as a prolonged round-the-world voyage, and Paul entered the firm in March 1893 as holder of Power of Attorney. On 1 July of that same year, Max M. Warburg was admitted as a partner.

The years from 1893 almost to the outbreak of the First World War coincided with a long-term upward swing of the world economy, a movement that was interrupted only briefly in the years 1900 and 1907. Based largely on a significant increase in South African gold production and on a rapid expansion of world trade, the economic boom meant for Germany, and for the German banks in particular, a steady expansion of business as they moved to satisfy the ever-growing capital needs of

* See Max M. Warburg, *Aufzeichnungen*, p. 14.

† See *Aufzeichnungen*, p. 14. One of the bank's older employees recalls in his memoirs that each day throughout the epidemic two bottles of Hennessy cognac were distributed among some thirty employees at the firm's expense; when the cholera ended, so did the ration of cognac. See Max Hamlet, unpublished *Aufzeichnungen* (Tel-Aviv, 1940), p. 18.

established as well as new industries, and of foreign trade. The sums of capital now required to finance the growth of major industries began to outstrip the resources of even the largest banks, and the movement of expansion and amalgamation within the banking sector, in which many private banks merged with the big joint-stock banks, gathered momentum. M. M. Warburg & Co., with established international connections and newly-forged family links with New York and other major financial centres, was in a solid position to participate in the new upsurge of German economic power, and the new generation of Warburg partners was eager to exploit fresh opportunities, particularly in the new-issue side of the bank's business.

As full partner of the family firm, Max Warburg now launched himself with spirit and great energy into the competitive maëlstrom, travelling extensively in Scandinavia and elsewhere, endeavouring to obtain for the bank an improved position in issuing syndicates, not merely as sub-participant, but in its own name. The first significantly large transaction of the firm's burgeoning issue business came in 1900, when it placed 80 million marks in Reich Treasury Bills in the United States. The firm received the ultimate accolade in 1905, when it was admitted '*en nom*' to the honorific and lucrative Reich loan consortium, the inner circle of about fifty representatives of the German *haute banque*. Long before that point, however, the patient efforts to build up the firm's position – not least through a careful policy of granting syndicate sub-participations to brokerage houses of proven placing power – had resulted in a substantial increase in its issue business generally, as well as in the designation of Warburgs as paying agent and fiscal agent for various issuers. That such designation required careful campaigning and steady effort is illustrated by a letter of Max Warburg's to the St. Petersburg International Trade Bank:

> We took the liberty yesterday of repeating by telegram our request that you exert your considerable influence with Mendelssohn & Co. in Berlin so that agencies for the issue and conversion as well as coupon payments of the new Russian Railways First Mortgage Loan be established in Hamburg. . . . The gentlemen of the Hansemann and Bleichröder firms would be agreeable, but it is Mendelssohn & Co. primarily who will make the decision this time. Although we enjoy very good relations with Mendelssohn & Co., we nonetheless believe we could have no better advocates with that firm in this matter than yourselves. . . .*

* Max M. Warburg to A. Rothstein, 9 December 1895.

While issue business was of increasing importance, M. M. Warburg & Co. improved its position in every phase of its activity. The classic trade acceptance and foreign-exchange business was carried on with many banks in Germany and abroad, and added to it was a brisk activity in securities arbitrage, primarily with Berlin and Frankfurt, where transactions for joint account strengthened relationships with such firms as Löwenherz and Merzbach. Although these joint-account transactions often yielded only small profits, they represented a source of steady income, and laid the foundations for an extension of the firm's placing power. The main foreign houses with which joint-account business was transacted, aside from the 'special relationship' firm of Kuhn, Loeb & Co., were A. Keyser & Co. and S. Japhet & Co. in London, Albert Kahn in Paris; and in Copenhagen, R. Henriques, Jr., whose senior partner, Otto R. Henriques, was a staunch friend of the firm and on excellent personal terms with Max Warburg, whom he met frequently in Copenhagen or in Hamburg.*

Cultivation of relationships with Scandinavia was one of Max Warburg's major personal responsibilities. The older generation of Siegmund and Moritz Warburg had avoided travel to the Scandinavian countries because, as Max Warburg wrote, 'Grandmother was afraid they would not eat kosher food there. I did not labour under this handicap.'† The business connection with the Stockholms Handelsbank (later the Svenska Handelsbanken) was a particularly close one, based as it was on a truly fraternal friendship between Louis Fränkel, Managing Director of the Handelsbank, and Max Warburg. Fränkel, of German-Jewish origin, had since 1893 transformed his bank into a powerful competitor with the Stockholms Enskilda Bank of the Wallenberg family, and he made M. M. Warburg & Co. the main foreign business connection of the Handelsbank, which was a source of much attractive financing business from Denmark and Norway, as well as Sweden.

The competition for Scandinavian loan business evolved into a two-sided struggle in which the Stockholms Enskilda Bank under K. A. Wallenberg, allied with the Crédit Lyonnais of Paris, the Danske Landmansbank in Copenhagen and L. Behrens & Söhne of Hamburg, ranged itself against a Warburg-Handelsbank-Henriques group. The Warburg group enjoyed a competitive advantage when the London market had a demand for

* The Henriques family were remotely related to the Warburgs.

† Max Warburg, unpublished notes on the firm's history.

Scandinavian issues as did the Wallenberg syndicate when the French market could offer more placement possibilities. An arrangement was ultimately reached between the rival groups, and a formal agreement was signed in January 1910 after negotiations lasting since the previous summer. This confidential 'Nordic Arrangement' provided for an alternation of the leadership in Scandinavian business, no matter from what source it might come, and for the participation of all the banks in each transaction. The 'Nordic Arrangement' came to an end when the First World War made it unworkable.*

Although the issuing side of the bank's affairs continued to receive careful attention, the established business in bills and foreign exchange continued; M. M. Warburg & Co. had by the turn of the century become the leading Hamburg acceptance house and an important factor in foreign exchange trading. Commercial bills in substantial volume were traded actively on the Hamburg exchange, and large orders for securities and commercial paper of all kinds were executed on a regular basis for foreign purchasers. Foreign banks bought large quantities of German trade bills on a commission basis usually one-sixth to one-fifth of the prevailing official discount rate, and brisk trading developed through Rothschilds and other London friends in trade bills denominated in Marks, considered such an excellent investment for foreign banks that they came to be called *Zuckerbrot* ('sugarbread').

International currency arbitrage was also highly developed in Hamburg, and cultivated with care as an important branch of M. M. Warburg & Co.'s business. Recalling this activity, Max Hamlet wrote: 'The technique of calculation was painstaking; traders had to work quickly and accurately, with their fingertips, as it were. Logarithmic tables and calculating machines are a later invention; they have mechanized the process of calculation and probably impaired the acumen of individual traders.'†

The year 1898 brought with it the firm's centenary, a milestone which was celebrated quietly, but which gave the partners much gratifying

* Writing to K. A. Wallenberg on 27 August 1909, Max M. Warburg pointed out: 'You know what we bring to the alliance. . . . As far as our other international relationships are concerned, we have I believe demonstrated to you that we are not dependent on one group alone, but can at any moment be entirely flexible. I consider the tripartite tie between you, Fränkel and ourselves very fortunate in itself, since through this grouping complementary alliances will doubtless develop. . . .'

† Hamlet, op. cit., p. 5.

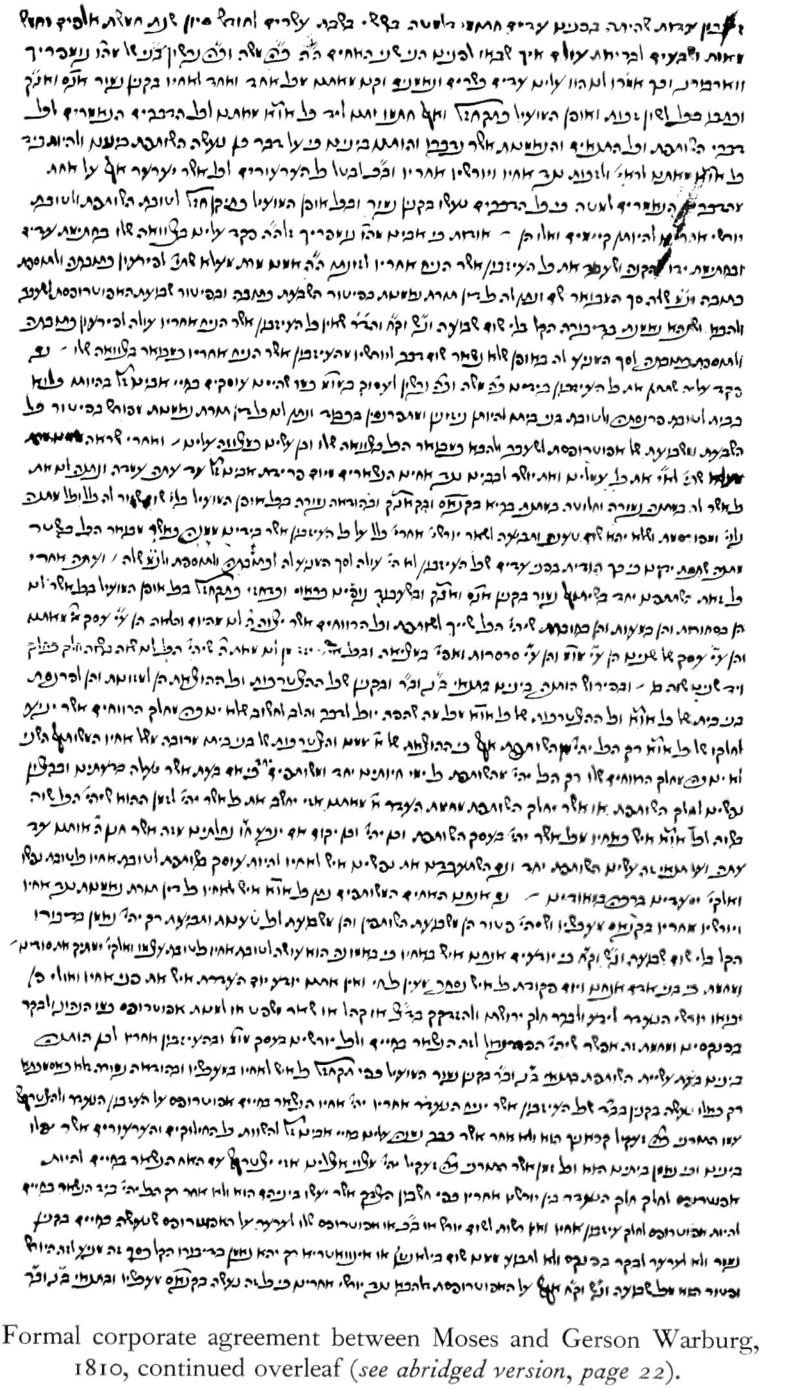

Formal corporate agreement between Moses and Gerson Warburg, 1810, continued overleaf (*see abridged version, page 22*).

בכל אופן השותפין בכל השותפות ועל תנאי זה נעשה השותפות ביניהם על כל הנאמר והנזכר הנ"ל / והנה כה"ר שלמה עזרא ואחיו

כה"ר נתן כי אין אדם יודע עתו ורגעיו ואולי יעבור הוא את פני אחיו וכה"ר נתן אחיו הצעיר יהי' אפוטרופוס על

חלקו ועל כל יורשין אחריו עד [illegible] כל [illegible] ולכן העני [illegible] ועשות [illegible] כי הבני [illegible] בקנס [illegible]

מוספת [illegible] [illegible] כה"ר שלמה מוספת על [illegible] עד סך אלף [illegible]

בין הכל חוץ [illegible] והעובדין וכל התפיסין אשר יש לה [illegible] באופן [illegible] שישאר [illegible]

סך שני אלפים [illegible] ואם [illegible] יותר עסק שלשת אלפים [illegible] עד סך אלף

[illegible] והמותר הכל [illegible] ואם לא [illegible] כסף הזה [illegible] חוק אחר ואם [illegible]

והרבות [illegible] ובבנות [illegible] חוק [illegible] עד סך אלף [illegible] ומוספת [illegible]

ולא יותר · [illegible] בקנס · [illegible]

[illegible] כה"ר נתן [illegible] אפוטרופוס על כל [illegible] עד אשר [illegible]

עד אשר [illegible] / [illegible] השותפים [illegible]

או [illegible] או [illegible] אפוטרופס

או [illegible] או [illegible] הקהלה כי על כל דברי התנאים והנאמרות הנ"ל נעשה השותפות וכל

הנ"ל נעשה בקנין וכל אופן המועיל בכל הקנינים כבי' תקה"ז וכל אשר [illegible] או [illegible] על התנאים

[illegible] על [illegible] ודברים הנאמרים והתנאים הנ"ל

[illegible] כה"ר [illegible] ואחיו כה"ר גרשון [illegible] גומפריך [illegible]

[illegible]

גרשון בן כה"ר גומפריך ז"ל

[illegible]

Sara Warburg (1805–84)

Moritz Warburg (1838–1911), *ca.* 1908, with four of his sons (*from l. to r.*)*:* Paul (partner, Kuhn, Loeb & Co., New York); Moritz; Aby (founder of the Warburg Institute, now of the University of London); Max (partner, M. M. Warburg & Co.), and behind, Felix (partner, Kuhn, Loeb & Co., New York).

The five sons of Moritz Warburg at their last joint meeting in Hamburg, 1929 (*from l. to r.*): Paul (chairman, International Acceptance Bank, New York); Felix (partner, Kuhn, Loeb & Co., New York); Max (partner, M. M. Warburg & Co.); Fritz (partner, M. M. Warburg & Co.), and Aby.

The firm's premises in Ferdinandstrasse, Hamburg: *left*, 1836–1913; *below*, from 1913 to the present.

Dr. Carl Melchior (1871–1933).

Dr. Rudolf Brinckmann (1899–1974).

evidence of the esteem in which M. M. Warburg & Co. was held in Germany and abroad. Looking back on the year, Max Warburg wrote in his private Annual Report:

> Although we refrained from any large-scale ceremony to mark this centenary, we received from almost all our business friends, the staff and the public authorities as well remarkably friendly marks of esteem. The year's results were extraordinarily favourable, but in this context it must not be forgotten that the most profitable revenues ... must be characterised as windfalls. ... Our employees numbered 36, of whom four hold Power of Attorney, 23 are banking staff, three apprentices, three servants and three volunteer trainees. Total turnover this year was M 5,100,000,000. The issues that yielded the most noteworthy results were: Hamburger Electricitätswerke ... Continentale Ges. f. electr. Intern. ... Union Pacific Reorganisation Syndicate. Aside from the several issues in which we were active on behalf of friends, we ourselves were underwriters in the following issues: M 2,000,000 share of Hamburg. Electric. Werke at 142, M 5,580,000 3½% Hannover State Loan at 101½%, M 20,000,000 3% Hamburg State Loan of 1897 at 95.90. ... Our holdings of securities for our own account amounted to M 9,205,000 on 31 December 1897, our syndicate account for 1897 was M 2,760,000. Our gross profit was M 1,575,288.01, after deduction of expenses, that is a profit of 27⅝% on the capital of M 5,700,000 with which we began the year. ...

It was also an eventful year in more personal terms: on 29 December Max Warburg became engaged to Alice Magnus, member of a family related to the Altona branch of the Warburgs and for long close friends of the Hamburg family. The couple were married in March 1899. Engagements and marriages of other members of the family followed in rapid succession; several of these added personal links to long-standing business relationships with a number of leading banking houses in Germany and elsewhere in Europe.

Within Hamburg itself, the respected position of the firm and its partners was reflected in the election of Max Warburg in 1897 to the office of Commercial Judge and of his brother Paul in 1901 into the élite ranks of the Hamburg *Bürgerschaft*, or Freemen, an honour which was to come to Max himself in February 1903. Paul Warburg enjoyed his membership of the *Bürgerschaft* for only a short time, however, before moving to New York in 1902, where he joined his brother-in-law Jacob H. Schiff as a partner of Kuhn, Loeb & Co. Looking back on the ten years that he and Paul had worked together in Hamburg, Max Warburg later remarked: 'We worked together very happily, and father took particular pleasure in driving with these two ponies in tandem.'* Despite their geographic separation, the two brothers continued their intimate cooperation: Paul remained a partner of M. M. Warburg & Co., spending several months each year in Europe, and the connection with Kuhn, Loeb & Co. became deeper, developing into a link of the first importance for the Hamburg branch of the family.†

The departure of Paul Warburg and the growing volume and complexity of the bank's affairs led later in 1902, at Max Warburg's request, to the appointment of a permanent legal adviser, Dr. Carl Melchior. Born in Hamburg on 13 October 1871, Melchior had studied law and attained the office of District Judge when he was offered the post with Warburgs. He joined the firm as counsel, became holder of Power of Attorney in 1911, and was admitted as a partner in 1917 – the first person not a member of the family to attain that position – a recognition of the extraordinary confidence that the Warburgs reposed in him.‡

Physically, too, the firm was expanding: in the autumn and winter of 1903 the bank building in Ferdinandstrasse was reconstructed, and the necessarily protracted process of acquiring neighbouring properties for further expansion was begun. The bank was hemmed in on one side by a fishmonger's; looking back to that time, Max Warburg wrote: 'We went so far as to instigate one of our employees to marry the rather elderly proprietor of the fish shop, but despite working on both victims the marriage did not take place.'§ This property and two others were ultimately purchased in 1906; in 1912 a new building was erected on the enlarged site and the bank moved into its new quarters in two stages, in June 1913 and one year later. A small corner property housing a pharmacy

* Max M. Warburg, unpublished draft memoirs.

† An intensive and varied correspondence linked the brothers when apart, each bringing potential business opportunities to the attention of the other. For example, Max wrote to Paul on 25 February 1902: 'Sacha [de Günzburg] is of the opinion that pig iron can very profitably be imported into America from Russia, and believes he can arrange such business in the near future. I understand as much about pig iron as Erich [his baby son] does of Kant, which adequately describes my knowledge of the matter, but since one usually earns most from things that one understands least, please from now on be good enough to look into pig iron in addition to your other preoccupations, and see how one might profitably import the stuff from Russia to America.'

‡ See *Carl Melchior, Ein Buch des Gedenkens und der Freundschaft* (Tübingen, 1967), and Max M. Warburg, *Aufzeichnungen*, pp. 49–52.

§ Max M. Warburg, unpublished draft memoirs.

was incorporated into the main premises only after the First World War, by which time the entire building was able to house a staff of 300 employees on its three floors.

Tensions in the Far East, culminating in the outbreak of war between Russia and Japan in February 1904, had unsettling effects on world markets, which brought the firm substantial losses in its securities portfolio. Max Warburg's report for 1903 was nevertheless able to list participations in a number of new issues. In the wake of Japan's success in inflicting a decisive defeat on Russia, the first Imperial Japanese Government loans were floated on the international markets, which was a significant development in the growth of M. M. Warburg & Co. as well as a milestone in Japan's rise to the status of a great power.

The first Imperial Japanese Government loan, an issue of £10 million at 6 per cent, was issued on 11 May 1904 by an Anglo-American group of banks jointly led by Kuhn, Loeb & Co. and associates in New York, and by the Hongkong & Shanghai Banking Corporation, Parr's Bank and the Yokohama Specie Bank in London. The loan, following shortly after Japan's first decisive victory on the Yalu River, was highly successful on both sides of the Atlantic, and was followed in November by another 6 per cent sterling loan for £12 million, which was equally successful.* With the Russian surrender at Port Arthur in January 1905 and the steady advance of Japanese troops in Manchuria, the international investing public developed a growing interest in Japanese loans, and it was possible for a financial operation of greater scope to be contemplated.

The American group, led by Kuhn, Loeb & Co., thereupon turned to M. M. Warburg & Co. with a request to sound the willingness of the German market to accept Japanese securities. Describing his response, Max Warburg later wrote:

> I did what every upstanding banker has to do in such cases, I went to the Foreign Ministry in Berlin. Under-Secretary of State Zimmermann of the Foreign Ministry was very much taken with the idea of admitting [to listing on the Berlin Stock Exchange] a Japanese bond issue, and I received permission to negotiate with representatives of the Japanese Government concerning the German tranche of the loan.†

* For a description of these loan transactions, see Cyrus Adler, *Jacob H. Schiff: His Life and Letters* (New York, 1929), Vol. I, pp. 213–30.

† Max M. Warburg, unpublished draft memoirs.

Max Warburg proceeded to London, where he entered into negotiaitons with the Anglo-American group and with the Japanese representative, Baron Korekiyo Takahashi, then Vice-Governor of the Bank of Japan and Financial Commissioner of the Japanese Government to London and New York.* The discussions were completed within a few days, and on 28 March 1905 an Imperial Japanese Government 4½ per cent sterling loan of £30 million was issued, half of which was underwritten by the American group. M. M. Warburg & Co. received from the London group an underwriting participation of £1 million. 'As yet unaccustomed to such amounts in a secure piece of business,' Max Hamlet later wrote, 'we gave away all but £100,000 in Germany (with an underwriting commission of 1½%) in order to achieve German subscriptions for the London consortium. We made ourselves very popular *urbi et orbi* in the German banking community with the participations which were enthusiastically received, and thereby strengthened our position.'† Although £30 million was a very large amount by prevailing international capital market standards, the loan was a great success.

On 11 July a second issue, also for £30 million, was launched, divided in equal tranches between England, the United States and Germany. M. M. Warburg & Co. shared the leadership of the German syndicate with the Deutsch-Asiatische Bank, and once again the loan was highly successful, being over-subscribed about ten times. The Japanese loan transactions, profitable in themselves, also brought M. M. Warburg & Co. considerable prestige in international banking circles as well as in Japan itself, where several leading finance and commercial houses now established cordial personal and business friendships with the Warburgs.

It was therefore with considerable satisfaction that Max Warburg was able to report:

The year 1905 meant for our firm a further strengthening, in fact an enhancement of our standing. We were for the first time officially included in the Reich loan consortium, and were then able through our links with our New York friends to assume a leading position for the German group in negotiations for

* Takahashi was later President of the Yokohama Specie Bank, Minister of Finance and Premier of Japan. Max Warburg, with whom Takahashi remained on excellent personal terms, described him as 'much the best at figures among all the many finance ministers with whom I have had dealings in my life. Even at moments of the most difficult negotiations he always remained polite and absolutely trustworthy.' Max M. Warburg, *Aufzeichnungen*, p. 20.

† Max Hamlet, op. cit., p. 9.

the issue of two Japanese loans. . . . We were able to conclude a successful bridging finance operation with our old friend Sweden, which brought us relatively small profits, but further raised our prestige in that country, since we were able at a critical juncture for Sweden [the separation from Norway] to put large sums on favourable terms at their disposal. . . .*

At mid-point in the year following that of the Japan issues, Moritz Warburg wrote to his son Max, then in Paris: 'With the best will in the world I have no idea what to report to you, since business here is absolutely dead.'† The senior Warburg's report was excessively gloomy, however: although the firm had some losses on investment account, the year brought with it an increased turnover, a balance sheet total of M 103,175,352, and several transactions which brought added prestige. These included leadership in a $50 million issue of Pennsylvania Railroad 4 per cent notes placed in Paris, and an attempt to establish a French-American bank with the participation of the Banque de Paris et des Pays-Bas, Société Générale, Kuhn, Loeb & Co. and Sir Ernest Cassel, the Cologne-born banker who had made a fortune in the City of London and was a close friend of Jacob H. Schiff – as well as of King Edward VII. The difficult negotiations aimed at establishing the new bank foundered at the last moment on account of the opposition of one of the proposed French participants, and although the disappointment in Hamburg was initially keen, hindsight subsequently demonstrated that the time would not have been propitious for such a project.‡

Perhaps most significant for M. M. Warburg & Co. in 1906 was its inclusion for the first time *en nom* in the Hamburg–America Line syndicate, which arranged a capital increase for the Line from 100 to 125 million Marks. This transaction, like many others in subsequent years, reflected the close personal and business friendship between Max Warburg and Albert Ballin, the highly respected managing director and indeed the creator of the Line, which was then rapidly attaining the status of the largest shipping company in the world. Ballin and Warburg conferred and corresponded often, and saw each other almost daily when both were in Hamburg; their mid-day joint appearance on the Stock Exchange was

* Max M. Warburg, Annual Report, 1905.

† Moritz M. Warburg to Max M. Warburg, 10 July 1906.

‡ The atmosphere of the Paris negotiation is captured in a letter Max Warburg wrote to his brother Fritz on 26 May 1906: 'The indiscretion here is simply unbelievable, and I should not at all be surprised if I read our final contract first in the newspapers, before we sign it!'

a feature of the Hamburg scene, and their offices were linked by a private telephone line.* Warburg introduced Ballin to Sir Ernest Cassel in June 1908, and the acquaintance between these two men ripened into a friendship which was to have business and political consequences: Ballin was a valued confidant and personal adviser to Kaiser Wilhelm II, as was Cassel to King Edward VII.†

The effects of the world economic crisis began in America in the autumn of 1907 rapidly spread to Europe; they were felt in Germany primarily in the money and securities markets, where heavy losses were suffered, and new issue business dropped sharply. M. M. Warburg & Co., with its close New York ties, also suffered investment losses, though its standing remained unaffected. Reporting on the year, Max Warburg was indeed able to write that new clients, including the Russian State Bank, had been acquired and old friends sustained in a period when the local Hamburg branches of the big Berlin banks had been unable to advance credits to their customers. A particularly noteworthy transaction in this crisis year was Warburgs' sale on behalf of the Swedish State Bank of 30 million Marks in German treasury notes in order to permit the State Bank to save an important Swedish bank that was in payments difficulties. This service was gratefully acknowledged in Stockholm, and raised the firm's standing in Scandinavia. Despite the difficult conditions, M. M. Warburg & Co. also arranged issues and Stock Exchange introductions in Hamburg for thirteen issuers, which brought the bank for the first time into the top rank of Hamburg issuing houses, on equal standing with the Norddeutsche Bank.

The business of M. M. Warburg & Co. was indeed evolving more and more towards the issuing side of banking activity. While within the German economy generally the metallurgical, engineering, chemical and electrical industries were developing most rapidly, Warburgs was devoting its greatest attention to such sectors as shipping, colonial enterprises and other foreign financing. A significant reflection of Max Warburg's concern with the wider world situation was the speech he made to the German Bankers' Convention on 5 September 1907 on the subject of

* See Lamar Cecil, *Albert Ballin: Business and Politics in Imperial Germany 1888–1918* (Princeton, 1967).

† Max Warburg described Ballin as 'a man of considerable stature, a constructive thinker, energetic, far-seeing, clever, amusing, kind and warm-hearted'. *Aufzeichnungen*, p. 25.

financial war-readiness. Although Warburg clearly saw the necessity for the German authorities to include the financial aspect in their contingency planning, he was later to confess: 'I was in no sense aware that these matters could so soon become urgent reality.'*

Increased international tensions resulting from colonial conflicts and Anglo-German naval rivalry now formed the backdrop to M. M. Warburg & Co.'s own steadily expanding foreign business. Max Warburg's summary for the year 1909 emphasized the overseas and colonial aspect of the bank's affairs:

> In 1909, we worked for the first time closely with the Foreign Ministry in Berlin on detailed transactions. The Chinese Railways business that was originally confided to the Deutsch-Asiatische Bank group became the point of departure for a German-English-French-American cooperative effort in which the foreign ministries had more to do with the fixing of terms than the financial groups. We succeeded through our good offices, in constant contact with Washington and the Wilhelmstrasse, in achieving an understanding between America and Germany. . . . The interest in colonial assets continued to become stronger. Long-standing Hamburg merchants' relationships overseas brought many possibilities of business, and we thus established a department devoted exclusively to working on projects of this sort brought to us by local and foreign friends. At the moment, we are dealing with an expedition† to the Far East, an expedition to Morocco and one to the Bismarck Archipelago; in all these enterprises, we shall not be able to dispense with the courage to incur costs – nor with the need for extreme caution.

In an attempt to interpose a counterweight to the growing English trade in Liberia, Warburgs sent an emissary there on behalf of a Hamburg group in order to explore commercial possibilities for joint German-American account.

Max Warburg summarized these colonial developments as follows: 'I daresay that no banking firm in Germany took as keen an interest in Germany's colonial activities as did ours. Indirectly as well, through my membership of the Chamber of Commerce, I supported colonial efforts wherever it seemed possible. I was able to make many contributions: once with the foundation of the Colonial Institute in Hamburg, again with

* Max M. Warburg, *Aufzeichnungen*, p. 23.

† Max M. Warburg, *Aufzeichnungen*, p. 24. Cf. Alfred Vagts, 'M. M. Warburg & Co. Ein Bankhaus in der deutschen Weltpolitik 1905–1933', *Vierteljahrschrift für Sozial- und Wirtschaftsgeschichte*, Bd. 45 (Stuttgart, 1958), pp. 289–388.

repeated support for the Institute of Tropical Hygiene in Hamburg, which was twice rescued from financial difficulties thanks to our intervention. I was a friend of Dernburg, the Minister for the Colonies.'*

On 28 January 1910 Moritz Warburg died. With his passing Max M. Warburg became the titular head of the firm, still supported by his brother Fritz and his cousin Aby S. Warburg, who was in fact senior to him in age. Dr. Fritz Warburg continued to devote himself to the bank's credit business, but was also active in developing a new department that dealt in non-ferrous metals, primarily copper, lead and tin. By 1911 the copper business alone had attained a turnover of some 21,000 tons and yielded a profit of 139,000 Marks.

Partly inspired by the search for new mining possibilities, M. M. Warburg & Co. concentrated its colonial efforts in Morocco, where since 1905 German trade and industrial interests had come into increasing conflict with the French, who wanted to declare a protectorate over the territory. In 1910 the firm had established the Hamburg-Marokko-Gesellschaft with Dr. Carl Melchior as chairman and Dr. Wilhelm Ch. Regendanz, a former member of the Colonial Department at the Foreign Ministry, and then holder of Power of Attorney at Warburgs, as managing director. Partly as a riposte to the French occupation of Fez in May 1911, Regendanz, a forceful personality given to personal initiatives of some boldness, arranged with the Foreign Ministry that a German emissary should be despatched to Morocco in order to establish a German presence and ascertain on behalf of the Warburg group and the Mannesmann interests whether there were workable bodies of mineral ores. The German representative, a mining engineer, departed in June 1911 to pursue his explorations in the sensitive neighbourhood near the harbour of Agadir.

On 1 July 1911 the German gunboat *Panther* arrived at Agadir with Regendanz aboard, ostensibly to protect German nationals in a troubled area, but actually to frighten the French, if possible, into making concessions to Germany in Morocco. However, the sole German national in the area – the hapless mining engineer – arrived at Agadir only three days after the *Panther*, thus somewhat diminishing the credibility of the official reason for the *Panther's* presence in Morocco.* The repercussions of this incident were immediate and severe: while the press in France and Germany whipped up strong nationalist feeling, French banks withdrew credits *en masse* from German clients, and the Berlin and other German stock exchanges suffered severe price falls on 2 and 4 September.

* See Vagts, op. cit., p. 321.

Secret negotiations were meanwhile initiated between the Wilhelmstrasse and the Quai d'Orsay, and ultimately an agreement was reached in November whereby France gave Germany a strip of territory in the Congo in exchange for official recognition of France's paramount influence in Morocco. Although Regendanz received a decoration for his part in the Agadir affair, it was quite apparent that Germany's attempt to acquire territory in Morocco by threats had failed. Worse still, the crisis had exacerbated English fears of Germany, fuelling the accelerating tension over naval programmes; and the precedent represented by the French withdrawal of credits as a political weapon was an ominous one for the future.

Political events such as the Agadir crisis, Italy's declaration of war on Turkey, the outbreak of the first Balkan war and the overthrow of the Manchu dynasty in China significantly disturbed markets in the second half of 1911. The last-named event in fact nullified a Chinese currency reform loan that had been signed in April 1911 with an Anglo-French-German-American banking group, after several years of tortuous negotiations in which M. M. Warburg & Co., in close coordination with the German Foreign Ministry, had been instrumental in integrating the American banking group into the four-power syndicate whose nominal German leader was the Deutsch-Asiatische Bank.

Despite political upheavals and their financial repercussions, the bank's business continued its steady expansion: the balance-sheet total at year-end of 1911 was M 104,863,573; for 1912 it declined to M 95,771,124, by the end of 1913 it had climbed to M 118,141,853. One reflection of new development was Max Warburg's nomination in 1911 to the Board of Blohm & Voss, the leading German shipbuilders. In the same year Dr. Melchior joined the Board of the Norddeutsche Hütte in Bremen. These board appointments represented a new departure in Warburgs' history, and were the first of many which were added in subsequent years. Construction of the Ferdinandstrasse bank building continued, and the bank premises began to assume their present form. To strengthen its ties further with British friends and clients, M. M. Warburg & Co. established a representative office in London under the management of a Dutch national, Pieter Vuyk. In Paris, where for several years M. Lionel Hauser had represented the bank's interests, his office was reorganized as a limited company, Lionel Hauser & Cie.

In addition to its traditional business in commercial paper and currencies – the trade bill portfolio amounted to M 14,769,503 at year-end 1911 – Warburgs continued to expand the issue side of its affairs, participating in several large loan operations for the Hamburg–America Line for the construction of giant steamers, and in both debt and equity transactions for such other concerns as Siemens-Schuckertwerke, the Deutsche Bank, Gelsenkirchener Bergwerks-AG, Disconto-Gesellschaft, Deutsche Orientbank, and a number of Scandinavian and other foreign issuers. Also noteworthy were participations in issues of treasury notes and longer-term loans on behalf of the State of Hamburg.

The disturbances in the Balkans in 1912 led to two special transactions on which Max Warburg reported as follows:

> We had two transactions to carry out in connection with the Balkan troubles. It was first suggested to us, through Bourke, Schiff & Co. in London, that we should advance money to the Bulgarians against Treasury bills. I travelled to Berlin to confer with the Foreign Ministry. Following the wishes of the Foreign Ministry, we declined to make an offer, but were able as a substitute to succeed in being admitted to the German consortium for Bulgarian business. At the end of November I was called to Vienna by the Kreditanstalt to negotiate with the Austrian Finance Ministry concerning a Treasury bill transaction. The meetings, in which Melchior also took part, led on 9 December to an issue of $25 million of Treasury bills with an average maturity of 18 months on a basis of almost 7%. The terms were hard, but the transaction was heartily welcomed in Austria, because Austria urgently required funds, and foreign markets had dried up.*

Despite such impressive gestures as the establishment in 1911 of the King Edward VII Foundation, an Anglo-German fund for the support of needy German nationals in England and their counterparts among British subjects resident in Germany – initial subscribers to the Foundation included Sir Ernest Cassel, Albert Ballin and Max M. Warburg – naval and colonial rivalries between Great Britian and Germany grew steadily more intense. Alarmed by the prospect of war, Sir Ernest Cassel and Ballin took the initiative in arranging for the visit to Berlin in February 1912 of Lord Haldane, the British Secretary of State for War. Haldane's mission failed to produce any agreement to curtail the naval armaments race; the mission had in any case been immediately preceded by the introduction of a supplementary naval bill in the Reichstag calling for large increases in naval manpower, as well as the formation of an entirely new battle squadron.

* Max M. Warburg, unpublished draft memoirs.

The stalemate on the question of naval limitation did not, however, preclude progress in taking the heat out of two other areas of contention in Anglo-German relations: the general colonial question and railways in Mesopotamia. In the course of slow negotiations the complex issues surrounding these subjects were gradually resolved, and Anglo-German understandings crystallized in several agreements – although these were to come to nothing with the outbreak of war in 1914. Warburgs were intimately concerned with several of these.

England and Germany found common ground most easily in the joint conviction that Portugal's vast colonial possessions in Africa were neglected, mismanaged and ripe for a more appropriate system of administration. In August 1913 a secret Anglo-German treaty was signed to provide for a division of the Portuguese colonies into English and German spheres of influence if Portugal were to request an international loan to be secured on her colonial revenues. At the initiative of Dr. Regendanz of Warburgs, an Overseas Study Syndicate* was established in 1913, of which the Hamburg members included M. M. Warburg & Co., the Hamburg-America Line, the Woermann shipping line, F. Rosenstern & Co. and the Norddeutsche Bank. To these were added a Berlin bank group – the Berliner Handelsgesellschaft, Deutsche Bank, Disconto Gesellschaft and Brisk & Pohl – and Fried. Krupp AG of Essen. In the course of 1912, Warburgs had arranged several transactions in Chinese and Turkish treasury bills for Krupps, relations with whom, despite their other banking connections, were becoming closer.

Both the German Colonial and Foreign Ministries took a keen interest in the Syndicate: their representatives attended its meetings and participated in its decisions.† It was therefore with the blessing of the Wilhelmstrasse that the Overseas Study Syndicate, after obtaining the agreement of British African interests, mounted an expedition of engineers and representatives of the banks and the Imperial Government that went to Mossamedes in Portuguese Angola in order to assess the feasibility of a railway from the coast to connect with railways in German South-West Africa. The expedition was still in Angola when war broke out, and the projected railway was never built.

* Uebersee-Studiensyndikat.

† Cf. F. W. Pick, *Searchlight on German Africa: the Diaries and Papers of Dr. W. Ch. Regendanz* (London, 1939), p. 109: 'The protocols of the meetings show clearly that once again the Hamburg group, though formally acting on its own account and initiative, was actually the arm of the Imperial Government.'

More significantly, the Hamburg group, again led by M. M. Warburg & Co. with the strong backing of the Foreign Ministry, had succeeded by the time the war began in acquiring for Germany a far greater prize than a mere railway concession: no less than virtual sovereignty over a colony nearly as large in area as Great Britain.* The colony was the northern part of the Portuguese East African colony Mozambique, known as Nyassaland. Directly adjacent to German East Africa (now Tanzania), and still largely unsurveyed, Nyassaland had an area of some 189,875 square km. It was owned by a chartered company, the Companhia do Nyassa, which possessed a monopoly on the region's economic exploitation as well as almost total sovereign rights, including the right to levy taxes on the population. The majority of shares in the Companhia do Nyassa was held by a British company, Nyassa Consolidated Ltd., which had paid no dividends since its incorporation in 1908 and had also done almost nothing to exploit the vast riches of the territory under its control.

The Hamburg group and Dr. Regendanz conceived a scheme for acquiring on behalf of the Imperial German Government the majority of shares in Nyassa Consolidated; but in order to help raise the funds required it was necessary to enlist the support of a Berlin banking group. A syndicate was formed to advance the £150,000 required for the purchase, in which the Deutsche Bank and the Berliner Handelsgesellschaft each participated as to 25 per cent; M. M. Warburg & Co. and the Disconto Gesellschaft each 16·66 per cent, and Mendelssohns and Bleichröders each 8·34 per cent. The management remained with the Hamburg group, which was prepared to undertake the risk of the share purchase without assurance of reimbursement from the Government. The Berlin banks, however, were adamant in regarding their advance as a loan to the Reich to be repaid with interest, and their view carried the day. The Imperial Government, whose representatives had been involved throughout the negotiations, reluctantly agreed to reimburse the bankers by annual instalments of £15,000 out of the secret fund of the Foreign Ministry, in return for which the Government would acquire all the sovereign rights vested in the Companhia do Nyassa and thus exercise the right to administer the new colony in harmony with the practice in German East Africa.† On 28 May 1914 the transaction was completed in

* See Vagts, op. cit., p. 350.

† Repayments were to be made out of secret funds to avoid voting regular budgetary funds in the Reichstag, which would have wounded Portuguese sensibilities. See Vagts, op. cit., p. 351.

London, with the consent of the British Foreign Office, and the British-owned Nyassa Consolidated shares were sold to the London representative of Warburgs, Pieter Vuyk, who was listed as transferee in order to avoid undue publicity. Two months after the successful completion of Regendanz's plan came the war, and the Nyassa Consolidated shares were confiscated by the British authorities as enemy alien property.

Yet another Anglo-German understanding was shattered by the war: the plans for formation of an Anglo-German bank in Morocco, for which both Max Warburg and Regendanz had been negotiating with Lord Milner since February 1914. The bank, first projected as the Anglo-German Bank of Africa and then to be known as the Bank of North-West Africa, was to have had a capital of £200,000, half to be provided by a German group led by Warburgs, and half by a British group. The Milner-Warburg agreement was printed and ready for signature by the fateful summer of 1914; when war came it was shelved and never subsequently revived.

In the last months of peace, Max Warburg was frequently preoccupied with Anglo-German relations. The Morocco and Nyassa Consolidated negotiations brought him to London in February 1914; and in May, on the occasion of the departure on its maiden voyage of the Hamburg–America Line's new giant liner *Vaterland*, the Chancellor, Bethmann-Hollweg, expressed his satisfaction to Warburg with the improvement in Germany's relations with England.* In June Warburg was three times in London to deal with aspects of a Brazilian loan led by Rothschilds, and was able to note that agreements were being reached in hitherto controversial areas of Anglo-German competition in Africa and Turkey, notably the Baghdad Railway in which Warburgs were interested as participants in a syndicate led by the Deutsche Bank.

Late in the same month of June, the Kaiser took the occasion of a private dinner in Hamburg to discuss the general situation with Max Warburg, who wrote that the Kaiser appeared both nervous and depressed at the prospect of war:

> He complained that we had too few railways on the Western front against France; oppressed by his worries, he even wondered whether it might be better to strike first rather than wait. I did not in fact have the impression that he was thinking seriously of a preventive war, but his gloomy assessment of the situation caused me dismay. I replied that I nonetheless saw things differently.

* Max M. Warburg, *Aufzeichnungen*, p. 28.

Germany was becoming stronger with every year of peace. Waiting further could only bring us gains.*

A few days after this conversation, Max Warburg wrote to his friend Sir Ernest Cassel, who had enquired whether Warburg would accompany the Kaiser to the annual Kiel Regatta:

I do not have time to go to Kiel, but I hear that a terrific love appears to have broken out between the Germans and the English, which let us hope will be a lasting one.

Two days later, on 28 June, Albert Ballin telephoned Max Warburg with the news that the Archduke Franz Ferdinand, heir to the Austrian throne, had been assassinated at Sarajevo. An era in the history of Europe and of M. M. Warburg & Co. had come to an end, although few suspected as much in the crowded weeks between the assassination and the formal declarations of war which followed in August.

† Ibid., p. 29.

6

WAR YEARS: 1914–1918

Although the fateful dimensions of the world crisis were not fully grasped in July 1914 – at most, a Russian-Austrian war was feared, England's neutrality being considered certain – M. M. Warburg & Co. attempted throughout the month to limit its new commitments, and to prepare for unforeseen contingencies by realizing some of its disposable assets. When the rapid drumfire of war declarations began on 28 July, the firm moved to withdraw its London representative to Amsterdam, from which point he was able to maintain cable communications with America when, on declaring war, the British Government severed the German cable link to New York.

With the closing of the Hamburg Stock Exchange on 30 July, and increasing indications of gold hoarding and spreading illiquidity, the firm extended itself to support brokerage and other houses with which it had long-standing business relationships, and made efforts to influence other banks and commercial houses to act generously and calmly in rapidly changing emergency conditions.* The immediate question of prime economic importance was whether a moratorium on debts should be declared. Max Warburg, who had been called to Berlin on 6 August with Albert Ballin and others to discuss with high Government officials various aspects of the war emergency, was firmly against the notion of a moratorium, and his view prevailed. Instead, war credit banks were established in order to extend credits to businesses requiring additional liquidity as a result of war conditions. Dr. Carl Melchior and Dr. Fritz

* Writing to Carl Otto Henriques of R. Henriques, Jr., in Copenhagen, one Hamburg business man described Max Warburg at this period as 'a hero; he stands like a rock amid the surf, and anyone who comes into contact with him feels the comforting calm that he radiates'. A. Rose to C. O. Henriques, 20 August 1914, Henriques Archive, Copenhagen.

Warburg were active in drafting the statutes for the Hamburgische Bank von 1914, which became the first such institution to be established and which was later to be widely imitated in Germany; Dr. Fritz Warburg became Vice-Chairman of the Bank's Board.

The second important task was the organization of food and other supplies for an economy that was by no means prepared for a war of any length. In cooperation with Albert Ballin and the administrative staff of the Hamburg–America Line, M. M. Warburg & Co. helped initially to establish the so-called Reichseinkauf, which acted as a department of the Ministry of the Interior for the importation of essential foodstuffs. However the Reichseinkauf proved unwieldy and inefficient, and Dr. Melchior was seconded by the War Ministry to the Ministry of the Interior in order to reorganize the entire enterprise. He did so by splitting the organization into the Zentral-Einkaufsgesellschaft m.b.H. with its seat in Berlin, and the Lager- und Speditions-Gesellschaft m.b.H. in Hamburg, of which Max Warburg became Chairman. Both these companies issued bills to finance their purchases *(Kriegsrembourse)*, which were discounted by the banks in ever-growing volume, eventually reaching a peak of some half-billion marks. These enterprises and the Ministry of the Navy also did substantial business in foreign exchange with Warburgs, as did private clients with overseas interests. These were able to meet their foreign commitments by dollar remittances arranged through Warburgs' New York connections; such transfers amounted to over $50 million in the period from the summer of 1914 to March 1915. Maintenance of a link with New York also enabled the firm to arrange a $5 million Swedish Treasury bill transaction with Kuhn, Loeb & Co., and to act as agent for the transfer of large sums raised in the United States for the relief of the Jewish population in the war zones of Poland and Galicia.

By the end of the year 1914, the pattern of the bank's activity throughout the war had already been determined by Government financial measures: with vastly expanding military expenditures financed by resort to the printing-press, and with the decline of normal investment opportunities, the firm was compelled increasingly to invest its own and its clients' resources in war-finance paper of all kinds. The blockade meant the end of traditional international trading business, except to a limited degree with foreign neutrals. As Government intervention in all phases of the economy grew inexorably, normal issuing activity also ceased, and M. M. Warburg & Co. participated increasingly in Government loan issues, and in the establishment of such war corporations as the Seeversicherungsgesellschaft for marine insurance and the Kriegsmetallgesellschaft for the purchase of strategic metals.

Over forty of the bank's employees were called to the colours immediately upon the outbreak of war, and women were engaged in large numbers to replace the staff who had departed. The active assistance of the firm's senior members was also required from the very beginning by several Government departments. In 1915, Max Warburg undertook trips to investigate and report on conditions in Belgium and Holland, while Dr. Melchior travelled to Bulgaria and Rumania to negotiate important war-supply contracts on behalf of the Zentral-Einkaufsgesellschaft. The long-standing Scandinavian links of M. M. Warburg & Co. were turned to good account in several confidential missions: the Foreign Ministry requested Max Warburg to go to Sweden, which he did on three separate occasions in 1915, in order to try and influence the Swedish Government, through its Foreign Minister Knut Wallenberg, to adopt a more friendly attitude towards Germany. Although doubting the efficacy of such efforts, Warburg had several talks with Wallenberg, reporting his realistic conclusions in detailed letters to Berlin. Dr. Fritz Warburg moved to Stockholm with his family in order to assist in complicated barter negotiations with Sweden and Norway for essential raw materials; his stay in Stockholm, originally meant to last only a fortnight, was to be prolonged until the Armistice. His semi-official status, independent of the German Embassy in Stockholm although he worked in careful coordination with it, was to prove invaluable in delicate negotiations for loans and other essential war assistance.

Towards the end of 1915, much of Max Warburg's time was expended on long-drawn-out discussions at the Foreign Ministry designed to free the Transocean-Gesellschaft m.b.H. telegraph agency from the political influence of its heavy-industry majority shareholders, an effort in which Hamburg and other trading interests were enlisted. Warburg was also asked by Admiral von Holtzendorff for his opinion on the economic consequences to be anticipated from heightened submarine warfare. In writing his memorandum on this subject, Max Warburg referred to the vital necessity of maintaining the neutrality of America – an opinion ultimately rejected by the military, who failed to share his insight into the strength which America could add to the coalition of Germany's enemies.

As the conflict dragged on, the first symptoms of war-weariness became apparent: the blockade raised prices of all products, and every commodity was in short supply. The railway system, plagued by shortages of coal and rolling stock, nearly collapsed in the autumn of 1915, thus increasing the difficulties of feeding the population. The resultant unrest was reflected ominously in disorders which broke out in Hamburg and other cities and had to be forcibly suppressed.

Max Warburg was nominated in July to the Advisory Council of the Kriegsernährungsamt, the body charged with organizing civilian food supplies, and was active in the establishment of Deutsche Aussenhandel G.m.b.H. which was engaged primarily in trading business with Rumania. He corresponded tirelessly with the Reichsbank, the Treasury and the Ministry of the Interior on matters urgently affecting German payments abroad, and remained in close touch with war developments through Ballin and high-ranking friends in the Foreign Ministry and other Government departments. Melchior continued to be recruited for frequent missions to negotiate supply and other contracts for various Reich authorities. In Stockholm Dr. Fritz Warburg's special position was utilized by the Foreign Ministry, which authorized him to receive a Russian representative, a Duma member named Protopopov, for informal personal soundings on the possibility of a separate peace. Protopopov was himself disavowed by the Russian Government, and the chances of a separate peace, which Dr. Fritz Warburg had never assessed as very bright, evaporated entirely when the German Government recognized the independence of Poland.

Reporting on the year 1916, Max Warburg wrote:

> Daily business consisted chiefly of transactions of the Zentral-Einkaufsgesellschaft, the placement of war loans and local authority bills, and in arbitrage transactions in American and especially Nordic securities and Scandinavian coupons. . . . The total of our balance-sheet assets amounted to M 213 million as compared with M 131 million at 31 December 1915. The increase of about M 82 million is the consequence of our large loan transactions with the Reichsbank, in which the counter-value of the large amounts taken in from abroad was deposited with us, for the most part on long term.*

Despite such imaginative transactions as the placement of over $3 million of dollar-denominated treasury bills of the State of Hamburg in Scandinavia, the firm's scope for independent activity was steadily contracting. International business in the traditional form was long since past; the concentration movement in German finance and industry was growing apace; and Max Warburg regretfully acknowledged that 'even after the

* 1916 *Annual Report.*

war many matters that until now could still artificially be kept in Hamburg will have their centre of gravity in Berlin.'*

Looking back on the year from a later vantage-point, he saw clearly that

> Our financial fate was ever more closely linked with the political destiny of Germany. The fiction that an individual firm could maintain itself in wartime independent of the economic and political situation of the Empire was clearly revealed. There was probably no German private banking firm that issued guarantees on behalf of the German Empire to as great an extent as we did. To that degree it is certainly true that we partially co-financed the war; especially in connection with purchases made in neutral foreign countries, we had to give our guarantee.†

With wry humour, Max Warburg remarked to Dr. Melchior that if Germany were to lose the war and the Reichsbank should be unable to honour its guarantees *vis-à-vis* the firm, there would be nothing to do but insert the following newspaper advertisement: 'M. M. Warburg & Co. has suspended its payments on the field of honour.'‡

On 15 January 1917, the Hamburg Chamber of Commerce passed a resolution, against the most vigorous opposition from Max Warburg, calling on the Kaiser to unleash all-out submarine warfare. This counsel of despair, born of sheer frustration over the seemingly eternal deadlock on land, ultimately commended itself to the highest military authorities, with the predictable result that on 6 April the United States declared war on Germany. In both personal and business terms, this development had painful consequences for the Warburg partners: Felix Warburg, who had become a United States citizen, had to relinquish his partnership in M. M. Warburg & Co. Even before Felix Warburg left the firm, it had been decided to break with 120 years of tradition by admitting a non-member of the family, Dr. Carl Melchior, to full partnership. This recognition of Melchior's outstanding abilities was widely acclaimed by friends and clients of M. M. Warburg & Co. when it was publicly announced in March 1917.

The year's business was concentrated primarily in war loan participations and in numerous transactions with Sweden, in which Warburgs discounted Kr.51 million in Swedish bills and had credit lines with

* Ibid.

† Max M. Warburg, unpublished draft memoirs.

‡ Max M. Warburg, *Aufzeichnungen*, p. 46.

Swedish banks amounting to Kr.34 million. The firm participated in the establishment of the Spinnpapier-Gesellschaft & Kommandit-Gesellschaft with a capital of M 2.875 million, designed to counter Swedish attempts to raise the price of paper exported to Germany. Another enterprise that was founded in 1917 with the firm's active participation was the Zinn-Import-Gesellschaft, a purchasing syndicate of German tin importers.

Amid the myriad political and financial anxieties of the period, a moment of comic relief was occasioned by the request of old Carl Hagenbeck, who loved his famous collection of animals as much he loved his family, for a M 8,000 loan to finance their provisioning. Max Warburg, who had already advanced substantial sums for this purpose, initially refused the loan but ultimately relented, and wishing at least to enjoy some entertainment from the transaction, called in his legal adviser and announced solemnly that he had advanced a loan for M 8,000 secured by a first mortgage on one of Hagenbeck's rhinoceroses. The worthy jurist insisted that in view of the impossibility of registering the mortgage some visible sign of the Warburg lien be attached to the animal itself, or at least its cage. 'I told him,' recalled Max Warburg, 'that I already had so many rhinoceroses in my office that I would not inscribe "M. M. Warburg" on the zoo fence.'* A further demand was made that the life of the rhinoceros be insured, a condition Hagenbeck was only too glad to comply with. The unforeseen sequel to this episode was that the animal survived the war and was later sold to the Budapest Zoo, thus permitting repayment in full of the Warburg loan, much to the surprise of all the principals in the transaction.

Such light-hearted interludes were all too rare, however. In July 1917, Max Warburg made proposals to the Reichsbank and other authorities advocating the lifting of exchange controls and suggesting ways in which the German currency might be strengthened. Meetings with high Government officials on currency and war debts, on the position of Hamburg within the Reich, on foreign trade, and indeed on a host of other public issues continued to crowd Warburg's calendar even as the general situation steadily deteriorated. Dr. Melchior also gave freely of his time and energies, and was able in October, after protracted negotiations, to sign a German-Dutch barter agreement of large dimensions. An ominous development at the year-end was the nationalization of all banks by the

* Max M. Warburg, unpublished draft memoirs.

new revolutionary régime in Russia: this step directly threatened the value of the firm's sizeable portfolio of Russian bills.

Assessing the year's results, Max Warburg was able to concede that the financial outcome had been favourable, if not quite as satisfactory as in the preceding year. Earnings above the normal rate of interest were prudently allocated to a special reserve for the contingency, which was to prove all too real, of non-payment of Russian bills. Summarizing his conclusions, Warburg wrote:

> Although 1917 from a purely accounting viewpoint appeared successful, the future of the firm, so closely linked with the future of Germany, could only be regarded with concern. The statesmanship of the German Empire both externally and internally failed to clarify itself during the war years, but on the contrary became more muddled and aimless. There are still no signs that wise policy and strength of will can prevail in positions of authority.*

By 1918 Germany had been bled white of both material and human resources. The war nevertheless went on, with the statesmen 'still hoping for something, in a situation that had long since become hopeless.'† At the beginning of March the new Chancellor, Count Hertling, invited Max Warburg to Berlin and asked him to go to Holland in order to make contact there with the resident American Minister with a view to sounding out peace possibilities. Warburg undertook the mission out of a sense of duty, but the American Minister declined to receive a German representative; the atmosphere had been decisively altered since Warburg had received his commission by the harsh terms of the Treaty of Brest-Litovsk, signed on 3 March 1918.‡

Despite disappointments and political alarms, the work of the firm continued. A project of long standing designed to give Hamburg an enhanced position in the financing of overseas enterprises came to fruition with the founding in 1918 of the Aktiengesellschaft für In- und Auslands -unternehmungen, with a capital of M 25 million and the participation of many first-rank German trading concerns. Later in the spring of 1918 Warburgs participated in the establishment of the Cuxhavener Herings-fischerei-Aktiengesellschaft and the Spinnstoffeinfuhr G.m.b.H. Meanwhile, Dr. Fritz Warburg continued his labours in Stockholm, negotiating

* 1917 Annual Report.

† Max M. Warburg, *Aufzeichnungen*, p. 57.

‡ On this incident, see Prinz Max von Baden, *Erinnerungen und Dokumente* (Berlin 1927), pp. 242 ff., and Max M. Warburg, *Aufzeichnungen*, pp. 57–60.

agreements for credits and the delivery of Swedish ores and other commodities. On 15 June, Max Warburg gave a speech to Reichstag deputies who were visiting Hamburg on the subject 'Currency and Economic Policy after the War', on which occasion he met for the first time Friedrich Ebert, then Chairman of the Social Democratic Party and later to become President of the Republic.

As the war reached its most critical point, Prince Max von Baden, who had been asked to form a Government, summoned Max Warburg to him at Dessau and asked if he could count on his cooperation. Warburg replied that he could not take up a Cabinet post: as a Jew, he would be an unacceptable Finance Minister to certain elements within Germany, and the Social Democrats would see in him the personification of finance capitalism. He did, however, undertake to advise Prince Max whenever his assistance should be needed. The call came soon, and it came urgently: throughout the month of October Max Warburg was almost uninterruptedly in Berlin, where he saw Prince Max and his other advisers several times a day, and discussed with them what options still remained open to Germany in the ever-narrowing range of alternative policies. Despite Warburg's plea for more time, the panic mood at military headquarters swept all before it: on 5 October, Prince Max signed the request for an immediate armistice, and on 9 November he announced the Kaiser's abdication. The next day he himself resigned as Chancellor, and on 11 November the guns at last fell silent on all fronts.

In Hamburg, meanwhile, a Workers' and Soldiers' Council on the Soviet model had been constituted on 5 November. Despite the threat of general breakdown, Max Warburg pressed his fellow-members of the Chamber of Commerce for the establishment of contact with the Council, and meetings were eventually arranged. Lengthy negotiations with the Council's representatives revolved mostly around the issue of how Hamburg's financial independence and credit could be safeguarded. It was ultimately announced on 14 November that Hamburg continued to possess the rights and privileges of a juridical person, and that its Finance Department *(Finanzdeputation)* bore the ultimate responsibility for the finances of the city-state. By this means, the continuity and integrity of Hamburg's credit were assured, and it became possible to contemplate refunding operations for Hamburg obligations that had been placed with local and foreign banks.

Amid all the strains of a situation in which each day brought new calamities and dangers, perhaps the hardest blow for Max Warburg personally was the death on 10 November of his close friend Albert Ballin. With Ballin's death also died the hope that he could have lent his unique talents to the herculean task of the post-war reconstruction of his shipping empire and of the German economy generally.

On 16 November, still mourning for his friend, Max Warburg was requested to be the representative of the Reich Treasury in the forthcoming peace negotiations. He declined the offer, pointing out that, in view of the hard conditions that the victorious Entente would undoubtedly impose, it would be vital to constitute a larger delegation of experts. Warburg further proposed that Dr. Melchior be nominated a member of the peace delegation. After days of discussion and sleepless nights, a peace delegation was constituted under the chairmanship of the Foreign Minister, Count Brockdorff-Rantzau. Melchior was appointed a member of the principal delegation, and Max Warburg joined the financial delegation that accompanied the German negotiators to Versailles. Nearly six eventful months were to pass before the Allies presented their peace conditions to the German representatives.

7

UNEASY PEACE: 1919–1923

Hostilities had ended with the Armistice, but peace in any real sense continued to elude a defeated and exhausted Germany. The Allies maintained their strict blockade; men returning from the armed forces competed for employment in a labour market which had drastically shrunk because of the abrupt ending of war industry; food and raw materials were in extremely short supply; and tensions grew rapidly, especially in the big cities, where extremist parties attempted to drum up support among the unemployed. The new Republic came into being amid strikes, street disorders and threats of insurrection from both left and right. Administrative and legislative changes were introduced rapidly by the new authorities in a bewildering array of decrees and ordinances, and in the prevailing atmosphere of confusion and despair there seemed no firm ground on which a banking house could base its current business, let alone rational plans for the future. All calculations foundered on the inescapable fact that the value of the Mark was impossible to determine as long as the magnitude of the Allies' reparations demands remained unknown.

Max Warburg and his partner Carl Melchior were frequently in Berlin in the early months of 1919 in order to participate in the arduous preparatory work for the peace conference; in April, both men travelled with the German finance delegation to the Versailles negotiations, spending their time initially in strict confinement at the Château de Villette near Compiègne. After weeks of wearying labours under high pressure, the suspense of the delegates was ended with the presentation on 7 May of the Allies' peace terms. Although both Warburg and Melchior had been less than optimistic with regard to the Entente's position, neither they nor any of the other members of the German delegation had been prepared for the harshness of the terms demanded, whereby Germany was to lose 13 per cent of her pre-war territory and some 6 million subjects. Alsace and Lorraine were ceded to France, which also assumed jurisdiction for fifteen years over the vital coal-mining area of the Saar; important territories in the East were given to Poland and Lithuania; all Germany's colonies and investments overseas were lost, as was much of the merchant navy. Most serious from the economic and financial standpoint was the imposition of an indeterminate liability to pay war reparations: while the Allied Reparations Commission was deliberating as to the final figure, Germany was required to make substantial deliveries of goods, raw materials, gold and convertible currencies on account.

After two days of anxious study of the Allied terms, Max Warburg wrote despairingly to his wife: 'Well, we have not yet come to terms with our fate. Only one thing is certain: *that* peace we can *never seriously* sign.' He added, characteristically: 'One must not however lose one's nerve!'*

In discussions within the German delegation, a proposal of Melchior's and Warburg's for an initial negotiating offer to the Allies of a total of 100 billion gold Marks in reparations, to be paid interest-free in annual budget-linked instalments, was unanimously approved. But there were to be no negotiations on this issue: the final note of the Entente was presented to the Germans on 16 June, and that evening the delegates departed for Weimar, their cars running the gauntlet of verbal abuse and stone-throwing from the bitterly hostile French populace. In the overheated atmosphere of Weimar, there were endless Cabinet meetings and frantic attempts to avoid the inevitable. 'Total confusion reigned,' Max Warburg wrote. 'No one knew what he wanted, and above all, the experts were not permitted to speak at all.'† The financial experts unanimously submitted their resignations on 18 June, thus emphasizing their conviction that the Allies' terms were impossible of fulfillment and if signed would lead to Germany's economic ruin. The ultimate decision to accept the treaty conditions was taken only after further turmoil within the Government and an agonized national debate; on 28 June 1919 the war formally came to an end with the signature of the peace treaty in the Hall of Mirrors at Versailles.

The war was over, but it was to no atmosphere of peace that Warburg and his colleagues returned from the negotiations. On the contrary,

* *Aufzeichnungen*, p. 79.

† Ibid., p. 85. For an appreciation of Melchior's activity at Versailles by a leading member of the British delegation, see John Maynard Keynes, 'Dr. Melchior: a Defeated Enemy', in *Two Memoirs* (London, 1949).

hatred of the victorious Allies had increased, and was projected by scurrilous newspapers and pamphlets also on to all those who had in any way been connected with the 'Peace of Humiliation', despite the well-known fact that the German delegates had all struggled valiantly against acceptance of the imposed peace conditions. Warburg and others had to contend with a rising tide of abusive letters, threats and public attempts to cast aspersions on their patriotism and loyalty.

Although still cut off from many of its pre-war connections, and hampered by the painfully meagre prospects of any international trade, M. M. Warburg & Co. slowly picked up the threads of its traditional business. Returning personnel had to be re-integrated into the firm, investment clients advised anew, old contacts re-established and, if possible, new friends won. The firm's chief concern was the repayment of its debts owed abroad, and the fashioning of some machinery that could assist Germany's reconstruction effort by financing the import of essential raw materials, primarily from America.

In July and August 1919, Max Warburg was in Switzerland where, despite the continuing uncertainty, he was able to discuss with Swiss bankers the notion, later to become reality, of organizing an international acceptance bank that could enable Germany to have access once again to sources of international capital for financing her trade. In the autumn, Warburg participated in meetings in Amsterdam at which John Maynard Keynes was also present, discussing with American, Dutch and French bankers the tangled issues of inter-Allied debts, reparations, and the revival of the German economy. In correspondence with friends in Germany and elsewhere, Warburg initiated a campaign for the rehabilitation of Germany through the advance of a large-scale international loan and her admission to the League of Nations.

But with all these energetic efforts, Max Warburg was forced to acknowledge that 'one can look back on 1919 only with deep disappointment . . . the merchant navy, colonies, rich territories were all taken away from Germany . . . the future appeared more worrying and difficult than at the end of 1918.'* Writing privately at the year-end to his old friend Carl Otto Henriques, Warburg observed wryly: 'One is only wise when things are going badly. That is why I am now so clever.' †

* Unpublished draft memoirs.

† Max M. Warburg to Carl Otto Henriques, 22 December 1919, Henriques Archive, Copenhagen.

For the Warburg firm, 1920 saw the beginnings of a slow upward movement: with the gradual recovery of foreign and domestic trade, the old business in commercial bills revived; stock exchange activity quickened as established companies raised their capital, mergers became more frequent and new groups were established. Notable transactions in the old style included the successful reorganization after lengthy negotiations of Hochofenwerk Lübeck Aktiengesellschaft, and substantial capital increases under the firm's leadership for the Norddeutsche Versicherungs-Gesellschaft, in which a leading Swedish insurance group then took a participation, and for Oelwerke Stern-Sonneborn A.G. and the Cuxhavener Hochseefischerei. Another example of the recovery was the firm's role in placing M 25 million of a new capital issue of M 100 million of the Allgemeine Elektrizitäts-Gesellschaft of Berlin with the metals firm of Guggenheim Brothers in New York, a transaction arranged through Kuhn, Loeb & Co. In February, Max Warburg realized a long-cherished ambition when the Deutsche Waren-Treuhand A.G. was founded by M. M. Warburg & Co. with a group of Hamburg houses and Mendelssohn & Co. of Berlin. This new enterprise, Warburg recognized, would contribute only modestly to the bank's earnings, 'but fills a need, acting as a trusted intermediary for those credits that foreign lenders may in due course extend to Germany.'*

The financial results of the year were unexpectedly favourable: in particular, very substantial advances made during the war to the Reichsbank under the Warburg guarantee were largely repaid. Large paper profits were in fact illusory, however; the background to all transactions and all calculations was the relentless and rapidly increasing depreciation of the German Mark. M. M. Warburg & Co., as a long-established private bank, was in a unique position to observe the moral as well as material effects of this creeping catastrophe: 'The disintegration of Germany is becoming evident on all sides,' wrote Max Warburg at the year-end.

> Periodicals, learned societies, cultural enterprises of every kind that were nurtured for decades have had to be given up. It is with great difficulty that we are managing to keep afloat even those institutions in which we have for decades taken an interest. . . . Sons and daughters can no longer be educated to the standard that had formerly been taken for granted. Fine houses and old family heirlooms must be sold. There is a silent poverty that is developing

* 1920 *Annual Report.*

which, in the case of pensioners, *rentiers* and all those dependent on a fixed income, is proving utterly hopeless.*

The crisis over reparations simmered meanwhile from conference to conference; in July 1920 at Spa the carefully-prepared negotiating positions of Dr. Carl Melchior and other experts were swept aside by the French representatives, and an ominous note was introduced into the embittered controversy by Hugo Stinnes, thc Ruhr coal magnate, who published a letter referring darkly to a number of German representatives at Spa who 'out of a foreign psychology had broken German resistance against shameful unreasonable demands'. Agreement over the reparations figure eluded the assembled experts again at a meeting in London in March 1921. Finally, on 27 April the total German reparations debt payable was fixed by the Allied Reparations Commission at 132 billion gold Marks, a figure considerably in excess of any yet offered by Germany. A schedule of payments was communicated to Berlin on 5 May, with an ultimatum threatening occupation of the Ruhr if the schedule were not accepted. The German Government thereupon resigned and it was left to the new Chancellor, Dr. Joseph Wirth, to accept the Allied terms and authorize the first cash payment by August, in the amount of one billion Marks.

Wirth's fulfilment policy was, however, doomed to failure: the Mark, which by the beginning of 1920 had already lost nine-tenths of its pre-war value, dropped steadily, and it became clear despite harsh fiscal measures that it was impossible to attain a budgetary balance, let alone a surplus. Meanwhile the obligation to transfer large amounts of gold and convertible currencies put a further strain on Germany's slender reserves and made foreign bankers more reluctant than ever to extend either long- or short-term credits to German borrowers. Max Warburg and his partners were convinced that only a large-scale international loan could save the German currency and satisfy the reparations obligation. Such a loan remained a chimera, however, as long as the printing presses continued to roll and money itself became more and more worthless as a measure of value.

Amid all the gloom one brighter note was struck by the establishment in the course of 1921 of the International Acceptance Bank (IAB) in New York. With Paul M. Warburg as Chairman, and access to important sources of funds, the IAB rapidly developed a substantial business in the

* 1920 *Annual Report*.

financing of international trade.* An early successful transaction was the financing through M. M. Warburg & Co. and the IAB of a $9,000,000 contract with the Getreide-Einfuhr-Stelle for the import into Germany of essential foodgrains. The growing volume of foreign-currency business with and through the IAB was to constitute an important part of Warburgs' business throughout the critical inflation period and afterwards.

The ever-quickening tempo of the inflation dictated frequent capital increases for old clients: Oelwerke Stern-Sonneborn A.G., Cuxhavener Hochsee-Fischerei, Hochofenwerke Lübeck and others turned to the firm in 1921, and there were participations in new equity and loan issues for Fried. Krupp Aktiengesellschaft, Daimler Motoren Gesellschaft, the Hamburgische Elektrizitätswerke and other enterprises. By the end of 1921, M. M. Warburg & Co. had still not managed to liquidate all its pre-war foreign commitments, but those which had caused greatest concern to the partners had all been repaid. In order to protect its clients, the bank was compelled to invest a large part of its capital and profits in foreign currencies, thus partly escaping the worst consequences of the Mark's depreciation, and providing foreign-currency reserves against foreign debts both on pre-war and current account.

In chaotic money market conditions, and with a swelling volume of new regulations to be complied with, every individual transaction became inordinately complicated and required greater attention than ever before. The book-keeping for many transactions had to be carried on in dollars and other foreign currencies, thus imposing an additional burden on the secretarial and accounting staffs. Inevitably, the number of employees grew steadily, and all of them worked long hours. Fortunately, the Ferdinandstrasse premises that had been completed shortly after the war began proved adequate to house the bank's multifarious activities. Describing the hectic atmosphere of the year 1922, Max Warburg later wrote:

> The rapid devaluation of the Mark made it impossible to calculate in a business-like manner. We had many orders from foreigners to purchase large share-

* Founding shareholders in the IAB were M. M. Warburg & Co.; the First National Bank of Boston; A.B. Svenska Handelsbanken and Skandinaviska Kreditaktiebolaget, Stockholm; Sir Ernest Cassel, the National Provincial Bank, and N. M. Rothschild & Sons, London; Schweizerische Kreditanstalt, Zürich; Les Fils Dreyfus & Cie. and Schweizerischer Bankverein, Basel; Hope & Co. and Nederlandsche Handels-maatschappij, Amsterdam. In 1928, the IAB was merged with the Bank of Manhattan Company, now the Chase Manhattan Bank.

holdings for their account. As desirable as the participation of foreign countries in the German economy might have been, the bargain-basement sale of German capital now appeared questionable. Profiteers and new so-called 'banks' cropped up all over the place, rapidly earned enormous amounts (and then as quickly lost them again). These people did great damage to respectable businessmen.*

In January 1922 Wirth, the Reich Chancellor, summoned Dr. Melchior to Berlin to discuss with him preparations for the forthcoming European economic conference at Genoa which had been initiated by the British Prime Minister, Lloyd George. The Chancellor wished Max Warburg to accompany Melchior to Genoa, but Warburg declined, writing to Melchior:

> . . . I consider it *de facto* incorrect for our firm to be too strongly represented in this conference. . . . I should like only to ask in advance that you immediately leave the room if in connection with an international loan there is a demand for financial supervision of Germany. I do not wish under any circumstances to see us linked with the abdication of our financial independence, quite aside from the fact that I expect no results from such supervision.†

The sudden news of the German-Soviet Treaty signed at Rapallo on 16 April struck Melchior and his fellow financial expert Geheimrat Cuno like a thunderbolt: neither had been informed by the Foreign Minister, Rathenau, of the behind-the-scenes negotiations. Put thus into an impossible situation, Melchior and Cuno returned to Germany. The Genoa conference had in any event little effect on Germany's financial plight: the international experts agreed that an international loan to stabilize the Mark could only be raised if the reparations issue were definitively settled. Any attempt to put reparations on the Genoa agenda had, however, been blocked by the French Government.

Despite the failure to resolve the reparations dilemma at Genoa, the atmosphere within Germany seemed to clear in the wake of the conference. However, the calm was deceptive; on 24 June the Foreign Minister, Rathenau, was assassinated. Just four weeks before his death, he had tried again to press Max Warburg into joining the Government, and when Warburg had expressed his misgivings about the wisdom in the prevailing atmosphere of having two Jews in the same Cabinet, Rathenau had admitted receiving countless threats to his life.‡ Max Warburg wrote sadly to his brother Paul in New York:

* Draft memoirs.

† Max M. Warburg to Carl Melchior, 20 March 1922. M. M. Warburg Archives.

‡ *Aufzeichnungen*, p. 107.

This murder is shameful because it again makes plain the degeneration of German *mores*; one again feels the oppressive atmosphere that precedes a storm – it is the consequence of that disintegration that is spreading throughout Germany. All the dissatisfied, in fact despairing groups, among whom there is only misery and no hope, are becoming 'desperadoes'.*

Shortly after Rathenau's murder, Warburg himself received warnings from the Chief of Police in Hamburg of possible danger to his life; he was required to alter his daily routine, to have a police bodyguard, and ultimately to leave Germany and stay for a few weeks in Holland.

Early in the autumn, Max Warburg travelled to the United States for the first time since the war, restoring the firm's personal links with bankers and industrialists and at the same time putting Germany's case on the reparations issue to many leading Government and financial figures. In a move that foreshadowed ultimate American involvement in regulating the reparations tangle, Warburg attempted to organize the despatch by Barnes, the President of the United States Chamber of Commerce, of a small unofficial commission to Germany whose purpose would be to make an objective assessment of Germany's ability to pay reparations claims. The time was too early for such an initiative, but American awareness of the link between the reparations question and inter-Allied war debts was growing apace.

At the end of December 1922 the threat which had long hung over Germany became a reality when the Reparations Commission declared Germany in default on a routine delivery of timber. On 9 January 1923 a default in coal deliveries was declared, and two days later French and Belgian troops began to occupy the Ruhr. The new Reich Government under Geheimrat Cuno organized passive resistance measures in the Ruhr, but the enormous financial burden these entailed for Germany gave the *coup de grace* to the Mark, which plunged downward at unprecedented speed.

A speculative fever born of desperation now gripped large sections of the population: everyone who still received an income rushed to spend his money before it became utterly worthless. At M. M. Warburg & Co., currency quotations were chalked up almost minute by minute on a large board in the firm's foreign-exchange trading room; when it was noticed that the employees of the Hamburg–America Line were observing the

* Max M. Warburg to Paul M. Warburg, 24 June 1922.

quotations with binoculars from their offices on the other side of Ferdinandstrasse, the firm's large windows were curtained. Secretaries and clerks ran during their lunch hour to the counters of the big Karstadt department store to exchange money for goods; Hamburg sailors returning from foreign ports were virtually mobbed at the dockside for the foreign currency they might be prepared to exchange.* 'The Mark,' Max Warburg recalled, 'completely ceased to deserve the appellation "currency"; it became simply an illusion. Worthless scraps of paper, each nominally representing one million Marks and stuffed into huge sacks, dominated the market. Amid the torrent of events cascading down one after another, the firm's arrangements whirled in confusion.'†

Ominously, the Legal Department of M. M. Warburg & Co. worked overtime throughout the year 1923: the attempts of the tax and other authorities to stem the growing chaos by issuing a flood of new regulations meant an endless series of difficult problems for the bank's legal staff. Delayed payments, the revaluation of mortgages, arbitrage conditions and the proliferation of new types of blocked currency; all these and other problems added to the complications to be dealt with.

The 6th January 1923 was the 125th anniversary of the founding of M. M. Warburg & Co., but in the prevailing atmosphere of crisis the milestone was celebrated quietly. Instead of the large party that could have been expected in normal times, a small dinner was held at the house of Aby S. Warburg, to which only senior and long-serving employees were invited. The prevailing mood was one of gratitude for the bank's survival through perilous times and of guarded optimism in assessing an obscure future.

With the wiping out of the entire savings of the German middle class – a true social revolution in every sense – and the steady impoverishment even of those workers who still had jobs, bitterness and insecurity spread among all classes and assumed ever more threatening forms. Beneficiaries of these social tensions were extremist groups on the right and left, which steadily gained adherents. Defamatory attacks against M. M. Warburg & Co. and individual members of the firm were no longer a rarity. In one case, the editor of the anti-Semitic paper *Hammer* was forced by proceedings initiated by Max Warburg to retract allegations that the Warburg bank had, among other nefarious activities, financed the Russian revo-

* Reminiscences of Herr August Behrmann, former holder of Power of Attorney at M. M. Warburg & Co.

† *Aufzeichnungen*, p. 112.

lution.* Other attacks were suffered in silence: it was useless, for example, to expect redress from a Bavarian court against slanders printed in the *Völkischer Beobachter*.

The fever-chart of the Mark's long dying showed 100,000 Marks to the dollar on 13 June 1923, 200,000 Marks to the dollar one month later; and by the end of July one dollar fetched one million Marks. That appalling figure, however, was by no means to be the end. On 12 August the exhausted Chancellor Cuno resigned and Gustav Stresemann formed a new Government. By September the dollar quotation had reached 100 million Marks, and normal banking business as it had traditionally been understood in Germany had virtually ceased.

Even as currency values crumbled, M. M. Warburg & Co. continued to be appealed to by clients who relied on the bank to mobilize funds on their behalf. The firm arranged one advance of £50,000 sterling to the State of Hamburg in order to permit payment of the salaries of the port workers. That measure proved insufficient to meet other demands, however, and late in September the Hamburger Bank von 1923 was organized under the aegis of Warburgs, the Norddeutsche Bank and the Dresdner Bank. The new bank, in which most of the leading Hamburg trading and industrial concerns were represented, issued emergency currency expressed in terms of gold, thus permitting the payment of Hamburg's maritime workers. The Hamburgische Bank von 1923 was later the first German financial institution to receive dollar rediscount facilities through Warburgs with the International Acceptance Bank in New York.† Other foreign currency loans totalling $2,000,000 were made through Warburgs to the Hamburg–America Line; and other enterprises were assisted to meet their foreign-currency commitments through the firm's overseas contacts.

The Stresemann Government officially announced the end of the disastrous passive resistance policy in the occupied Ruhr on 26 September 1923. On 9 November Adolf Hitler's attempted putsch in Bavaria failed. Having survived this and other attempts at subversion, the Government was in a position to push through the desperately needed stabilization of the currency that had so long eluded previous régimes. A new currency, the Rentenmark, nominally based on land and industrial values, was

* *Aufzeichnungen*, p. 115.

† For a description of the rôle of M. M. Warburg & Co. in financing the State of Hamburg, see Leo Lippmann, *Mein Leben und meine amtliche Tätigkeit* (Hamburg, 1964), pp. 494–7.

introduced in mid-November. Backed by the psychological prop of a mortgage on agricultural property and industrial resources, the Rentenmark rapidly gained acceptance. The appointment of Hans Luther as Finance Minister and Dr. Hjalmar Schacht as Currency Commissioner to supervise the financial reforms assured energetic administration of the new rationalization measures. Recovery was remarkably rapid, and with the revival of economic life throughout Germany, fears that the Rentenmark would go the way of its predecessor proved unfounded, although many of those who had speculated on continued currency chaos and had built up paper empires of industrial and other property were swept away under the new conditions of stability. With the French Government's agreement at the year-end to participate in an enquiry into Germany's capacity to pay reparations, and the association of United States experts with the scheme, the way was at last cleared for dealing with Germany's international financial problems in a realistic and positive atmosphere.

M. M. Warburg & Co. had survived a critical period that had seen the collapse or disappearance through mergers of many old family firms in Hamburg and elsewhere in Germany. Surveying the maëlstrom through which the bank had been piloted, Max Warburg wrote to Carl Otto Henriques:

> I have become a philosopher; that is the only way of preserving one's pleasure in life, one's appetite and sense of humour – some of the few things that are not taxed. The inflation was such a disaster that now one has managed through a few desperate somersaults to attain some respite ... we shall probably not again fall into that catastrophe. There will nonetheless still be considerable convalescent pains before we even approximately manage to put our economic house in order.*

* Max M. Warburg to Carl H. Henriques, 30 December 1923. Henriques Archive, Copenhagen.

8

RECOVERY AND FRAGILE PROSPERITY: 1924–1929

The introduction of the new stabilized currency initiated a slow growth of confidence and a renewal of economic activity throughout the Reich. However, this recovery was accompanied by severe strains and complex problems in many sectors of the economy; the 'convalescent pains' that Max Warburg had predicted not infrequently took the form of crises within individual firms and entire branches of industry and commerce. As money became abruptly dearer, trade and industry were confronted with an acute shortage of credit, which the banks had the utmost difficulty in attempting to satisfy out of their own drastically diminished resources. The Reichsbank, in a stern effort to prevent any repetition of inflationary pressures, refused from April 1924 to extend further rediscount facilities to the banking system, thus thrusting the banks back upon their own slender means, and intensifying the search for foreign sources of credit.

Internationally, too, Germany's position had changed: with the establishment of a more favourable internal atmosphere and the advent of a new French Government, it was now possible to discuss the reparations question in a businesslike and objective manner. An inter-Allied conference, presided over by the American experts Charles Dawes and Owen D. Young, met in London early in 1924 and issued its report in April that year, recommending regular annual reparations payments, and a transfer system designed to protect the German currency from the risk of devaluation. The Dawes scheme provided further for the pledging of certain Government revenues for the payment of debts, for Allied controls over the Reichsbank and the railways, and for the appointment of a Reparations Agent to oversee Germany's capacity to pay. Although these provisions were strongly criticized as an invasion of German sovereignty, they in fact paved the way for a renewal of international confidence in the

German economy, and the widespread recognition that Germany's economic growth would redound to the benefit of her reparations and other creditors as well as to that of the German people themselves. Despite the bitter campaigning against the Dawes scheme as a 'second Versailles', it was adopted by the Reichstag in late August, and its provisions were swiftly carried into effect.

Among these new measures was a banking law that established a newly independent Reichsbank and defined the new Mark strictly in terms of gold. Limits were placed on the Reich Government's capacity to borrow from the central bank, and an independent advisory board *(Generalrat)*, to which Max Warburg was elected, was appointed to the Reichsbank. The first concrete evidence of the confidence engendered by the new course was the great international success in October of the 800 million gold Mark Dawes Loan, the proceeds of which were used to replenish the Reichsbank's reserves. The success of the Dawes issue and the appointment of the American S. Parker Gilbert as Reparations Agent led to the re-establishment of German credit on the international capital market, and a consequent interest in German investment on the part of foreign banks and industrial enterprises.

For M. M. Warburg & Co. the stabilization meant that 'we returned from the dollar to the Mark, from extortionate to normal interest rates, from speculation to calculation'.* The partners were able now to carry out a survey and to ascertain precisely what was left of the bank's resources after the ravages of war and inflation. Beginning with the Rentenmark and then with the introduction of the new Reichsmark, it became possible to calculate in German currency and to plan rationally for the future development of the bank's business. The most difficult aspect of adjusting to the new conditions was the unavoidable necessity for reducing costs: the 'liberation from Lilliputian accounts, from scribbling zeroes' † required a reduction in the bank's staff, from 535 employees at the end of 1923 to 358 at the end of 1924. The expanded quarters in the Ferdinandstrasse building that were opened late in 1924 now seemed too large for the bank's needs, and parts of the premises were let to other tenants. In the next two years further reductions in personnel became necessary, and labour-saving machinery was introduced in several book-keeping and secretarial operations in the hope that its high initial cost would ultimately be recouped through lower expenses.

* *Annual Report*, 1924.

† Max M. Warburg, memorandum to senior staff, 1924.

The abrupt change in the economic rules of the game caught many bankers and businessmen unawares, however: speculation in currencies had become so normal that the profits of ordinary commercial transactions were minor in comparison with the gains anticipated from currency fluctuations. In the first half of 1924, many Hamburg trading and banking firms flung themselves rashly into large-scale speculations on the falling French franc; the speculators were oblivious of the risks involved, failing to recognize that the French Government would do all in its power to rescue its currency, and that the new conditions in the international currency markets made a stabilization of the franc far more likely than previously. The crisis broke in May: as immense losses from franc speculation threatened to overwhelm house after house, Max M. Warburg organized a support fund of £110,000 in which the major Hamburg banks participated. This timely and large-scale support action rescued several long-established firms from difficulties and prevented a far bigger catastrophe from affecting a significant part of the Hamburg trading fraternity.

Although dramatic events such as the franc crisis occupied the centre of the stage, Warburgs' ordinary business went forward, and several new projects were embarked upon. In April the firm arranged a rediscount credit of $5 million, later raised to $25 million, for the Golddiskontbank with the International Acceptance Bank in New York; Max Warburg was at the same time elected to the Board of the Golddiskontbank. Due to the influence of Paul M. Warburg, American banks that had hitherto held aloof from German business joined the New York syndicate which participated in this important transaction, a symbol of growing American interest in German investments. Other credits in foreign currencies were arranged on behalf of the Hamburg–America Line and the Hamburgische Bank von 1923, as well as for other clients; with the revival of the internal capital market, Warburgs participated in a growing number of share and loan issues listed on the Hamburg and Berlin Stock Exchanges. Noteworthy also were the negotiations initiated by M. M. Warburg & Co. that culminated in the merger of the Ossag-Werke with the Royal Dutch Shell group, and the successful Western Union-Commercial Cable-Deutsche Kabel-Gesellschaft talks on a new cable link via the Azores between Germany and America.

In October Warburgs established – jointly with Kuhn, Loeb & Co., Dillon, Read & Co., the International Acceptance Bank and other houses – the American and Continental Corporation. With an initial capital of

$10 million, the new corporation was designed to grant credits and make industrial investments in Germany. Although American and Continental did not ultimately fulfil all the hopes of its founders, it made a number of valuable transactions in Germany, extending credits in its first year of life to Köln-Rottweiler A.G., Oberschlesische Oberkoks and other such concerns.

If 1924 was characterized chiefly by the recovery of the German currency, 1925 was the year in which the German economy in general was restored gradually to health, but again not without several severe crises, the chief of which resulted from the payments difficulties of the mammoth and over-extended Stinnes empire and the subsequent shock waves which submerged many smaller concerns and banks. The energetic intervention of the Reichsbank led to a painful but rapid overcoming of this liquidity crisis, and towards the end of the year share markets recovered and money became plentiful enough for the banking system to extend substantial industrial and local government credits.

For M. M. Warburg & Co., 1925 was a busy year with a series of major transactions, many of them involving the arrangement of American credits for German industrial enterprises and municipalities. At the request of the German Government, which was anxious to expand Soviet-German trade, the firm participated in a banking consortium that extended a £300,000 trade credit to a Russian manganese trading company (Jurt-Gesellschaft). The newly-founded American and Continental Corporation advanced more than $9 million through Warburgs to a variety of German companies, and an investment company, European Shares, Inc., was established in New York by Warburgs and Dulles, Hayden Stone & Co. with a capital of $6 million to invest in German securities.* Yet another international investment company was founded in London at the initiative of the firm, Industrial Finance and Investment Corporation, Ltd. Among the influential group of foreign shareholders interested in this vehicle for German portfolio investments were N. M. Rothschild & Sons, the Prudential Assurance Co., Kleinworts, Japhet, Sir Alfred Mond and the International Acceptance Bank of New York.

Despite all the heightened activity, the financial results of the year were meagre: competition was keen from both foreign and German banks, and costs remained too high in relation to the reduced number of clients

* European Shares, Inc., did not attain the performance record hoped for it, and was liquidated shortly after its incorporation.

and the relatively modest earnings on individual transactions. The numbers of staff continued to decline, reaching 327 at the year-end; new positions were found for almost all of those who had to leave the firm. Writing to a New York correspondent in mid-year, Max Warburg thus summarized the bank's position:

> Despite all the unfavourable conditions in which we live, we have thus far managed – touch wood! – by dint of adroit juggling to develop further and to earn a profit.*

Each individual transaction, however, required greater effort and consumed more time than in the halcyon pre-war days.

The Locarno Agreements initialled in October 1925 and Germany's subsequent admission to the League of Nations inaugurated a significant improvement in the country's international position. Trade and other agreements were thereupon concluded with a number of countries, the flow of goods and capital increased, and the pace of German economic growth perceptibly quickened. Carl Melchior was appointed as the sole German representative to the Finance Committee of the League of Nations; although this appointment meant that Melchior was to be more frequently absent from Hamburg, the honour was particularly gratifying to the partners of M. M. Warburg & Co.

Commenting on the firm's circumstances early in 1926, Max Warburg wrote to his brother Paul:†

> Everything is in flux, and the conclusion I draw is that, without necessarily believing in the end of the world, one cannot be too careful in individual transactions. I also come repeatedly to the conclusion that we should diversify a larger proportion of the firm's capital, i.e. we for our part should invest more in America, and it would be entirely appropriate on the other hand if the Americans at the same time carefully invest a portion of their surplus in Europe.

Max Warburg gave repeated warnings, both public and private, of the dangerous consequences for the German economy of the ever-increasing volume of borrowing abroad, especially from American sources. Nonetheless, with German interest rates pegged at high levels compared with

* Max M. Warburg to Lucien Nachmann, International Acceptance Bank, 15 August 1925.

† Max M. Warburg to Paul M. Warburg, 11 February 1926.

other European countries and with the United States,* it proved impossible to stem a vast influx of credits, many of them short-term; German banks, industries, states and municipalities were besieged by importunate would-be lenders, frequently at high rates which heavily discounted future earnings prospects.

The most notable transactions of 1926 for M. M. Warburg & Co. were a $5 million one-year Hamburg Treasury Bill issue, as well as two further long-term Hamburg loans in the amounts of $10 million and £2 million respectively. A Westphalia loan was placed in London in conjunction with Rothschilds, the first German issue since the Dawes Loan to be introduced officially in London. Another state issue, the Rheinprovinzanleihe, was placed by Warburgs in the Netherlands. Industrial financings included capital increases for the Hamburg–America Line and I.G. Farbenindustrie, and substantial loan business with Rudolph Karstadt A.G. The firm participated in nineteen new loan issues for various municipalities and industrial enterprises, as compared with only two such issues in the previous year. Negotiations for the introduction of Knorr brakes into France were initiated, and resulted ultimately in a marketing arrangement with Westinghouse interests. Warburgs continued to take part, not without considerable caution, in expanding business with the Soviet State Bank and with Rawack & Grünfeld in the Jurt-Gesellschaft, with which a syndicate of German banks was associated under a Reich Government guarantee of political risks involved in exporting to the Soviet Union. In all these and other business transactions, the efforts of the firm's partners and personnel were directed consciously to the strengthening of Warburgs' international friendships: the links with New York through the International Acceptance Bank and Kuhn, Loeb & Co., and with London primarily through N. M. Rothschild & Sons, remained of paramount importance for the development of the bank's affairs.

Responding to the increasing volume of business transacted in and through Berlin, M. M. Warburg & Co. established early in 1927 a presence there, initially in the form of an apartment for the accommodation of visiting partners and the entertainment of Berlin-based clients and

* In 1925, the average German interest rate for one- to three-month money was 9·13 per cent; in the same year the average of foreign rates for such money was 3·74 per cent. This gross disparity in rates, partly caused by the influence of the Dawes Loan floor under German interest levels, persisted throughout the period 1924–30, and made foreign investors prefer to lend funds short-term in Germany rather than invest them at perhaps longer term in their own countries.

associates. This modest *pied-à-terre* proved its value, and within the following year it was expanded into a small Berlin office with a resident staff to which associates from Hamburg were regularly seconded.

Meanwhile, the flow of foreign capital into Germany continued unabated: loans at high interest rates, sometimes for projects of dubious intrinsic merit, became the order of the day for municipalities and industrial enterprises previously unknown on international markets. The hectic atmosphere of Berlin was reflected in a report by a Vice-President of the International Acceptance Bank, who wrote to New York in the spring of 1927:

> During the negotiations one night in a restaurant, there were fifteen separate groups of American bankers, all there after the same business and glaring at each other. This is typical of Europe today.*

M. M. Warburg & Co. for its part experienced a decrease in turnover for the first time since the currency stabilization: 1927 turnover was RM 14,004 million as against RM 18,890 million in 1926. Part of the explanation of the drop in turnover lay in the bank's refusal to engage in large-scale foreign currency operations for its own account. Describing the policy that had been followed, Max Warburg wrote at the year-end:

> We must adhere to the principle of taking in money only at the lowest possible rates, since it is of the greatest importance for us not to appear greedy in the market. We have thus far declined to accept foreign monies in large amounts against Mark loans, but have just now undertaken a modest enlargement of our positions in foreign currencies.†

The remarkably rapid recovery which characterized the post-Locarno years continued also in 1928. Loan funds still poured into Germany, contributing to a favourable balance of payments, but over half this debt was in the form of short-term credits revocable at the first sign of political or economic difficulty. At the initiative of S. Parker Gilbert, the Reparations Agent, discussions leading to a new investigation of the reparations problem were begun at Geneva in September 1928, and led ultimately to the convening of an international committee of experts in Paris in February 1929. The general elections held in May 1928 brought a defeat for extremists on both sides of the political spectrum and a gratifying success for those parties which unequivocally supported the

* Hugh Knowlton to James P. Warburg, 27 April 1927.

† *Annual Report*, 1927.

Republic. Real stability, however, continued to elude Germany: unemployment remained high, agricultural producers were in increasing difficulties, and domestic investment was falling. Max Warburg tersely characterized 1928 as a year of 'high interest rates, heavy burdens, strikes'.*

The most significant event of the year for M. M. Warburg & Co. was the merger in December of the International Acceptance Bank with the Bank of the Manhattan Company, New York. The IAB, which in the seven years of its existence had achieved a leading position in the international acceptance business – its 1928 volume of acceptances totalled $60 million – complemented the industrial financing activity of the Bank of the Manhattan Company, a much longer-established institution. The merged bank, with its substantially increased resources, represented a source of considerable financing business for all its shareholders, including Warburgs.

As part of its continuing effort to attract foreign capital for long-term investment in German industry, Warburgs established in Amsterdam an international investment trust, the N.V. Nederlandsche Crediet- en Financiering-Maatschappij, with a capital of 12 million guilders. This institution, modelled on the American & Continental Corporation in New York and the Industrial Finance & Investment Corporation of London, was incorporated by Warburgs, Mendelssohn & Co. and the Nederlandsche Handels-Maatschappij with a substantial group of international shareholders, including Dutch, Swiss, Austrian, German, English and American banks.

Another noteworthy transaction in 1928 was the successful conclusion under the firm's auspices of lengthy negotiations for a merger of Cuxhavener Hochseefischerei A.G. with the Nordsee-Fischerei-Gesellschaft in Bremen. The Cuxhavener Hochseefischerei possessed a large fleet, while Nordsee had the more developed sales organization; the merged company represented one of Germany's major fishing enterprises, and Warburgs' continuing interest in its affairs was marked by the appointment of Dr. Melchior to the Board as Vice-Chairman.

The bank's turnover for 1928 attained RM 23.418 million, a substantial increase over 1927, and the year was an active one in issuing business, with Warburgs appearing *en nom* in thirteen issues, including those for I.G. Farbenindustrie, the rapidly expanding Kreuger & Toll

* *Annual Report*, 1928.

concern and Rudolf Karstadt A.G., which increased its capital from RM 51 million to RM 70 million. With a staff now stabilized at the figure of 289, a large and growing number of directorships and an increasingly busy Berlin office, Warburgs was well placed to seek new financing opportunities to replace the declining volume of traditional trade finance.

The year 1929 was dominated by preoccupation with the protracted negotiations over revision of the Dawes Plan. The international committee of experts met in Paris in February, under the chairmanship of Owen D. Young, formerly vice-chairman of the Dawes Committee; Dr. Carl Melchior was the official German Government representative at the meetings. After prolonged discussions, the Young scheme was elaborated, providing for German reparations payments until 1988, in the total amount of RM 110.7 billion. In return for these payments, Germany was to regain her financial independence–with abolition of controls over transfers, the railways and the banking system. Despite a furious campaign in opposition to it, spearheaded by Alfred Hugenberg and his German Nationalist party, the Young Plan was accepted in principle in August 1929. It was signed by President Hindenburg only in the spring of 1930, however, by which time the world economic situation had altered radically for the worse.

The Young Plan, like its predecessor the Dawes scheme, had optimistically assumed for its success a prolonged period of economic growth and political stability in Germany. As early as May 1929, however, it was apparent that these pre-conditions were not to be met: largely as the result of abrupt withdrawals of short-term credits on the part of French and other foreign banks, Germany's gold reserves sank to a critical low point, and the Reichsbank was forced to decree harsh credit restrictions and a sharp rise in interest rates. Despite these record rates foreign credits were not attracted to the German market, and the shakiness of German prosperity was demonstrated all too clearly by the collapse in August 1929 of the Frankfurter Allgemeine Versicherungsgesellschaft and a new wave of precautionary mergers, including, in the banking sector, the large-scale fusion of the Deutsche Bank with the Disconto-Gesellschaft.

M. M. Warburg & Co. marked the beginning of 1929 by admitting as partners its former senior associates Dr. Ernst Spiegelberg and Eric M. Warburg, son of Max Warburg, and the first representative of the fifth generation of the family to be so admitted, at the same time granting single Power of Attorney to Dr. Hans Meyer and to Siegmund G. Warburg. In September, Warburgs departed from precedent by establishing in Amsterdam a limited company, Warburg & Co., with a capital of 5 million guilders, and with the task of representing M. M. Warburg & Co. and the International Manhattan Company, New York – the securities subsidiary of the Bank of the Manhattan Company and the International Acceptance Bank – in the international issue and securities business. Before the First World War, M. M. Warburg & Co. had maintained representatives in Paris and in London, but had always concentrated its forces in Hamburg, refraining from the establishment of a full-fledged banking firm even in Berlin. If a departure from long-established policy was now initiated, it was in recognition of the fact that for the foreseeable future Germany would no longer be a capital-exporting centre, and that if Warburgs wished to be assured of a continued place in the international issuing business, it would have to do so from a vantage-point outside Germany. However, Warburg & Co. Amsterdam was not destined to achieve the aims of its founders: the world-wide economic crisis which began shortly after its establishment drastically curtailed both new issue business and international trade, and the firm had its period of greatest activity in catering for the credit and investment requirements of M. M. Warburg & Co.'s clients in the years of emigration from 1933 to the outbreak of war.*

Although new issue business in Germany fell off by 50 per cent in 1929 by comparison with the year before, M. M. Warburg & Co. was active in transactions for the Reich Government, Rudolf Karstadt A.G., Lübecker Hochofenwerk, and a series of state, municipal and provincial entities. Later, Max Warburg was able to write:

> We were at last indisputably the leading banking firm in Hamburg. The expansion of our business was demonstrated *inter alia* by the fact that our 1929 balance sheet totalled 382 million Marks; the total for the Vereinsbank was 127 millions and that of Schröder's Bank 191 millions, so that the two sole independent banking houses of standing in Bremen and Hamburg had combined assets of 318 millions. Our assets therefore exceeded those of both other banks together by some 20 per cent.†

The Wall Street stock market crash of October 1929 sent shock waves round the world, but in Germany its effects were particularly disastrous,

* After the occupation of the Netherlands in May 1940, no new business was undertaken. Warburg & Co. went into liquidation in March 1941 when its Jewish partners and staff were compelled to emigrate.

† Max M. Warburg, unpublished notes for the firm's history.

and were felt almost immediately; there were no longer American funds available for investment in Germany, and German stock markets slumped dramatically, despite the attempts of an intervention consortium of leading bankers to shore up rapidly crumbling prices. With nearly 2 million unemployed, the German Government was faced with the urgent need for increased revenue, but the only hope of attracting foreign funds was to make a success of the reparations loan provided for by the Young Plan. That success, however, seemed more and more elusive as conditions on the international capital market continued to deteriorate.

The essential artificiality of the post-Locarno prosperity in Central Europe was harshly illuminated by the collapse in October 1929 of the Boden-Kredit-Anstalt, once the wealthiest and among the most highly respected banking institutions in Austria. In an attempt to salvage something from the wreckage, the Österreichische Creditanstalt took over the Boden-Kredit-Anstalt, thus assuming a burden beyond its own strained resources, and setting the stage for the crisis that was to overwhelm the entire Austrian and German banking world in the summer of 1931.

9

CRISIS YEARS: 1930–1933

On 3 January 1930 a second conference was convened at The Hague for the purpose of giving final consideration to details of the Young Plan. The German Government entered upon these talks conscious of the critical need for reducing the reparations burden at a time when tax revenues were steadily declining even as the demand for Government-supported unemployment benefits was rising dramatically: over 1,500,000 unemployed workers had been on relief in December 1929, and during January their number grew by nearly another million.

When the wearisome negotiations were concluded on 30 January, Germany had accepted a total future reparations obligation of RM 110.7 billion, to be paid in annual instalments until 1987. The German negotiators had nevertheless secured several important concessions: the first annuities payable were RM 800 million less than those contemplated by the Dawes Plan; and, most important of all, on ratification of the Plan, the French occupation of the Rhineland was to cease and reparations payments were to be made through the newly-founded Bank for International Settlements in Basel, rather than through a Reparations Agent with far-reaching control over the German economy. The withdrawal of the Reparations Agent meant, however, that his function of protecting Germany's transfer capacity also ended: two-thirds of each annual instalment of the Young Plan now had to be paid unconditionally, regardless of the German balance of payments situation in any given year.

The Young Plan and the Hague Agreements were bitterly debated in the Reichstag, but ultimately adopted on 12 March by a vote of 266 to 193, and signed by President Hindenburg on the following day. While the Reichstag was still deliberating over the Young Plan, Dr. Hjalmar Schacht tendered his resignation as President of the Reichsbank, citing as his reason the minor changes that had been made at The Hague to the

Young Plan provisions originally agreed at the first Paris conference. As a leading member of the Reichsbank Advisory Board, Max Warburg felt keenly his responsibilities at this juncture; it was he who made the initial soundings that resulted in the appointment of Dr. Hans Luther to succeed Schacht as President of the Reichsbank.*

In order to raise funds for the first annual payment due under the Young Plan, an international loan in the amount of $351 million was floated in June. M. M. Warburg & Co. participated as to 4 per cent in the underwriting syndicate for a German tranche of RM 36 million, and Warburg & Co. in Amsterdam was a member of the group of Dutch banks underwriting the Netherlands tranche of the Young Loan. The issue was far from a success, however: the $5\frac{1}{2}$ per cent bonds which were issued at 90 per cent could not be firmly placed under prevailing conditions, and almost immediately declined below the issue price on all markets, involving the underwriters, including both Warburg firms, in considerable loss. Moreover, the failure of the Young Loan issue further weakened Germany's international credit standing and dashed any hopes that the German Government could cover its rapidly increasing budgetary deficits or future reparations payments by long-term foreign borrowing.

The steadily worsening economic situation now sharpened the political conflict within the governing coalition between the Social Democrats and the People's Party over how the increasing burden of unemployment benefits was to be borne. Despite intensive inter-party discussions, no compromise proved possible between those advocating a sharp reduction in unemployment benefits and the proponents of increased contributions by employers to the by now deficit-ridden unemployment insurance system. On 27 March Chancellor Müller and his Government resigned, and three days later Dr. Heinrich Brüning of the Centrist Party succeeded in forming a new Government which, without the Social Democrats, was unable to command a parliamentary majority and was thus compelled increasingly to rely on rule by Presidential decree.

The economic policies on which the Brüning Government now embarked rested upon the then conventional wisdom that the way to deal with the economic crisis was to balance the budget by reducing Government spending, raising taxes and if possible forcing down prices. Germany's reparations obligations were seen by Brüning as the chief obstacle to his hopes for greater financial manoeuvrability; and he hoped that by

* See Max M. Warburg, *Aufzeichnungen*, pp. 140–1.

making punctual payments on reparations account and pursuing a policy of rigorous Government economy, he would be able to demonstrate to Germany's reparations creditors that they were being given first priority, but that reparations were now simply beyond Germany's capacity to pay. Germany's political debts, however, were only a fraction of her dangerously heavy total of foreign debt. Net German foreign indebtedness at the end of 1930 amounted to RM 15.9 billion, some 39 per cent of which had been lent from United States sources, 18 per cent from the Netherlands, 15 per cent from Great Britain, 13 per cent from Switzerland and 5 per cent from France.* The threat represented by this vast accumulation of debt was made still more acute by the fact that RM 14.8 billion of the total was in the form of short-term credits with maturities ranging upwards only to a limit of ninety days.†

Chancellor Brüning pressed forward with his financial programme regardless of opposition, enacting new tax measures as emergency decrees, which were promptly rejected by the Social Democrats in the Reichstag. In consequence, the Reichstag was dissolved and new elections were held on 14 September 1930, in which Brüning's Government coalition was barely able to hang on, but in which Adolf Hitler's National Socialists achieved a resounding success, returning 107 members to the Reichstag.

The dramatic and ominous triumph of the Nazis in the September elections shocked world opinion, and in particular shook foreign bankers' confidence in German political stability. After several days of anxious waiting, foreign banks and other creditors withdrew vast amounts of short-term credits from Germany, and large holdings of German shares and bonds were dumped on all the major financial markets. Prices on the German markets themselves slumped by some 10 per cent. Moreover, the almost universal fears over Germany's future course were reflected in a significant flight of German capital abroad; the Reichsbank lost some RM 640 million by the first week in October. By the time Chancellor Brüning had formed his new Government, foreign opinion had somewhat calmed and it became possible for the Government to cover its immediate deficit by issuing $125 million of one-year Treasury notes which were placed as to 85 per cent outside Germany by a banking consortium led by Lee, Higginson & Co. of New York, Mendelssohn & Co. and the

* Karl E. Born, *Die deutsche Bankenkrise 1931* (München, 1967), p. 18.

† Born, op. cit., p. 19.

Nederlandsche Handelsmaatschappij in Amsterdam, along with a number of other Dutch, English and Swedish houses. M. M. Warburg & Co. participated as to $1,250,000 in the German portion of this bridging credit operation.

Describing the results of the year 1930, Max Warburg later wrote:

> After the elections and the failure of the Young loan, the worries for our firm also increased. Foreigners withdrew a great deal of money from Germany. We to some degree accelerated these repayments, in order not to display weakness abroad. It was gratifying that when foreign money was offered us, it was always at ¼ to ½ per cent lower than sums offered the big D-banks. But in fact, as a result of the political situation large sums were withdrawn from us also. Many of our clients found themselves in difficulties and had to suspend payments. We suffered large losses, even if these were substantially less than those of most other German banking firms. We had a number of clients who had assessed Germany's recovery far too optimistically and had committed themselves much too heavily.*

The increasingly cloudy outlook in Germany led the Hamburg partners to a decision to expand Warburg & Co. in Amsterdam: in October, Max Warburg travelled to New York to discuss with his brothers Paul and Felix the possibility of injecting further capital into the Amsterdam firm, a step that was later taken. In a generally troubled and unsatisfactory year, the successful flotation by Warburg & Co., Amsterdam, of a 5 per cent 40 million kroner issue for the Norges Kommunalbank was one bright exception; the issue was well received, and represented a considerable achievement for the fledgling Amsterdam outpost.

By the end of January 1931, the number of unemployed in Germany had reached 4,900,000 and Chancellor Brüning, anxiously persevering with his highly unpopular financial programme, determined to court greater domestic approval by pursuing a more energetic and assertive foreign policy. One aspect of this new departure was revealed on 21 March by a surprise announcement in Vienna and Berlin that the Austrian and German Governments had initialled an agreement for a customs union between the two countries. The proposed customs union was greeted with approval in Germany, but met suspicious hostility and protests abroad, particularly in France. Within the few weeks that followed the fateful announcement, French financial institutions reacted by withdrawing short-term credits from Austria in very substantial amounts,

* Max M. Warburg, draft memoirs.

thus laying bare the critical dependence and essential illiquidity of the Austrian banking system.

The withdrawal of foreign funds and a steady decline in Austrian stock markets were followed on 11 May by the sudden collapse of the largest bank in Austria, the Österreichische Creditanstalt. This highly respected bank, which had moreover been backed by the Vienna Rothschild house, had incurred vast losses when it acquired the bankrupt Boden-Kredit-Anstalt at the insistence of the Austrian Government, which in its turn now had to intervene with a purchase of Creditanstalt shares and other assistance measures that it had little prospect of financing except through massive foreign borrowing. The path to such borrowing appeared blocked, however, by the attitude of the French and other governments to the proposed Austro-German customs union.

The shock waves of the Creditanstalt crisis spread rapidly throughout the Austrian and German banking system. Withdrawals of foreign credits from Germany itself now accelerated; German securities, even those denominated in non-German currencies, were hastily sold at ever-decreasing prices on markets throughout the world. The distrust with which foreign lenders now regarded all German credits was further heightened by the disquieting announcement in mid-May that the large department store concern of Rudolph Karstadt A.G. was in serious difficulties. At the end of the month there came news that the big Nordstern insurance company had suffered losses of RM 28 million. Near panic overtook foreign creditors when the Reichsbank itself revealed in its first report for June that over RM 1 billion in gold and foreign exchange had been withdrawn from its reserves, which now stood perilously near the legal minimum. The calling of loans and drawing down of deposits went steadily on.

Events now overtook one another; the sheer rapidity of developments added tension to an already critical situation. A decree of the Reich President, announced on 5 June for the purpose of making further budget economies and introducing new taxes, was unfortunately accompanied by a public demand, designed primarily for domestic consumption, that Germany be relieved from 'unbearable reparation payments'. This statement provoked further uneasiness abroad; in the first four days after the announcement, the Reichsbank had to make RM 400 million available to pay foreign creditors who had called loans outstanding to German banks.*

* Born, op. cit., p. 71.

The situation was temporarily improved by a rise on 13 June in the Reichsbank discount rate from 5 to 7 per cent. The resultant quieting of the agitated money and other markets lasted only briefly, however; for on 17 June came the alarming announcement that the huge Nordwolle textile concern, whose primary banking connection was the Darmstädter- und Nationalbank, had collapsed with debts of some RM 100 million, after having deliberately misled creditors and shareholders over a period of years as to its true financial position. This news led to a further calling of foreign loans; on 19 June alone the Reichsbank lost some RM 70 million in foreign exchange, leaving the German currency only RM 100 million above its legal minimum coverage.* But at this critical juncture the United States President, Herbert Hoover, dramatically offered a one-year moratorium on all inter-Allied debt payments, on the condition that the Allies for their part should suspend reparations claims for the same period. However, the profound relief and the improved atmosphere which greeted this announcement in Germany did not last long; the French Government approved the moratorium only on 6 July after a stubborn rearguard action, and the panicky calling of German loans by French, Dutch and Swiss banks increased yet again.

A last-minute attempt on 10 June by Luther, the President of the Reichsbank, to arrange central bank credits in London and Paris was a failure. On 11 July, a Saturday, the German Government was informed that the massive deposit withdrawals of the past days had made it impossible for the Danatbank to open for business on the following Monday. Almost simultaneously, the Government learned of the complete illiquidity of the Landesbank der Rheinprovinz.

Feverish discussions now ensued among representatives of the Government, the Reichsbank and the leading private and joint-stock banks. As a result of the talks, in which Carl Melchior represented M. M. Warburg & Co., it was decided to announce a Government guarantee of the Danatbank's deposits. The emergency decree giving effect to this decision was no sooner issued on Monday 13 July than a panicky run on all the banks began, attaining such dangerous proportions that all banks were compelled to close their doors by noon. Chancellor Brüning was unable to do more than acknowledge unpalatable facts by declaring first two bank holidays and then a series of them; normal payments were resumed only on 5 August, and the hastily closed German stock exchanges

* Born, op. cit., p. 76.

did not open again until 3 September. Emergency decrees of all kinds were now issued, extending Government controls over foreign credits and exchange, tightening tax regulations, and establishing on 26 July the Akzept- und Garantiebank A.G. with a capital of RM 200 million and the task of making further credit available, especially to the hard-pressed savings banks, by discounting bill and acceptances.

Informal international attempts to deal with the grave issues posed by the worldwide crisis were succeeded by a full-scale conference held in London from 20 to 23 July between Germany and her creditors including the United States. While talks were proceeding at Government level, Melchior and Gustav Schlieper of the Deutsche Bank und Disconto-gesellschaft met at the behest of the Reichsbank with two leading London bankers in order to explore the possibility of preventing further panicky withdrawals of foreign credits still outstanding in Germany.

These preliminary talks were followed by substantive negotiations to which those German banks that still enjoyed a good reputation and extensive connections abroad were invited to send representatives. Dr. Ernst Spiegelberg represented Warburgs in the meetings, out of which emerged a standstill agreement – initially for six months, but later repeatedly extended. The London Conference had, however, failed to solve basic trade and currency problems of the major financial powers; the impasse was ultimately to force even the United Kingdom, after months of steady haemorrhaging of foreign exchange, to go off the gold standard in September. Country after country now adopted protectionist measures of all kinds in a vain attempt to export its economic difficulties; world trade, already drastically shrunk, continued to shrink still further.

'What we have just experiened,' Carl Melchior observed prophetically at the conclusion of the standstill agreement, 'is the destruction of the ground-rules of the capitalist system. Yet the system depends on the strictest observance of these very rules. This is the first time that I have had to refuse to fulfil an obligation to which I had freely committed my name simply because the state required me to refuse. The capitalist system in Germany will not survive such a deviation from its rules. For the deviations will constantly increase, and the system will accordingly dissolve.'*

The Brüning Government persisted doggedly meanwhile in its policy of attempting to overcome the internal economic crisis by cutting public

* Quoted in Erich Eyck, *A History of the Weimar Republic* (Cambridge, Mass., 1964), Vol. II, p. 323.

expenditures and raising taxes. The most radical of the Government's measures was the emergency decree of 8 December 1931 which forced sweeping decreases in certain prices and in interest rates, wages and salaries, and provided further for a series of new taxes. These included a flight tax *(Reichsfluchtsteuer)* that was ultimately to serve as the chief confiscatory instrument of the Nazi régime in despoiling emigrants forced by its policies to leave the Reich. The far-reaching emergency decree, which had an electrifying effect inside and outside Germany, was designed also to persuade Germany's creditors that payment of the unconditional reparations annuities provided by the Young Plan would have to be deferred. Accordingly, after Chancellor Brüning had paved the way with intensive diplomatic soundings, the Bank for International Settlements convened a Special Advisory Committee, on which Germany was again represented by Carl Melchior, to consider Germany's request for a postponement of reparations payments. The Committee reported on 23 December, giving a detailed account of Germany's financial crisis and recommending the governments concerned to accede to Germany's request. The French and British Governments accepted the Committee's report, and suggested that a conference should be held in Lausanne to discuss again the entire reparations issue in the light of the new conditions which the Young Plan had so entirely failed to foresee. The permanent settlement of the contentious question came ultimately at Lausanne in June 1932, and brought with it the definitive end of reparations. But the beneficiary of this long-sought and tenaciously argued goal was not the Brüning Government, which had strained every nerve and endured unremitting hostility to demonstrate its international good faith *vis-à-vis* Germany's creditors, but the Government of von Papen.

Chancellor Brüning, his position undermined on all sides, was dismissed by President Hindenburg on 30 May, only sixteen days before the Lausanne Conference. Brüning's fall marked a crucial turning-point in the disintegration of the Weimar Republic and its institutions: with his departure the National Socialist tide was now uncontained, and Germany's fate henceforth rested in the hands of those who trustingly believed they could tame the Nazis in return for the calculated conferment of political favours.

'In a battle soldiers must die, in a financial panic banks must lose money,' wrote Max Warburg philosophically some years after the great crisis.* M. M. Warburg & Co. was not spared sizeable losses in the course

* Max M. Warburg, unpublished draft memoirs.

of the turbulent years 1930–2; but the firm's continued existence and reputation were never in question, either at home or abroad, where Max Warburg's uniquely close relationship with his American brothers assured access to important sources of capital which could supplement the bank's own resources. M. M. Warburg & Co. had always been above all a family firm, and the *sauve qui peut* attitude of most overseas banks towards their German correspondents was unthinkable where Paul and Felix Warburg were concerned with the house in which they had been partners.

When Max Warburg travelled to America in the autumn of 1930, he foresaw a severe economic crisis ahead, but he – in common with many others – could not gauge the vast dimensions it was to assume. 'People were prepared, and I too was prepared,' he recalled, 'for certain possible symptoms of a crisis – withdrawal of funds on the order of 10 or 15% or more as happens in a panic; but I never reckoned with the simultaneous paralysis, withdrawal of funds and depreciation of assets that we actually experienced.'* When the storm broke, it was of proportions for which there had been no precedent, and assumed forms that made all previous attempts at defence largely irrelevant. The bank found itself confronted with large losses in its credit business, where substantial and complex credit lines were outstanding to industrial and commercial clients whose ability to service their debts had been severely limited or destroyed by the overall downward plunge in the German economy. The severe decline of securities prices, particularly for Reich and municipal bonds, diminished the value of the firm's investment portfolio; and there were in addition withdrawals of funds by foreign and some domestic clients.

Despite their essentially pessimistic assessment of the political as well as economic future in Germany, Paul and Felix Warburg agreed to meet the extraordinary demands of the situation by infusing more capital into the family firms in Hamburg and Amsterdam. James P. Warburg, then Vice-President of the merged International Acceptance Bank and Bank of the Manhattan Company, spent the summer months of 1931 in Hamburg, working with his German cousins during the exceptionally busy time while frozen commitments were being liquidiated, further withdrawals met, and several of the bank's clients and banking friends tided over during periods of temporary difficulty.†

* Max M. Warburg, unpublished notes for the firm's history.

† See James P. Warburg, *The Long Road Home* (New York, 1964), pp. 91–2.

Later, in the autumn of 1931, M. M. Warburg & Co. embarked on negotiations with the Berliner Handels-Gesellschaft, one of the few major banks to have withstood the crisis without difficulties. These negotiations, conducted largely by representatives of the younger generation on both sides – James P. Warburg and Siegmund G. Warburg with Hans Fürstenberg of the Berliner Handels-Gesellschaft – resulted in an arrangement for the placement with the Warburg group of a block of RM 5 million of Berliner Handels-Gesellschaft shares, in return for the transfer by Warburgs of certain assets, including shares of an *ad hoc* corporation in which both banks were equal partners. By placing this substantial block of shares in firm and friendly hands, the Berliner Handels-Gesellschaft added to its liquidity and freed itself of the potentially damaging obligation to intervene in the market for its own shares, while Warburgs gained a closer relationship with the most important of the remaining independent major banks, the only bank in its class that had not been forced to seek Government assistance. Max Warburg became a member of the Berliner Handels-Gesellschaft management board, and several joint transactions ensued. The entire range of mutual benefits anticipated from the new relationship could not ultimately be realized, however, since the two banks were essentially conducting the same type of business and competing for similar clients. In a friendly arrangement agreed some years later, the banks' joint corporation was dissolved and the block of shares retransferred to the Berliner Handels-Gesellschaft, which was able in the much improved market conditions then prevailing to place them firmly among a wider investing public.*

Reflecting later on that stormy year, Max Warburg wrote: 'The experiences of 1931 demonstrate how strongly the individual is influenced by features of the contemporary scene, and cannot liberate himself from them despite being animated by internal principles that should keep him aloof from actions shaped by the contemporary mood.' † Wisdom after the event indicated that the bank had been unduly sanguine in some of its engagements; the ensuing losses were large, although some losses which in 1931 seemed total were later diminished as clients were able in improved conditions to marshal some assets for partial repayment of their debts. M. M. Warburg & Co. had nevertheless been able to maintain its own

* See Hans Fürstenberg, *Erinnerungen* (Wiesbaden, 1965), pp. 245–6, and Rolf E. Lüke, *Die Berliner Handels-Gesellschaft in einem Jahrhundert deutscher Wirtschaft* (Berlin, 1956), pp. 227–8.

† Max M. Warburg, unpublished notes for the firm's history.

liquidity and freedom of manoeuvre. The year led to a close relationship with one of the major Berlin banks, but not to any structural alteration in the Hamburg firm nor to any loss of independence. Keeping its sails still close-reefed against the economic storms, the firm entered 1932 determined to continue its traditional business in all branches.

The new year began, however, with a heavy personal blow for the partners: on 24 January Paul M. Warburg died in New York, thus depriving his brothers of his wise counsel at a still critical time, when the German banking structure was being shored up only with Government help, and the outlook for classic private banking business seemed bleaker than at any time in the firm's history.

The big branch banks, still reeling from the massive deposit withdrawals of the summer, were mostly unable at the beginning of 1932 to resume their credit business because they were uncertain as to the extent of their own commitments or the dimensions of the Government help they could expect. The prolongation in January of the Standstill Agreement with foreign creditors for a further year clarified somewhat the foreign business position. The continuing intervention of the German Government came in the form of capital injections, and a strong impetus towards further concentration in the banking sector: in February the Dresdner Bank was merged with the illiquid Danatbank: the new Dresdner Bank which thus resulted was to all intents and purposes a State institution. Further Government assistance was extended elsewhere in the economy: to the shipping companies in the form of Reich loan guarantees, and to the steel industry through share purchases. Despite growing Government intervention in major economic sectors, the number of unemployed failed to subside; their misery fuelled a social discontent that benefitted the increasingly bold advocates of totalitarian solutions to Germany's problems.

The economic situation was at its worst in the summer of 1932; by autumn the first signs of an overall improvement were visible at last, although the banks continued to suffer from the actual or threatened bankruptcy of many major industrial and commercial debtors. The Government stepped in once more by founding the Deutsche Finanzierungs-Institut A.G. (Finag) and the Tilgungskasse für gewerbliche Kredite (Tilka). Finag helped the banks to realize their frozen loans by advancing credits against securities which the banks had accepted in lieu of loan repayments; Tilka, provided with a Government guarantee fund, was able to help the banks amortize their loan losses over a period of years, thus preserving the integrity of their reserve funds. Despite all these measures, the toll among banks was a heavy one: there now remained only five major Berlin banks instead of six; the number of provincial and local banks had fallen from 211 in 1929 to 157 in 1932, and of private banks over the same period from 1,100 to only 709.*

For Warburgs the year 1932 meant a further contraction in loan business, although there was some revival of activity in the new issue and securities business. Many old loans were liquidated, and others were reduced; new American and English credit lines made available to the firm were used exclusively to finance imports of commodities, mostly cotton and coffee. Although there were no major losses, the profit margins on such credit business as there was shrank nearly to vanishing point as the Government and Reichsbank exerted relentless pressure on all the banks to lower their interest rates; in some cases the profit on a transaction barely covered costs, which continued to remain high largely because the Standstill Agreement and the complexity of Government regulations required the maintenance of a substantial technical staff. Writing his *Annual Report*, Max Warburg concluded:

For 1932 there is no point in making observations on individual departments of the firm. We were everywhere in a defensive position; on the one hand, we had to press for liquidity, and on the other we tried not only to retain our old, good clientele but also to acquire new clients of standing. It was work that was not directed toward a particular goal; essentially defensive, but including a seizing of such opportunities as were offered in a time of crisis.†

Despite all the grave economic difficulties, the chief threat to the firm's future lay in the political sphere. With his usual perspicacity, Carl Melchior had diagnosed the situation before grim forebodings had become dread reality. Writing on 25 August 1932 to Dr. Hans Meyer of Warburg & Co., Amsterdam, he observed:

I am occupied at the moment less with economic affairs than with matters of public *mores*, for it is in these matters that I see the most dangerous development for us. I really do not know where things are going with us when the leaders of our largest political party declare their solidarity, doubtless out of inner conviction, with men who – at least from what one reads in the newspapers – have committed murder in the usual sense of the Penal Code, and thus should have been condemned to death even by an ordinary tribunal. It seems to me

* Born, op. cit., p. 174.

† *Annual Report*, 1932.

that the Government has until now calmly been doing everything to oppose this confusion of public morality. With passions whipped up to fever pitch, however, the Government's task is terribly difficult. At any rate, it seems to me that this problem, which lies entirely outside the economic and technical-political sphere, has become the most important one for us. In the final analysis, one can only hope that our people, who are after all decent and reasonable, will succeed at last in overcoming these fever symptoms. However, as long as we live in conditions of such moral confusion and inner strife, I fear we shall be unable to make any progress in other areas.*

On 30 January 1933, Adolf Hitler became Reich Chancellor, heading a coalition Government with Hugenberg's Nationalists that could not command a majority in the Reichstag. Subsequent developments all too clearly demonstrated the impotence of Hitler's opponents, who either collapsed into silence, were arrested or were forced into exile or hiding. The way was thus open for the assumption by Hitler of total power, and the rapid, systematic destruction of the rule of law inside Germany.

* Max M. Warburg, *Aufzeichnungen*, p. 145.

10

DEFENCE OF A TRADITION: 1933–1938

The coming to power of the National Socialist régime was ultimately to pose for M. M. Warburg & Co. the stark question of survival in any form; but initially the fateful consequences of Hitler's takeover were not fully grasped by all the partners at Ferdinandstrasse. Writing later, Max Warburg confessed that in 1933 he had seen the change in régime as merely the result of the self-seeking political intrigues of von Papen and his friends, and had completely under-estimated the mass support which Hitler had been able to exploit: 'I considered it absolutely inconceivable that this man could ever become sole ruler of one of the most creative, industrious and powerful of peoples.'*

As the first measures of the new government were promulgated with the swiftness and audacity that were to become the hallmark of Nazi policy, the Warburg family and the bank's partners were divided in their several assessments of the new circumstances. Despite advice to the contrary from several quarters, Max Warburg resolved firmly to remain in Hamburg and to continue the bank's business in all its aspects as long as that might be possible:

> I was determined to defend my firm like a fortress. My family was of the opposite opinion. My American brother Felix, who always regarded my fate as if it were his own, did everything conceivable to persuade me to liquidate the firm and emigrate. My wife and son also believed that the time for our emigration had come: they were convinced that I was in great danger. But I remained steadfast. They stood by me, and I was still convinced that such a sacrifice would some day not have been in vain.
>
> Melchior considered the situation much more serious than I did, perhaps only because he in any case tended towards pessimism. I had no doubt that we

* *Aufzeichnungen*, p. 140.

were at the beginning of one of those many periods of suffering that the Jews in particular have had to undergo; but it was my firm belief that this period would be limited in duration. From this belief I drew the strength that enabled me to carry on.*

But even before the Act permitting the Government to rule by decree was promulgated on 24 March, the signs multiplied that M. M. Warburg & Co. was not going to be permitted to carry on its business as before. On 14 March, Max Warburg learned in the course of a friendly visit from one of Hamburg's leading bankers that the Finance Department of Hamburg would not henceforth be consulting the firm in financial matters as it had done for many years previously. The Mayor and other officials had been receiving a stream of letters protesting against the alleged financial 'dictatorship' of M. M. Warburg & Co. in Hamburg, and now felt compelled to yield to the threats expressed or implied by these letters. Shortly after this interview, the Hamburg State Councillor Leo Lippmann called at Ferdinandstrasse to report that he had just been abruptly dismissed from the Finance Department, without a word of thanks or recognition for his decades of outstanding service to Hamburg.† Max Warburg's laconic comment at the time on the day's revelations was simply: 'Death rides fast.'‡

Pressures of all kinds mounted insidiously on the bank and its clients. Acts of outright physical intimidation or hooliganism such as were organized against large Jewish-owned department stores were, to be sure, avoided; the firm was spared the cruder aspects of the SA-inspired boycott on 1 April 1933 of all Jewish businesses. But privately inspired boycotts and a subtle atmosphere of threat made the doing of business with Warburgs inadvisable for many firms and individuals, whatever their standing *vis-à-vis* the régime. Nazi Party functionaries in Hamburg had Max Warburg and certain of his partners followed by photographers who recorded those who stopped to exchange greetings with them; the number of those willing to be thus publicly marked dropped steadily. Likewise, there was a sharp decline in the number of clients wishing to call personally at Ferdinandstrasse to transact business.

Although the firm's employees behaved in exemplary fashion, even going so far as to resist for some time the election of a works council as

* *Aufzeichnungen*, p. 147.

† See Leo Lippmann, op. cit., pp. 620–5.

‡ *Aufzeichnungen*, p. 148.

'recommended' by the new labour regulations, there could be no doubt of the growing isolation in which the bank now found itself. Honorary offices and Board memberships of all kinds had to be given up, one by one, with a consequent shrinking of the bank's business connections, and thus not merely a loss of deposit and credit business but exclusion from new issue and securities transactions as well.

When members of M. M. Warburg & Co. were voted off corporate Boards, good form was sometimes observed; but in many cases a deliberately insulting manner of imparting the news was chosen. When Max Warburg was deprived of his Supervisory Board seat in the Hamburgische Wirtschaftsdienst, which he had founded, the news was conveyed to him by a very junior employee whom he did not know; in the case of several other Boards a curt letter was the reward after many years of association. In only one case, that of the Kiel Institut für Seeverkehr und Weltwirtschaft, was there a demonstration of solidarity by two other Board members, who expressed their disgust at the new measures by tendering their resignations to take effect along with Warburg's.

Max Warburg was ousted from the Advisory Council of the Reichsbank, a body that was in any case cast aside in October 1933. When he was voted off the Board of the Hamburg–America Line, an attempt was made to soften the blow by requiring the resignations of two elderly Board members, the Chairman Max von Schinckel and Baron Rudolf von Schröder, at the same time. The regular Thursday breakfast Board meeting at which these resignations were made official was the occasion of a tragi-comic episode: the remaining Board members were so shamefaced over the proceedings that Warburg himself gave not only the traditional farewell speech, but also the reply that his former colleagues were too timid or embarrassed to give, emphasizing that M. M. Warburg & Co. had on several occasions come to the rescue of the Hamburg–America Line when other banks had failed to do so, and that it was his firm that had given the line the means to equip the new Ballin class of vessels with which it was able to resume operations after its war losses.*

Despite protests from its American bankers and shareholders, the Deutsch-Atlantische Telegraphen-Gesellschaft compelled Max Warburg to leave its Board; the Hamburg Chamber of Commerce, which a few short years before had conferred on Warburg its gold medal in recogni-

* See *Aufzeichnungen*, pp. 149–50.

tion of long and distinguished service, now turned him out, as did the Philharmonic Society, the Board of Higher Education and other institutions. Dr. Carl Melchior was ousted from several corporate Boards as well as from official boards such as that of the Bank for International Settlements in Basel. The firm ceased as a matter of course to be consulted in financial matters by any public authority in Berlin or in Hamburg itself.

Of the 108 Board seats which members of the bank held at the beginning of 1933, eighteen had to be given up in the course of that year. The number of the firm's clients, which in 1930 had been 5,241, declined by the end of 1933 to 1,875. Foreign exchange transactions for the firm's own account were made extremely difficult by reason of Germany's overall strained foreign-exchange position; the once considerable and lucrative business with foreign state banks stopped completely. However, export credits were in many cases still possible to arrange, frequently through Warburg & Co. in Amsterdam.

Under these circumstances there was no new issue business or significant long-term financing activity for the firm in 1933. An enterprise that was to play a major role in financing the emigration of a large part of the German Jewish community was, however, founded jointly by Warburgs and A. E. Wassermann of Berlin. Known as Palästina-Treuhand-Gesellschaft m.b.H. ('Paltreu'), it enabled emigrants to transfer funds to Palestine by paying Marks to exporters in Germany through Paltreu, and obtaining from importers in Palestine the countervalue in Palestine pounds, through a parallel organization to Paltreu, Haavara Ltd. of Tel-Aviv. The capital transfers thus accomplished through the sale of so-called 'emigrant blocked Marks' *(Auswanderer-Sperrmark)*, under conditions that were more favourable than those available to non-Palestine-bound emigrants, were an important factor in building many key commercial and agricultural enterprises within the burgeoning Palestine economy. For Warburgs, the activity with Paltreu meant a series of highly complex tasks in dealing with many individual transfers: the multiple documentation required of an emigrant from the tax authorities alone required most painstaking processing. Paltrau transfer work also gave the firm an insight into the fate of many smaller Jewish enterprises, which had often been in existence for generations, and which were now going into liquidation or being sold in efforts to realize some capital for starting anew outside Germany.

Despite the most intensive efforts by its partners and staff, the bank's financial results for 1933 showed a substantial loss. Refusing nevertheless to concede defeat, Max Warburg wrote at the year-end:

> The past year was one of retrenchment. Since a recovery is not possible for the moment, we can only defend our fortress in the meantime, by trying to retain our clientele in Germany and abroad. In this connection, small measures may to some degree be of importance: no Board seat that is taken from us should be regarded as definitely lost, and every opportunity should be seized to regain these positions, even if success may yet be far off.*

'In general, however,' he concluded, 'the firm's capacity to survive has been demonstrated, thanks to the devoted work of all concerned, despite sometimes colossal difficulties.'†

The year, which had been overshadowed by many losses and partings, came to a sad end with the deaths on the same day, 30 December, of Aby S. Warburg and Dr. Carl Melchior. To Aby S. Warburg, with his long years of experience as senior partner of the firm and his shrewd knowledge of men and affairs, had fallen many of the responsibilities for dealing with personnel matters at Ferdinandstrasse; he had also devoted much effort, particularly in his last years, to looking after the traditional Warburg interests in community and charitable institutions. Dr. Melchior, literally worn out by his ceaseless travels and strenuous negotiating efforts on behalf of Germany, died from a heart attack. Just a few days previously, preparing with his customary orderly calm for a development he felt to be inevitable, he had given a personal Power of Attorney in case of his arrest by the Gestapo to a trusted friend and colleague, Dr. Kurt Sieveking.‡ The deaths of Aby Warburg and Melchior meant not merely the severing of yet another link with a happier past, but also the loss of vastly experienced and valued counsellors at a critical juncture in the affairs of M. M. Warburg & Co.

Throughout 1934, Max Warburg and his remaining partners divided their attention between business affairs and the increasingly urgent appeals of the Jewish community. As Chairman or Board member of such national organizations as the Reichsvertretung der deutschen Juden and the Hilfsverein der deutschen Juden, as well as a number of Hamburg communal bodies, Max Warburg was fully occupied in assisting his

* Max M. Warburg, draft memoirs.

† Ibid.

‡ See Sieveking foreword in *Carl Melchior, ein Buch des Gedenkens und der Freundschaft* (Tübingen, 1967).

Jewish fellow-citizens to organize tolerable existences under gravely deteriorating conditions. In an effort to obtain at the highest level some moderation of the Government's anti-Jewish policy, he called on Vice-Chancellor von Papen in Berlin on 28 June. After hearing Warburg's exposition of the problem, von Papen undertook merely to do what he could. Two days later, he himself narrowly escaped death in Hitler's infamous purge of potential opponents, and whatever slight influence he may have wielded up to that point entirely vanished.*

Although hope of an eventual improvement in the political climate was still not abandoned, elementary prudence now required the firm reluctantly to wind down its activities within Germany. Credit engagements were deliberately reduced, and shrank in the course of the year from RM 62.4 million to RM 54 million. Long outstanding credits to Rudolph Karstadt A.G. were partly realized with the reorganization of that concern after protracted, difficult negotiations. Karstadt and other department store groups such as Wertheim and Tietz significantly increased their liquidity by selling off parcels of real estate, thus benefitting their bank creditors, including Warburgs.

An attempt was made to compensate for the shrinking of the firm's business within Germany by devoting greater effort to expanding its outposts abroad. After long preparatory negotiations with banking friends in several countries, the Dutch International Corporation was established in Amsterdam, which in its turn founded the New Trading Company in London, with a capital of £120,000. Warburgs gradually withdrew from Dutch International and took a larger participation in New Trading Company, on whose Board Siegmund G. Warburg, a partner in M. M. Warburg & Co. since 1930, was the most active member. The intention was to found a series of small organizations which could service Warburgs' clientele within Germany from abroad, and could be useful as well to those former Hamburg clients who had already emigrated and were starting new enterprises in England and elsewhere. Developing from this original context, the New Trading Company devoted an increasing share of its financing business to medium-sized British enterprises of all kinds: the later City of London house of S. G. Warburg & Co. was ultimately to emerge from these modest beginnings.

Throughout 1934, as in the preceding year, Warburgs was active in arranging Palestine transfers, and in this connection was able, after four

* See *Aufzeichnungen*, p. 154.

months of negotiations, to arrange financing for large-scale exports of Palestine Jaffa oranges for the 1934–5 season, a transaction which resulted in further emigrant transfer possibilities, and a substantial turnover for the firm in so-called *Orangenmark* ('orange Marks'). Other transfers were made possible on this pattern through the financing of essential imports from Turkey. The complex activities of Paltreu and a series of financial advisory commissions on behalf of enterprises whose owners wished to liquidate or sell their assets with a view to emigration represented for M. M. Warburg & Co. one source of new clients and new business, but also a grim reminder that any long-term prognosis for its own future must inevitably be cautious. Characterizing the firm's business position at the end of 1934, Max Warburg wrote that after the buffetings of the crisis years the bank had now come to the point where it might in ordinary times have reasonably expected to embark on a programme of constructive expansion: 'The road to recovery would have been open, but was blocked by National Socialist policy.'*

The enactment in September 1935 of the Nuremberg Laws established the legislative basis for the subsequent exclusion of Jews – as defined in a hastily-issued and often confused set of supplementary decrees – from wide areas of German life. Initially, however, the laws were viewed by the official spokesmen of the German Jewish community as potentially opening the way towards a tolerable if circumscribed existence for most of their number. However, these slender hopes were belied by steadily mounting pressures within the Nazi Party for a full-scale attack on Jewish participation in all aspects of German life, and most particularly in the economy. What made such an assault impolitic at this juncture was the bleakly unavoidable fact that interference with Jewish economic activities still posed a possible threat to Germany's economic recovery, and therefore to the stabilization of the régime. The Reichsbank and the Reich Economics Ministry understood that the disruptions caused by an attempt to uproot Jewish enterprises from Germany would have serious repercussions abroad, and that Germany's still critical shortage of foreign exchange for the import of many urgent necessities dictated a prohibition on 'spontaneous actions' such as the nationwide boycott of 1 April 1933. Moreover, with the approach of the 1936 Olympic Games, any potential threat to Germany's constructive new image was to be avoided.

Despite all these factors tending toward a stabilization of the situation, smaller Jewish enterprises, particularly those serving the domestic market,

* Max M. Warburg, draft memoirs.

found themselves subjected to a crossfire of relentless pressures from public authorities, suppliers, customers and sources of credit. The numbers of such enterprises dwindled steadily from 1933 onwards, and their proprietors were frequently forced to move from villages and smaller cities to the big cities or abroad. Larger Jewish-owned businesses, especially those which in some way contributed to Germany's foreign-exchange earnings, had in most cases managed to stay in business, even at a reduced volume, without being threatened with outright liquidation.*

M. M. Warburg & Co. for its part continued to fight a stubborn rear-guard action: the annual report for 1935 speaks in a few brief sentences of a steady shrinking in most branches of the bank's business. Quite aside from official anti-Jewish measures and the steady coercion exerted on the firm and its clients in quasi-legal and indeed in illegal ways, there were decreasing opportunities for private bankers of any kind to engage in large-scale transactions within an economy increasingly dominated by the State and its financing programme. Although a series of new credits was extended to old clients and some new ones, the total volume of credits outstanding continued to decline as credit engagements of long standing were progressively liquidated, and the average size of individual credits continued to fall. An important and complex part of the bank's activity consisted in assisting foreign banks and exporters to liquidate their commitments within Germany: many American and English accounts in blocked Marks were successfully covered through German exports, even though in most cases this was possible only with losses to the foreign creditors.

The years 1936 and 1937, relatively quiet ones as far as anti-Jewish agitation was concerned, enabled M. M. Warburg & Co. to maintain its holding operation and in some limited respects even to improve its essentially defensive position. Speaking to the staff on 16 April 1936, Max Warburg was able to report that even with a reduced overall volume of business the number of clients had increased from 1,807 in 1934 to 2,183 in 1935. The Credit Department had successfully undertaken a series of difficult but rewarding tasks on behalf of Hamburg exporters and importers; the Documentary Department had been fully engaged with the various transfer operations and other documentary transactions; and even the business in trade bills and acceptances had

* See Helmut Genschel, *Die Verdrängung der Juden aus der deutschen Wirtschaft* (Göttingen, 1966), pp. 136–8.

shown a gratifying increase.* Later that year, on 12 November, again speaking to a staff meeting, Max Warburg once more expressed gratitude in his general report for the faithful efforts of all at Ferdinandstrasse, and ended with the words:

> But it is our difficult and – precisely because of that – exciting task to steer our firm successfully through this period also. Therefore, no exaggerated conclusions regarding the future, but on the other hand, no excessive doubts either.†

As long as Dr. Hjalmar Schacht remained in office, the official policy of the Reich Economics Ministry – which, to be sure, frequently brought it into conflict with other Ministries and with organs of the Nazi Party – was to maintain most Jewish enterprises unhindered in the exercise of their business; one example of his relative weight *vis-à-vis* his adversaries was that on 1 April 1938 there were still almost 40,000 Jewish-owned businesses in Germany.‡ But with Schacht's departure in the autumn of 1937 and the assumption of his main functions by the officials of Goering's Four Year Plan, the way was clear for the introduction of a much harsher policy against Jews in the German economy, however damaging this might be from the point of view of Germany's foreign exchange balances or her relations with foreign trading partners. The end of the so-called Jewish 'close season' came in December 1937 with a large-scale Christmas boycott in Nuremberg organized by Gauleiter Julius Streicher. Significantly, this boycott was unopposed by any official reprimand. Jewish enterprise of all kinds was now made increasingly difficult by local propaganda and boycotts, the conspicuous marking of shops and factories, arbitrary tax measures and outright prohibitions on trading. With even more fateful consequences, the 'aryanization' process was now put on an official footing; it was organized systematically by the reconstructed Reich Economics Ministry and often financed on behalf of the 'aryanizing' enterprises by credits arranged through the big banks.§

For M. M. Warburg & Co. and its staff the period in which some semblance of normal business had been possible now also came to an end: the firm had arrived at a point where 'passive and active resistance blocked all freedom of manoeuvre, so that the maintenance of old relationships,

*Firm history notes.
† Ibid.
‡ Genschel, op. cit., p. 136.
§ Ibid., pp. 144–50.

let alone the establishment of new contacts, was impossible. It was a paralysis, a withering away.'* Sooner or later almost all the bank's 'aryan' business friends succumbed to a variety of threats and refrained from open involvement with Warburgs – some with expressions of regret, many in embarrassed silence. Between 1936 and 1938 another eighty Board seats were taken away from partners of the firm; one maritime company, in the founding of which Warburgs had played the leading role, considered it politic to re-name two of its vessels, previously called the *Melchior* and the *Max Warburg*, so as to efface all memory of the bank's activity on its behalf. As business volume continued to slacken, the numbers of staff also slowly declined: the attrition was most marked among the bank's Jewish employees who now, in growing numbers, sought refuge abroad for themselves and their families.

At Ferdinandstrasse the sombre atmosphere of the autumn of 1937 was further darkened by the death on 20 October of Felix Warburg in New York. His concern for the German Jewish community into which he had been born had been expressed since 1933 in ceaseless activity to make a new start possible for those able to emigrate, and to make the lives of those who could not leave Germany more tolerable. Felix Warburg's intense family loyalty ensured to the last his personal interest in the affairs and fate of M. M. Warburg & Co.

Toward the year-end in 1937, conditions had deteriorated to the point where, Max Warburg recalled:

> It became quiet in our firm. On my way to the bank I met not a single acquaintance, while in former times I was continually doffing my hat in greeting. To be sure there were, aside from Reusch,† others among my friends who displayed moral courage. The business days dragged monotonously by. There was hardly any foreign correspondence left because of the censorship, but even the German correspondence was sparse, since letters addressed to a Jewish house were compromising. After the meagre post had been read, there was an exchange of views between the partners and senior staff. There was no new business to discuss, but instead for the most part the winding-up of relationships that either were broken off entirely or were left intact in purely nominal form. The many new laws concerning Jews had to be studied with the help of the firm's eight lawyers.‡

In the last months of 1937 and the beginning of 1938, there was a sharp quickening in the pace of 'aryanization' of all businesses; directors,

* Max M. Warburg, draft memoirs.

† Managing Director of Gutehoffnungshütte.

‡ *Aufzeichnungen*, p. 153.

managers, salesmen and other employees were dismissed *en masse* from enterprises thus taken over, and swelled the ranks of the unemployed who were entirely dependent on the assistance available within the Jewish community. The fate of such Jewish-owned enterprises as remained became ever more precarious as credit and other restrictions steadily narrowed the possibilities of any normal trading activity.

Although the number of the firm's Board seats had by this time dropped to eighteen, M. M. Warburg & Co. remained a member of the Reich loan consortium, an exception which Max Warburg traced directly to the influence of Schacht, who had understood the importance of the Warburg name in the consortium for the successful placement of Reich issues.* Early in 1938, Schacht summoned Max Warburg to Berlin and informed him with regret that the firm could no longer be retained in the consortium for Reich issues. Warburg replied that in that event the firm would have to be liquidated; Schacht for his part said he had expected such a response.†

On his return to Hamburg, Max Warburg relayed Schacht's news to his partners, and it was reluctantly decided that the inevitable had now to be faced. A series of discussions was therefore initiated with the remaining friends of the firm – banks, overseas trading companies and a number of industrial enterprises – with a view to constituting a group that might take over the bank's assets and continue its business. Although local and national Nazi functionaries interested themselves in the bank's fate, the Warburg partners were successful in including in the takeover group only friends of the bank. A limited company was formed, in which the per-personally liable proprietors were Dr. Rudolf Brinckmann, holder of the bank's Power of Attorney since 1931, and Paul Wirtz, an experienced and able Hamburg overseas merchant.

The assets of the bank were transferred to the new group, which continued to do business under the style of M. M. Warburg & Co. K.G.: the retention of the old name was specifically requested by the authorities, who wished to exploit the firm's international goodwill even in the new circumstances. After deduction of taxes, a large reserve for trading risks, and a considerable sum representing 'a tax that had no name',‡ the Warburg partners were permitted to leave a silent participation in the new limited company. However, this investment was confiscated at the begin-

* *Aufzeichnungen*, p. 153.

† Ibid., p. 154.

‡ Ibid., p., 155.

ning of the war, and in 1941 the firm was required to change its name to Brinckmann, Wirtz & Co.*

Max Warburg's son Eric had preceded him into exile, to New York, where he founded E. M. Warburg & Co. to carry on merchant banking with the nucleus of former Warburg clients who had emigrated to America. Siegmund G. Warburg continued his activities in London. Other former partners and staff of the Hamburg house were scattered throughout the world: in Western Europe, Latin America, Palestine and the United States.

Max Warburg, his brother Fritz and the other partners who were leaving the firm bade farewell to their colleagues in a meeting at the end of May 1938. Speaking to the entire staff in the familiar large hall at Ferdinandstrasse, Max Warburg said, in a speech that all present heard with deep emotion:

'I do not need to tell you, my dear colleagues, how difficult this transformation of our firm has been for us. According to the law, the firm is the name under which the merchant carries on his business and issues his signature. But it can be more, it should be more, and for us it was much more. It is only because we and our ancestors felt the firm as a living unity, over and above its temporary representatives; because we did not regard it as only the source of a livelihood for those living from time to time, but as the remaining result of work accomplished, and the obligation to carry on further work; only because of that can we explain the firm's preservation through all sorts of crises and the vicissitudes of time. And this thought – that in such a firm there is a conceptual value that is independent of and far beyond its temporary proprietors – was one that became the *leitmotif* and ultimately the decisive impulse in the hard decisions we have had to confront in these past months.

'There were two paths between which we had to choose: either we had to give up the business, go into liquidation and transfer the clientele to another banking firm; or place the structure itself above persons and maintain the firm, departing ourselves and transferring the management to our successors. We chose the second path, because we did not wish this firm, which has been our life's work up till today, to be destroyed. Above all, however, we did not wish your community, in which you grew close in decades of work, to disintegrate. It is this thought that has guided us, and that will justify our decision.

'The firm and the working community embodied in it will continue to exist. The proprietorship and with it the management will be in the hands of Dr. Brinckmann, whom you have known for years, and Herr Wirtz, whose reputation precedes him as a successful Hanseatic merchant in the most distinguished

* Genschel, op. cit., pp. 237–8.

sense of the word. In both gentlemen you will have upright chiefs, far-seeing, wise, independent directors of the company. It is no light task that these gentlemen are assuming, and they can only accomplish it if you, our colleagues, stand by them with the same tirelessness, self-possession and devotion which you have given to us, which we have always felt as the good fortune of our work, and for which at this time we once again wholeheartedly thank you.' *

At the end of August 1938 Max Warburg and his wife sailed to New York, fully intending to return to Hamburg in the autumn so that he might resume once more the direction of the charitable enterprises to which he had been devoting much of his time since May; but his intention was overtaken by events, and he was not to see Hamburg again.

When the organized pogrom known as *Kristallnacht* burst over the whole of Germany on the night of 9–10 November 1938, Dr. Fritz Warburg, who had been on a visit from Sweden to look after Hamburg's beleaguered Jewish Hospital, was arrested by the Gestapo and his passport was confiscated. He was allowed to leave Germany again only in May 1939, after the personal intervention at Gestapo headquarters in Berlin of a partner in one of Hamburg's oldest Christian banking houses. It was henceforth clear, however, that any member of the Warburg family venturing to return to his homeland faced the virtual certainty of arrest at the frontier.

The new proprietors of the firm, Dr. Rudolf Brinckmann and Paul Wirtz, guided the bank prudently and successfully, at no small political risk to themselves, throughout the dark years of wartime destruction. When Eric M. Warburg, then a high-ranking officer in the United States Air Force, found the firm still carrying on amid the ruins of Hamburg in the Spring of 1945, he was able, initially as a non-resident of Germany, to resume the interrupted continuity of the family's involvement with the fortunes of the old house. From 1948 the Warburg family were financially interested in the bank, and in 1956 Eric M. Warburg returned to Ferdinandstrasse as a general partner. The bank rapidly rebuilt a substantial business in international underwriting, financing foreign trade, and the entire range of classic private banking business.

In January 1970, the long tradition begun in 1798 was re-established, and the historic name M. M. Warburg & Co. was restored to Hamburg. The firm now carries on its multifarious activities under the name of M. M. Warburg-Brinckmann, Wirtz & Co.

Max M. Warburg, *Aufzeichnungen*, p. 156.

GENEALOGICAL TABLES

- Simon von Cassel *d. ca.* 1566
  - Samuel *d. ca.* 1595
    - Jacob Simon Warburg *d.* 1636
      - Levi Juspa-Joseph Warburg *d. ca.* 1678
        - Jacob Samuel Warburg *d.* 1668
          - Moses *d.* 1701
            - Samuel *d.* 1759
              - Elias Samuel *d.* 1805 *m.* Jeannette Delbanco
                - Moses Elias
                - Samuel Elias 1759–1826 *m.* Mariane Meyer
                  - Abraham (Aby) 1798–1856 *m.* Sara 1805–1884
                    - Rosa 1833–1908 *m.* Paul Schiff ↓
                    - Siegmund 1835–1889 *m.* Theophilie Rosenberg — *Continued on facing page* (1)
                    - 1 da.
                    - Moritz 1838–1911 *m.* Charlotte Oppenheim — *Continued on facing page* (2)
              - Gumprich Marcus 1727–1801 *m.* da. of M. R. Heckscher
                - Moses 1763–1831 *m.* Röschen Hausen
                  - Sara 1805–1884 (*m.* Abraham (Aby), above)
                - Gerson *d.* 1825 *unm.*
                - Elias ↓
                - Simon ↓

1.

Siegmund Warburg
1835–1889
m. Theophilie Rosenberg

- Aby S.
  1864–1933
  m. Olga Leonino
  - Karl (Charles)
    1907–1972
  - 4 da.
- Rosa
  1870–1922
  m. Alexandre Baron de Günzburg
  - ↓
- Georges
  1871–1923
  m. Lucie Kaulla
  - Siegmund Georg (Kt.) 1902–
    m. Eva Philipson
    1 so., 1 da.
- 4 da.

2.

Moritz Warburg
1838–1911
m. Charlotte Oppenheim

- Aby Moritz
  1866–1929
  m. Mary Hertz
  - 1 so., 2 da.
- Max Moritz
  1867–1946
  m. Alice Magnus
  - Eric M.
    1900–
    m. Dorothea Thorsch
    - Max A.
      1948–
    - 2 da.
  - 4 da.
- Paul Moritz
  1868–1932
  m. Nina Loeb
  - James P.
    1896–1969
  - 1 da.
- Felix Moritz
  1871–1937
  m. Frieda Schiff
  - 4 so., 1 da.
- Fritz Moritz
  1879–1964
  m. Anna B. Warburg
  - 3 da.

NOTE ON UNPUBLISHED AND RESTRICTED SOURCES

The old firm of M. M. Warburg & Co. had in 1938 no archive in the real sense, but merely a comprehensive index of current business matters which was retained for ten years, according to then-prescribed regulations governing the preservation of records. In addition to these records which were required for active use, there were a few older books that were retained for their antiquarian interest; and the personal files of individual partners for those letters and other writings that were confidential and bore the designation 'Not through the Secretariat'. In this class of material, the personal papers of Max M. Warburg and Dr. Carl Melchior were preserved from routine or politically-motivated destruction by the efforts of Eric M. Warburg; also preserved in this way were the personal files that reflected the many public and honorary positions of the two men.

The old copy books that belong to the business affairs of the bank and which remain on the premises at Ferdinandstrasse 75 are listed and described as follows:

Large quarto volume I: 1892–6
Large quarto volume II: 9 October 1896–November 1898
Large quarto volume III: 17 January 1897–31 December 1901
Quarto private copy book of Max M. Warburg, 10 February 1892–December 1894
Quarto Jubilee copy book: Letters of thanks for congratulations received on 1 January 1898
Quarto copy book no. 2: 27 December 1894–31 July 1896
Quarto copy book no. 3: (Max M. Warburg) 11 October 1896–7 October 1897
Quarto copy book no. 4: 20 October 1897–October 1898
Quarto copy book no. 4A: 28 October 1895–23 December 1895
(Only 48 pages of this last book have been used, mostly in the handwriting of Max M. Warburg; on 9 December 1895 the first typewritten letter appears, addressed to the London and Hanseatic Bank, signed by Moritz Warburg.)

Small octavo copy book A: 25 March 1889–18 March 1890
Small octavo copy book B: 29 April 1890–5 December 1892

The correspondence was tolerably well indexed only in these two octavo books. Legibility is inadequate in almost all the copy books. Apparently, keeping the copy books up to date was not at this stage – as it was later – the first assignment for trainees.

Four quarto volumes covering the period from 1872 to 1877 contain a record of the securities business, entered and kept accurately by the staff responsible for those transactions.

The prescribed period for retaining material was not slavishly adhered to; many files relating to special relationships, e.g. that with the Berliner Handels-Gesellschaft, survived the dangerous years. The correspondence between Albert Ballin and Max M. Warburg, collected in five folders dated from May 1905 to November 1918, is especially noteworthy. In his book on Albert Ballin,* Lamar Cecil describes this material as 'disappointing', since it represents merely a supplement to almost daily conversations; but it is nonetheless valuable for the light it sheds on the business style of both Ballin and Warburg. Max M. Warburg's correspondence with Sir Ernest Cassel would have represented a historical resource of the highest importance; but the two volumes of these letters disappeared between the years 1938 and 1945, and there is also a blank on the English side.†

There are however other extant sources, in the form of memoranda and longer historical surveys, that go beyond the mere listing of business transactions and offer a lively picture of the firm's partners and the way its business was conducted.

The description written in 1914 by Aby S. Warburg, a partner from 1889 to 1933, takes pride of place in this class of material. In his later preface dated 15 January 1915, Aby S. Warburg writes: 'I have attempted to write a biography of my father, in which task Mr. Salomon von Halle, an old friend of our firm who was also active in the business for many years, rendered essential assistance.'‡

It is characteristic that this historically most valuable and sensitive depiction was written by a member of the firm whose training and talents

* Lamar Cecil, *Albert Ballin: Business and Politics in Imperial Germany 1888–1918* (Princeton, 1967).

† Letter from Countess Mountbatten of Burma to E. Rosenbaum, in the possession of Eric M. Warburg.

‡ Salomon von Halle died in Frankfurt am Main on 2 October 1918.

tended more toward a trustee's administrative activity than the entrepreneurial expansion of the firm's business. He was able to base his work on a most comprehensive collection of family papers and business files that his father, Siegmund Warburg, a partner from 1859 to 1889, had with remarkably sure instincts preserved from the daily round of business and family affairs. This material, which was brought by Charles (Karl) Warburg to England in 1933, is now in the carefully run archive that Eric M. Warburg established in Hamburg.

Dr. Fritz M. Warburg wrote a continuation of this memoir from his Swedish exile in Stockholm; he too, despite all his activities, was of a more contemplative character and inclined because of his legal training toward intuitive abstract thinking. His memoirs depict the development of the firm, the nature of its typical business transactions, and the character of those senior staff members who did not belong to the *Chefkabinett*. For those who still knew him personally, all this was supplemented by fascinating stories in which the European world of high finance from St. Petersburg to Paris, from the Scandinavian North to Austria, came vividly alive.

A further supplement to these presentations is the comprehensive report, in the nature of a souvenir, that Max Hamlet sent from Tel-Aviv on 30 June 1940 to Max M. Warburg in New York. In his notes on the firm's staff, Dr. Fritz Warburg writes of Max Hamlet, who began working at Warburgs on 1 October 1889, at the age of nineteen, and received Power of Attorney in 1903, that he was 'perhaps, of all the old senior staff, the most versatile in his training; his expertise in bills of exchange, securities, gold arbitrage, and above all new-issue business, enabled him to handle transactions in all these areas.' Accordingly, Hamlet's description is as accurate as it is lively; it depicts with great vividness the varied tasks that a multifarious banking business required, and shows what extensive activities were carried out by a relatively small staff. Among the unexpected ornaments of his report, there is a description of the goings-on at the Hamburg Stock Exchange with its unusual characters and its type of humour that is less comprehensible for us than it was for those whose daily work was enlivened by it.

The last work to be mentioned in this survey is the large manuscript that Max M. Warburg left when he decided in the summer of 1939, at the suggestion of Sir John Wheeler-Bennett, to write his memoirs. The essential points about this manuscript appear in the preface that Eric M. Warburg wrote to the selected memoirs that were privately printed in

1952. The writing of these memoirs was a heroic task, the success of which Max M. Warburg himself doubted, because he remained very much aware of the private banker's responsibility to avoid everything that might be construed as unwarranted disclosure. Thus a work was created whose author was himself always conscious that for some readers it might contain too much, and for others too little information. The selected memoirs ultimately printed resolved this dilemma, which the author entirely understood. In a letter written to E. Rosenbaum on 13 June 1944, Warburg said:

I have several purposes:
1. I want to show how a private banker works, what chances he has, what possibilities, and so on.
2. I want to show the values of the private banker by his personal connections and independence.
3. I want to show that I had many opportunities in my life and I want really to bring the truth about many points which has not been told up to now.
4. I want to show all that in a light way so that the reader gets convinced that very great decisions are often made only by chance and how, in fact, diplomatic, political and finance-political life has been during the last fifty years.

As I very often had the chance to express my opinion and to visualize things, I should like to say that, too, without being immodest, so that in the future not I but that particular period will speak by itself.

These are only a few remarks that I wish to make this morning as this is a very busy day . . .

The tone of these words may serve as an introduction to his incomplete work which, even in that form, represents a source that continues to speak to us.

SELECT BIBLIOGRAPHY

Achterberg, Erich, *Der Bankplatz Frankfurt am Main, Eine Chronik*. Frankfurt a.M., 1955.

—, *Kleine Hamburger Bankgeschichte*. Hamburg-Altona, 1964.

Adler, Cyrus, *Jacob Schiff: His Life and Letters*. New York, 1929.

Baasch, Ernst, 'Zur Geschichte der Handelskrisis von 1857', *Zeitschrift des Vereins für Hamburgische Geschichte*, Bd. 30, 81–105.

Baden, Prinz Max von, *Erinnerungen und Dokumente*. Berlin, 1927.

Bamberger, Ludwig, *Charakteristiken*. Berlin, 1894.

—, *Lebenserinnerungen* (ed. by Paul Nathan). Berlin, 1899.

(Behrens) *175 Jahre L. Behrens & Söhne*. Hamburg, 1955.

Bergengrün, Alexander, *David Hansemann*. Berlin, 1901.

Berghoeffer, Ch. W., *Meyer Amschel Rothschild, der Gründer des Rothschildschen Bankhauses*. Frankfurt a.M., 1922.

Bismarck, Otto Fürst von, *Gedanken und Erinnerung*. Berlin, 1932.

Böhme, Helmut, *Deutschlands Weg zur Grossmacht*. Köln, Berlin, 1966.

—, 'Wirtschaftskrise, Merchant Bankers und Verfassungsreform', *Zeitschrift des Vereins für Hamburgische Geschichte*, Bd. 54, 1968.

Bonn, Max Julius, 'Die Vorgänge am Edelmetallmarkt in den Jahren 1870–1873', *Münchner volkswirtschaftliche Abhandlungen*, Nr. 40. Stuttgart, 1900.

Born, Karl E., *Die deutsche Bankenkrise 1931*. München, 1967.

Bouvier, Jean, *Les Rothschild*. Paris, 1967.

Brunner, Frederick H., 'Juden als Bankiers – ihre völkerverbindende Tätigkeit' in *In zwei Welten. Siegfried Moses zum fünfundsiebzigsten Geburtstag*. Tel Aviv, 1962, 509–35.

Buckland, C. S., *Metternich and the British Government from 1809 to 1813*. London, 1932.

Büsch, Johann Georg, *John Bull der Jüngere oder: Über die neuesten Vorfälle der Londoner Bank*. Hamburg, 1797.

—, *Versuch einer Geschichte der Hamburgischen Handlung*. Hamburg, 1797.

[Bullion Report] *Report together with minutes of evidence, and accounts, from the Select Committee on the high price of Gold bullion*. London, 1810.

Burckhardt, Jakob, *Weltgeschichtliche Betrachtungen*. Stuttgart, 1929.

—, *Briefe* (ed. by Fritz Kaphahn). Leipzig, 1935.

Capefigue, Jean Baptiste Honoré Raymond, *Histoire des grandes opérations financières*. Paris, 1860.

Cecil, Lamar, *Albert Ballin: Business and Politics in Imperial Germany 1888–1918*. Princeton, 1967.

Compter, Wolfgang, *Bankbetriebslehre*. Darmstadt, 1967.

Crouzet, François, *L'Economie Britannique et le Blocus Continental (1806–1813)*. Paris, 1958.

(Davout) *Memoire de M. Le Marèchal Davout Prince d'Eckmühl Au Roi*. Paris, 1814.

Davout in Hamburg. Ein Beitrag zur Geschichte der Jahre 1813–1814. Von einem Freunde der historischen Wahrheit (by a friend of historical truth). Mülheim (Ruhr), 1892.

Eckardt, Julius von, *Lebenserinnerungen*. Leipzig, 1910.

Eckert, Christian. *J. H. Stein: Werden und Wachsen eines Kölner Bankhauses in 150 Jahren*. 1940.

Ehrenberg, Richard, *Das Haus Parish in Hamburg*. Jena, 1905.

Emden, Paul H., *Money powers of Europe in the Nineteenth and Twentieth Centuries*. London, 1937.

Eyck, Erich, *A History of the Weimar Republic* (2 vols.). Cambridge (Mass.), 1964.

Fay, C. R., *Great Britain from Adam Smith to the Present Day* (3rd ed.). London, 1932.

Feaveryear, A. E., *The Pound Sterling: a History of English Money* (2nd ed., revised by E. V. Morgan). Oxford, 1963.

Fürstenberg, Hans, *Erinnerungen*. Wiesbaden, 1965.

Gayer, Arthur D. (ed.), *The Growth and Fluctuation of the British Economy, 1790–1850*. Oxford, 1953.

Genschel, Helmut, *Die Verdrängung der Juden aus der deutschen Wirtschaft*. Göttingen, 1966.

Gilbart, James William, *The History, Principles and Practice of English Banking* (new ed., revised by Ernest Sykes, 2 vols.). London, 1907.

Gille, Bertrand, *Histoire de la Maison Rothschild* (2 vols.). Geneva, 1965, 1967.

Glagau, Otto, *Der Börsen- und Gründungsschwindel in Berlin*. Leipzig, 1876.

—, *Der Börsen- und Gründungsschwindel in Deutschland*. Leipzig, 1877.

Glückel von Hameln, *Denkwürdigkeiten* (ed. by Alfred Feilchenfeld, 4th ed.). Berlin, 1923.

Gombrich, E. H., *Aby Warburg: an intellectual biography*. London, The Warburg Institute, University of London, 1970.

Grunwald, Kurt, 'Railways and Jewish Enterprise', *Year Book XII*, Leo Baeck Institute. London, 1967.

Gutmann, Franz, *Das französische Geldwesen im Kriege (1870–1878)*. Strassburg, 1913.

Haarbleicher, M. M., *Zwei Epochen aus der Geschichte der Deutsch-Israelitischen Gemeinde in Hamburg*. Hamburg, 1867.

Halle, Ernst Levy von, *Die Hamburger Girobank und ihr Ausgang*. Berlin, 1891.

Hegel, G. W. F., *Grundlinien der Philosophie des Rechts*. 1820.

Heine, Heinrich, *Werke* (ed. by Oskar Walzel). Leipzig, 1910.

Holleiner, Karl, *The Imperial Loans*. Oxford, 1965.

Jantzen, Günther, 'Hamburg und Wien. Zur Geschichte hamburgischer Beziehungen zu Oesterreich im 19. Jahrhundert', *Mitteilungen der Handelskammer Hamburg*. Hamburg, 1967, 641 ff.

Jenks, Leland Hamilton, *The Migration of British Capital to 1875*. London, 1927.

Kellenbenz, Hermann, 'Der deutsche Aussenhandel gegen Ausgang des 18. Jahrhunderts' in *Die wirtschaftliche Situation in Deutschland und Österreich um die Wende vom 18. zum 19. Jahrhundert.* Stuttgart, 1964.

— (ed.), 'Öffentliche Finanzen und privates Kapital im späten Mittelalter und in der ersten Hälfte des 19. Jahrhunderts', *Forschungen zur Sozial- und Wirtschaftsgeschichte*, Band 16. Stuttgart, 1971.

—, *Sephardim an der unteren Elbe.* Wiesbaden, 1958.

Keynes, John Maynard, *Two Memoirs.* London, 1949.

Klein, Gottfried, *400 Jahre Hamburger Börse.* Hamburg, 1958.

Knapp, Georg Friedrich, *Staatliche Theorie des Geldes.* München, 1905.

— and Friedrich Bendixen, *Zur staatlichen Theorie des Geldes. Briefwechsel von 1905–1920*, selected and edited by Kurt Singer. Basel, 1958.

Krohn, Helga, *Die Juden in Hamburg, 1800–1850.* Frankfurt a.M., 1967.

—, *Die Juden in Hamburg. Die politische, soziale und kulturelle Entwicklung einer jüdischen Grossstadtgemeinde nach der Emanzipation, 1848–1918.* Hamburg, 1974.

Lévy-Leboyer, Maurice, *Les banques européennes et l'industrialisation internationale dans la première moitié du XIXe siècle.* Paris, 1964.

Lippmann, Leo, *Mein Leben und meine amtliche Tätigkeit.* Hamburg, 1964.

Lüke, Rolf E., *Die Berliner Handelsgesellschaft in einem Jahrhundert deutscher Wirtschaft.* Berlin, 1956.

Lüthje, Bernd, 'Eine neue Heimat in Hamburg', *Mitteilungen der Handelskammer Hamburg.* Hamburg, June 1966.

Marshall, Alfred, *Money, Credit and Commerce.* London, 1924.

Martin, Paul C., 'Rahmenordnung und Geldwirtschaft der Frühindustrialisierung' in H. Kellenbenz, *Öffentliche Finanzen und privates Kapital im späten Mittelalter und in der ersten Hälfte des 19. Jahrhunderts.* Stuttgart 1971.

Mathies, Otto, *Hamburgs Reederei 1814–1914.* Hamburg, 1924.

Max, Prinz von Baden. *See* Baden.

Carl Melchior, Ein Buch des Gedenkens und der Freundschaft (hrsg. vom Verein für Hamburgische Geschichte). Tübingen, 1967.

Mönckeberg, Carl, *Hamburg unter dem Druck der Franzosen. Historische Denkwürdigkeiten.* Hamburg, 1864.

Möring, Maria, *Joh. Berenberg, Gossler & Co.* Hamburg, 1962.

Nathan, Paul, *Lebenserinnerungen.* Berlin, 1899.

Nebenius, Carl Friedrich, *Der öffentliche Credit.* Karlsruhe Baden, 1820.

Nolte, Vincent, *Fünfzig Jahre in beiden Hemisphären.* Hambnrg, 1853.

Pick, F. W., *Searchlight on German Africa: the Diaries and Papers of Dr. W. Ch. Regendanz.* London, 1939.

Plenge, Johannes, *Gründung und Geschichte des Crédit Mobilier.* Tübingen, 1903.

Pressburger, S., *Österreichische Notenbank 1816–1966. Geschichte des Österreichischen Noteninstituts.* Wien, 1966.

Ricardo, David, *Works and Correspondence.* Cambridge, 1951.

Rosen, Friedrich, *Aus einem diplomatischen Wanderleben* (2 vols.). Berlin, 1930–2.

Rosenbaum, Eduard, 'M. M. Warburg & Co., Merchant bankers of Hamburg' in *Year Book VII*, Leo Baeck Institute. London, 1962.

Rosenberg, Hans, 'Die Weltwirtschaftskrise von 1857–1859', *Vierteljahreszeitschrift für Sozial- und Wirtschaftsgeschichte*, Beiheft 30. Stuttgart, 1934.

Rothschild, Constance de, *Reminiscences*. London, 1922.

Schinckel, Max von, *Lebenserinnerungen*. Hamburg, 1927.

Schumacher, Hermann, 'Geschichte der deutschen Bankliteratur im 19. Jahrhundert' in *Festschrift für Schmoller*, Bd. 1, Abhandlung VII. Leipzig, 1908.

Schumpeter, Joseph, *History of Economic Analysis*. New York, 1954.

—, *Business Cycles* (2 vols.). New York, London, 1939.

Sieveking, Heinrich, 'Die Hamburger Bank 1619–1875' in *Festschrift für Werner von Melle*. Hamburg, 1933.

—, *Karl Sieveking, 1787–1847. Lebensbild eines Hamburgischen Diplomaten aus dem Zeitalter der Romantik*. Hamburg, 1923–8.

Singer, Egon, *Die Entstehung der hamburgischen Staatsanleihen von 1801 bis 1857*. Hamburg, 1916.

Sliosberg, Henri, *Baron Horace O. de Gunzbourg, sa vie et son œuvre*. Paris, 1933.

Soetbeer, Adolph, *Beiträge und Materialien zur Beurtheilung von Geld- und Bankfragen mit besonderer Rücksicht auf Hamburg*. Hamburg, 1855.

—, 'Die fünf Milliarden. Betrachtungen über die Folgen der grossen Kriegsentschädigung für die Wirtschaftsverhältnisse Frankreichs und Deutschlands' in *Deutsche Zeit- und Streitfragen*, III. Jahrgang, Nr. 33. Berlin, 1874.

Sombart, Werner. *Der moderne Kapitalismus* (2 vols.). Leipzig, 1902; then in later editions with the supplement '*und in Anfang des 20. Jahrhunderts*', revised to 1925.

—, *Die deutsche Volkswirtschaft im 19. Jahrhundert*. Berlin, 1912.

Strousberg, Bethel Henry, *Dr. Strousberg und sein Wirken. Von ihm selbst geschildert*. Berlin, 1876.

Tiemann, Hermann, *Essays, Vorträge und Aufsätze aus vier Jahrzehnten*. Hamburg, 1975.

Tilly, Richard Hugh, *Financial Institutions in the Rhineland 1815–1870*. Madison, London, 1967.

—, 'Los von England. Probleme des Nationalismus in der deutschen Wirtschaftsgeschichte', *Zeitschrift für die gesamte deutsche Staatswissenschaft*, Bd. 124, Heft 1. Tübingen, 1968.

Toury, Jacob, *Die politischen Orientierungen der Juden in Deutschland. Von Jena bis Weimar*. Tübingen, 1966.

(Trinkaus) *175 Jahre C. G. Trinkaus. Tradition und neue Aufgaben*. Düsseldorf, 1960.

Vagts, Alfred, 'M. M. Warburg & Co. Ein Bankhaus in der deutschen Weltpolitik 1905–1933', *Vierteljahreszeitschrift für Sozial- und Wirtschaftsgeschichte*, Nr. 45. Stuttgart, 1958, 289–388.

Wagner, Adolph, *Die Geld- und Credittheorie der Peel'schen Bankacte*. Wien, 1862.

Wandel, Eckard, *Hans Schäffer. Steuermann in wirtschaftlichen und politischen Krisen 1886–1967*. Stuttgart, 1974.

Warburg, James P., *The Long Road Home: the autobiography of a maverick*. New York, 1964.

Warburg, Max M., *Aus meinen Aufzeichnungen*. New York, 1952.

Weiss-Wellenstein, Gustav, 'Ein altes Beispiel mitteleuropäischer Interessengemeinschaft' in *Mitteleuropäische Wirtschaft*. Wien, December 1927.

Wilson, James, *Capital, Currency and Banking* (2nd ed.). London, 1859.

Wohlwill, Adolph, *Neuere Geschichte der Freien und Hansestadt Hamburg, insbesondere von 1789 bis 1815*. Gotha 1914.

—, *Hamburg im Todesjahr Schillers*. Hamburg, 1905.

INDEX